What Some are Saying About
Ron Dunn: His Life and Mission

Here is a page-turner of a book about one of the most effective preachers the world has ever been given. Expect your own worldview to become credibly rounded off as you read Ron Owens's account of an utterly loved preacher whom the apostle Paul would have called "a messenger of the church and the glory of Christ."

Richard Bewes, O. B. E., former rector of All Souls Church,
Langham Place, London, England

When I shared Bible conferences with Ron Dunn, I used to think that he was so professional—smooth, competent, and effective. That view mellowed as I got to know him, and I came to realize that the secret of his ministry was that he was *real*. This book confirms that. It reveals in challenging detail the person behind the preacher, and I predict that it will be a means of great blessing to countless readers.

John Blanchard, preacher, apologist, and author,
Banstead, Surrey, England

When I read Manley Beasley's biography by Ron Owens, I knew who needed to write Ron's story. Kaye and I talked and agreed. This book is a treasure. It will give you insights into one of the greatest expositors of the twentieth century, a man with a dry wit and a great love for God.

Michael Catt, senior pastor, Sherwood Baptist Church,
Albany, Georgia

Ron Dunn's clear, biblical exposition, coupled with his keen understanding of the human situation, made Ron a powerful instrument in the hand of the Lord. His theology of the Christ-life shaped my understanding of what it means to be a follower of Christ. When I became a pastor, I wanted my churches to be exposed to the Spirit-anointed ministry of

Ron Dunn. I am profoundly grateful that my friend, Ron Owens, has preserved the life and ministry of a great saint in *Ron Dunn: His Life and Mission*.

Michael Dean, senior pastor, Travis Avenue
Baptist Church, Fort Worth, Texas

This book, like others penned by Ron Owens, is written out of years of friendship and ministry, sharing hard times as well as good. Ron Owens has a rare capacity that few possess—the ability to tap the heart of his subject and somehow let his life flow from pen to paper. You will find the portrait painted in this book to be an amazingly accurate rendering of my friend and our prophet, Ron Dunn.

Tom Elliff, president, International Mission Board,
Southern Baptist Convention

Ron Dunn was a man whose intimacy with God was obvious. No one walks by faith, prays with power, or preaches with such divine anointing unless he has learned to cling to the Vine as did this "prince among preachers." Ron Dunn lived his life in the crucible of sorrow and on the pinnacle of triumph, but he was always consistent in his surrender to Christ; and Ron Owens has marvelously captured the essence of the man with his poignant pen. This book will inspire you, challenge you, and very likely transform your life.

Gerald Harris, editor, *Georgia Baptist Index*

Future generations owe a huge debt to Ron Owens for putting Ron Dunn's life into perspective in this biography. Through it all, Ron, like Barnabas of old, "saw the grace of God and was glad." We would all do well, as the apostle Paul admonished, to imitate Ron Dunn as he imitated Christ. I love him and still miss him with each passing day and look forward to seeing him again "in the morning."

O. S. Hawkins, president/CEO, GuideStone Financial Resources

Why is it that I can't forget his voice or his sermons? Ron Dunn was used by Jesus to speak deeply and profoundly into my life and calling. He was impossible to forget once you met and heard him. I cannot wait to get my hands on this book. You are about to have the privilege of reading about one of God's greats!

Johnny Hunt, senior pastor, First Baptist Church,
Woodstock, Georgia

This wonderful book should be read by every preacher and every Christian who loves good preaching.

R. T. Kendall, former minister, Westminster Chapel,
London, England

As a gospel singer for more than fifty years, I have had the joy of serving with hundreds of our Lord's great preachers and Bible teachers, and Ron Dunn is my all-time favorite. Every time he spoke, living water flowed. Ron was a good friend who blessed and enriched my life. I miss him. My profound thanks to Ron Owens for writing this biography. It should be read by everyone in need of a blessing sent from heaven.

John McKay, gospel singer, Weatherford, Texas

As I read the draft, I thought of so many people we are praying for who need sections of this book right now to help them survive! I was sorely tempted to copy, paste, and send portions to those hurting so badly, but of course, I knew that would not be ethical. I predict this book will be a major force in God's hand to help weary pilgrims, preachers in particular, not to mention the rich preaching material it contains.

Don Moore, former executive director,
Arkansas Baptist Convention

When I read the manuscript of *Ron Dunn: His Life and Mission*, my heart was set ablaze! This book is a *MUST* for any preacher or layman who is hungering and thirsting for revival. As Ron Owens tells the story of the great awakening in MacArthur Boulevard Baptist Church, it once again created a hunger in my heart to see revival.

And it's a must for every discouraged pastor. As Ron Owens tells the story of all the dark days Ron Dunn went through, it will motivate you to keep the faith. If you feel that your prayers are unanswered and that God is silent, this book will be well worth the money to you. The sermons are challenging and encouraging. Ron lives on through this biography. It just has to be read!

Jimmy Robertson, founder/codirector,
Milldale Conference Center, Zachary, Louisiana

My heart has been touched, and I have been deeply moved as I have read this truly inspiring book on the life of my friend Ron Dunn. Ron Owens has done a remarkable job in piecing together the complex life and history of one of the twentieth century's favorite preachers. How can one not be moved again to be reminded of the challenges that Ron and Kaye had to face as parents—the spiritual battles fought, the victories won! If you never heard him preach or maybe have never even heard of him, please start turning the pages now and be gripped by this amazing re-telling of one of God's giants in the faith.

Phil South, director, World Action Ministries,
United Kingdom

You'll find people all over the world whose lives were transformed by the teachings of Ron Dunn. He was a man whose life matched his preaching, plain and powerful. Ron was my friend whom I trusted to the end. The visits late in his life were such as to form a reservoir of encouragement for the rest of my life. See you later, dear friend! Thank you, Ron Owens, for favoring the body of Christ with another powerful biography.

Jack Taylor, president, Dimensions Ministries,
Melbourne, Florida

This book is excellent. I wish I had heard Ron Dunn preach in person, but all I've heard are his tapes. He was a unique preacher. The hand of the Lord was truly upon him, and his messages made the "victorious life" plain and practical and encouraged us to trust Christ for the very best. Nobody can duplicate him, but anybody who knows the Lord can learn from him and turn trials into triumphs.

Warren Wiersbe, author and former pastor,
Moody Church, Chicago, Illinois

Ron Owens's biographical sketch of Ron Dunn's journey of faith in our God is amazing. He weaves Ron Dunn's heritage, marriage to Kaye, the brokenness of Ronnie Jr.'s death, his ministry, and messages into a tapestry that encourages the reader to thirst after the "much more" of the Christian life.

John L. Yeats, SBC recording secretary
and executive director of the Missouri Baptist Convention

Forewords by
Michael Catt & Tom Elliff

RON
D U N N

HIS LIFE AND MISSION

RON OWENS

PUBLISHING GROUP

Nashville, Tennessee

978-1-4336-8034-2

Published by B&H Publishing Group
Nashville, Tennessee

Dewey Decimal Classification: B
Subject Heading: DUNN, RON \ CLERGY—BIOGRAPHY \
JOY AND SORROW

Cover photo is taken by Kaye Dunn in Cape Cod, Massachusetts.

2 3 4 5 6 7 8 • 18 17 16 15 14 13

Dedicated to
Kaye, Stephen, Kimberly,
and to the memory of
Ronnie Jr.

Contents

✳ ✳ ✳

Foreword by Michael Catt   xv
Foreword by Tom Elliff   xvii
Acknowledgments   xxi
A Word from Kaye   xxiii
Introduction   1
Prologue   5

PART ONE: Beginnings

Chapter 1: From Fence Post to Fort Smith   9
Chapter 2: One + One = One   13
Chapter 3: Crossing the Red River   19
Chapter 4: Another Crossing   22
    Sermon: *Which Side of the Jordan?*   22

PART TWO: MacArthur Days (1966–1975)

Prelude   31
Chapter 5: A Providential Move   32
Chapter 6: A View from the Inside   36
Chapter 7: A Divine Encounter   39
    Sermon: *From Your Pastor's Heart: A Watershed Moment*   41
Chapter 8: Revival Years: A Place Shaken (1970–1975)   47
Chapter 9: The Birth of a Ministry   54

Chapter 10: When the Church Prays   59
    Sermon: *When the Church Prays* (Acts 4:23–33)   62

PART THREE: **The Best of Times and the Worst of Times**

Chapter 11: The Best of Times   71
Chapter 12: The Worst of Times   74
Chapter 13: Surprise, It's God! (Genesis 32:24–32)   79
    Sermon: *Surprise, It's God!*   80

PART FOUR: **The Dark Night of the Soul**

Chapter 14: Another Giant   97
Chapter 15: An Answer: Strangely Clothed   102
Chapter 16: Strange Ministers   106
    Sermon: *Strange Ministers*   107
Chapter 17: What Now?   110
    Sermon: *What Now?*   110
Interlude: Family   116

PART FIVE: **Going International**

Chapter 18: And Beyond   141
Chapter 19: The UK Calls   144
Chapter 20: LifeStyle Ministries—UK   151
Chapter 21: Don't Just Stand There, Pray Something   157
    Sermon: *Just Do It*   157
Interlude: Mentored and Mentoring   172

PART SIX: **Ron Dunn—Author**

Prelude   183
Chapter 22: Any Christian Can   184
Chapter 23: Faith Crisis   189
Chapter 24: When Heaven Is Silent   196
Chapter 25: Will God Heal Me?   206

Chapter 26: Surviving Friendly Fire   219
Interlude: Getting to Know You   229

PART SEVEN: A "Prince" Among Preachers

Chapter 27: Quick Start   239
Chapter 28: More Tributes to "The Preacher"   244
Chapter 29: *Chained to the Chariot* (2 Corinthians 2:12–17)   260

PART EIGHT: Heading Home

Chapter 30: Kaye's Medical Time Line   281
Chapter 31: One More Sermon!   287
    Sermon: *Knowing God* (Philippians 3:10)   289
Chapter 32: Back Home   300
Chapter 33: Earth Grieved as Heaven Rejoiced   305
Chapter 34: Will a Man Serve God for Nothing?   312
    Sermon: *Will a Man Serve God for Nothing?*   312

Epilogue   324
Appendix 1: Tributes and Testimonies   329
Appendix 2: Index of Tributes and Endorsements   337
A Continuing Legacy   339
Notes   340
Photo Gallery   343

Foreword

✳ ✳ ✳

Everyone needs a hero, a mentor, a friend, a wise sage who can speak into our lives. By the grace of God, I knew Ron Dunn as all of the above. Many men have influenced and impacted my life but none more than Ron Dunn. Ron taught me how to see and seek God in the struggles of life. He did so through his preaching, his counsel, and my personal observations of a man who lived many days in the valley. Yet regardless of the trial or test, he would ascend to the pulpit to preach of the victory we have in Christ. I was with Ron and Kaye the day his father died because Ron was preaching at Sherwood at the time. I was privileged to be with Ron in a variety of circumstances. These experiences were enough to know that this man lived what he preached.

My friendship with Ron was one of the great joys of my life. I knew he didn't like to talk on the phone, but he always took my calls. I lived with anticipation for every possible moment I could have with him during our annual Bible conference, which he preached for sixteen consecutive years. One of my funniest memories of Ron happened during that conference. We were having noonday services, and he was running late. I called him at the hotel, and he had fallen asleep (Ron found it impossible to sleep at night). He was scheduled to preach his final message on Habakkuk that morning. He took a deep sigh and said, "Michael, you know the message and my points. You just go ahead and preach it for me."

I rushed to my study, got my four pages of notes from that message, and did my best to impersonate Ron. He made me swear I would never tell Kaye. I didn't until years later.

When Ron died, I experienced a great void in my life. It impacted me more than the death of my own parents. He held such a place in my heart, my life, and my ministry that I couldn't imagine not being able to talk to him and seek his counsel. One of the hardest days of my life was preaching Ron's funeral. It really wasn't a funeral but rather a celebration of his life. Various preachers and friends spoke, and I did the final message. Over the years I find myself asking: "What would Ron think? What would Ron say? I wonder how Ron would feel about that."

Calling Ron Dunn my friend was one of the greatest privileges of my life. Now, because of the extensive work of his friend Ron Owens and the contributions of many pastors and family members, you have in your hands a book long overdue. Several years before he died, Ron asked me to write his biography. I was honored, but I knew I couldn't do it. When I read Manley Beasley's biography by Ron Owens, I knew who needed to write Ron's story. Kaye and I talked and agreed. This book is a treasure. It will give you insights into one of the greatest expositors of the twentieth century, a man with a dry wit and a great love for God.

These pages will also give you a glimpse into the life of a man who defined what it means to be an overcomer. As Ron said, "I've been to the bottom, and it's solid ground." Few people I've ever met have walked through more "dangers, toils, and snares" than Ron did. We are the recipients of what he learned from God in those moments. Read this book. Recommend it to friends. Give it as a gift.

—Michael Catt

Senior Pastor, Sherwood Baptist Church, Albany, Georgia

Foreword

Placing the phone down, I shook my head in disbelief. At first I hadn't even recognized his voice, although I had listened to it more than the voice of any other preacher for more than thirty years. Perhaps it was because I sincerely thought he was in the hospital, seriously ill and maybe even dying. Or maybe it was because his normally soft, sometimes slightly raspy, but always penetrating resonance was growing weak on this, his final stretch toward home. So it had taken a few seconds to awaken to the fact that I was speaking to "The Prophet."

Oh, I know well that most readers would agree that the foundational gift of prophesy, in the sense of foretelling future events, was set aside with the closing of the canon. But there is a definite and continuing place for the other side of prophesy, "speaking forth the Word of God," and that gift remains with the church today.

Over the years I have believed that God has raised up prophets, men who boldly proclaim the Word of God, uniquely fitted to each church I have pastored. This would be a man in whom my heart safely rested, someone the church both willingly heard and deeply respected. Of that man (and on one occasion two men) I would say to our congregation, "He is our prophet." Occasionally I would even remind him that, should God give him a specific message needed by our church, all he needed do was to call, and the pulpit was his as soon as he could get there. And so the prophet was calling.

> "I believe God has given me a message for the church," said Ron, his voice barely above a whisper. "And I think I'm to preach it this coming Sunday."

Fittingly, First Southern's pulpit was Ron's that Sunday morning, and the message he preached from the first chapter of Philippians would prove to be his last. As was said of Robert Murray McCheyne, Ron "preached as a dying man to dying men."

Shortly after that morning service, Ron returned to the Dallas area where he was soon admitted to the hospital in which he passed away only a few days later. All of us who shared in the memorial service and at the graveside found ourselves struggling to convey the appreciation we felt for the investment he had made in our lives. Ron's life and death left us with eternity in view.

Prophet was not the only term used to describe Ron. During one of our annual August Days of Refreshing that I jokingly referred to Ron as Southern Baptist's answer to Columbo, the disarming detective who had a knack for bumbling his way into the truth. The name stuck. Columbo, for those unfamiliar with the TV miniseries, was famous for his, "Oh, by the way . . ." statements that brought perplexity and fear into the hearts of his culprits. So was Ron. "Oh," he would say, with a telling pause punctuated by a long sigh, "Did I mention to you . . . ?"

Gifted with a spontaneous and unforced sense of humor, Ron was never shy about exposing his own foibles and idiosyncrasies. God often used this remarkable quality to strip bare the pretenses with which people often armed themselves, allowing the Word of God to penetrate their hearts. Our First Southern family often noted that Ron was "one of us," struggling to overcome the same challenges we faced in our own lives.

From the first time I heard Ron preach, I was captivated by his unique ability to mine truth from the Scripture. That ability, coupled with his openly transparent manner and remarkable capacity for practical application always seemed to leave Ron's audiences wanting to drink more deeply from the Word of God.

Ron Dunn's firm adherence to the Word of God enabled him to escape the theological flights of fancy that captivated the minds of other popular preachers and teachers in the earlier days of his conference ministry. He was a Bible scholar in the truest sense of the word. While never denying the mystical aspects of faith, Ron constantly brought personal experience back to the fundamental question: Does this correspond with the clear teachings of God's Word? This simple practice produced a trustworthiness in his life and ministry that is so desperately needed today.

As most readers will know, Ron and his wife, Kaye, shared a faith that was, on more than one occasion, severely tested. These were tests that might leave the average Christian questioning the sovereign wisdom and love of God. Ron and Kaye possessed a faith that had been hammered out on the anvil of their own experience.

Because Ron's was a tested faith, his audiences often included people searching for answers to their own very real struggles. Simply knowing that Ron and Kaye had also faced some of life's extremities gave his message an authenticity that can be gained in no other fashion. In such settings I often saw tears running down the cheeks of people whose hearts found a genuine hope in what he was sharing.

It is only fitting that Ron Owens write this biography of Ron Dunn. Ron, and his wife Patricia, often shared ministry in settings where Ron was a featured speaker. This book, like others penned by Ron Owens, is written out of years of friendship and ministry, sharing hard times as well as the good. Ron has a rare capacity that few possess, the ability to tap the heart of his subject and somehow let his life flow from pen to paper. You will find the portrait painted in this book to be an amazingly accurate rendering of my friend and our prophet, Ron Dunn.

—Tom Elliff

President, International Mission Board Southern Baptist Convention

Acknowledgments

✳ ✳ ✳

With deep gratitude I thank the following:

Kaye, Stephen, and Kimberly, for their encouragement and input, without which this story could not have been written. And to Dan Robinson who, out of his love for Ron and for Kaye, diligently prayed for and encouraged me throughout the writing of this biography.

Kaye and Michael Catt for giving me the honor of writing Ron's story.

Michael Catt and Tom Elliff for writing the forewords.

To Kaye and Joanne Gardner for the years of scrapbook ministry and family history that have been an immeasurable source of information.

Those who took time out of their busy schedules to participate in the "Friends of Ron Dunn" gatherings in Albany, Georgia, and Euless, Texas, from which many of the tributes have been taken.

The others who provided personal tributes to the man who not only impacted their lives while he was with us but who continues to influence them to this day.

My wife, Patricia, whose listening ear, seeing eye, and input have been invaluable.

Those who read the manuscript and kindly wrote endorsement blurbs.

Those who prayed and those who sat through multiple reading sessions.

Thanks be to our Lord for the precious memories Patricia and I have of times spent together with Ron and Kaye over twenty-five plus years, beginning at the Encouragers Conference in 1973 at MacArthur Boulevard Baptist Church.

A Word from Kaye

❋ ❋ ❋

"I thank my God upon every remembrance of thee." What a wonderful thing to be able to say when your sweetheart goes to heaven. Ron was a tremendous influence in my life because I was only sixteen years old when we married, and we spent forty-five precious years together, plus the two years that we dated. He had such a hunger for God and a love for His Word. After reading Jill Morgan's *A Man of the Word: Life of G. Campbell Morgan,*[1] he committed himself to expository preaching and spent hours each week studying for new messages, doing a careful exegesis of each passage as he prepared to preach. He handled God's Word with reverence, feeling a tremendous responsibility for his congregation that he get it right. Little did he realize that those same messages would still be going around the world years later.

Ron loved to preach, and he had a pastor's heart. Even when he went into an itinerant ministry, he called himself a "traveling pastor." He loved going back to the same churches year after year, encouraging the pastors and exhorting the people to godly living. He had a teachable spirit and was mentored by many godly preachers. Their influence on his life made him want to pour his own life into younger preachers.

Forty to forty-five weeks a year on the road was not easy for someone who loved home as much as Ron did. One of my joys was making our little motel rooms a "home on the road." We didn't stay in a lot of fancy places, so I would go to the nearest grocery store upon our arrival in a town, buy a bouquet of flowers, some fresh fruit, and candles in order to make our place cozy. When possible, we got two adjoining rooms with a connecting door so that one side could be used to spread out all his books for study and the other side as living quarters. That was important when most of Ron's studying was done on the road. We always had more suitcases of books than clothes with us.

Ron allowed me the privilege of being not only his partner in marriage, but also his partner in the ministry. We were a team and loved spending time together traveling from meeting to meeting. God took the simple but profound truths he preached, and these were sent out on cassette tapes all over the world. This opened doors for him to travel to many of those countries. He hated his "twangy" voice, a mixture of lazy Oklahoma, Arkansas, and Texas dialects; and yet God used that voice on tapes to spread the gospel. He was always amazed and humbled that he was invited to preach with men he thought of as "giants of the faith." How he loved to preach at the Keswick and Filey Conferences in England! He began reading sermons from the *Keswick Journals* as a young preacher and was thrilled when God opened that door through his friendship with Dr. George Duncan.

Ron, or course, would not have chosen the training school God put him through. The hurts and despair he thought were going to destroy him were the very thing that encouraged his listeners. How does a person living with heavy depression become known as a minister of encouragement? Only a sovereign, great God can do that.

Family was always important to Ron and he carved out time for us. Some of the most precious times we had together were during the summer at our farm in Arkansas. He loved to put a red bandana around his head, strap his pistol around his waist and mow on the tractor, shooting a few snakes along the way. Those were also special days of being with our extended family. He loved his children fiercely, and the legacy of his prayers of intercession for them are still before the throne.

Although Ron was only 5' 9" tall, he stood ten feet tall in my eyes because of his tenderness and gentleness toward me. I never doubted I was loved. I thank God for having put this special man in my life.

I heard him say so many times that God never wastes time or experience, and little did we know way back in the 1970s, when we met Ron and Patricia Owens, what an important part they would play in our lives. We not only had the joy of fellowship on the many international trips we made together, as well as ministering in Bible conferences through the years, but now I've had the great joy of working with Ron on this biography.

I believe he has beautifully and prayerfully captured the essence of my Ron's life and ministry on paper. You will get to know the real Ron Dunn through reading this book.

Introduction

❄ ❄ ❄

Nothing speaks so profoundly about a person's life as what is remembered of him or her after death. In reality we write our own obituaries while we are alive, and how encouraging and edifying it is to look back on the life of one who has fought the good fight, kept the faith, and finished well. Ron Dunn's life not only validated the message he preached, but it impacted thousands of lives while he lived, and it continues to reach around the world through CDs, DVDs, and books.

Ron mastered the art of communication in both speaking and writing. Anyone who heard him preach, or who has read his books, knows what I mean. There have been times in writing this biography that I have wished Ron were writing his own story, rather than me attempting to put his life on paper. Then I'm reminded that he is writing, or rather, has written his story and that this biography is but the extension of the life he lived.

But this is not only Ron's story; it is also the story of Rita Kaye Mitchell who, while still in high school, married Ronnie Louis Dunn, a young aspiring preacher boy. It is the story of two lives who were called on to traverse the deepest valleys and to climb the highest mountains together.

Ron was an insatiable reader. He loved books. He was one of the most widely read evangelicals of his day. His interests covered classic literature, both secular and sacred, theology, history, fiction, including

Louis L'Amour westerns. He read contemporary religious authors and not only those with whom he agreed. He was not afraid to read the works of those with opposing theological views, as he was secure enough in his own faith and doctrine not to be threatened by others' opinions, always placing those opinions against the plumb line of Scripture. This he found stimulating. It not only strengthened his own faith, but it helped him understand why those with opposing views came to the conclusions they did.

Among Ron's favorite authors was Charles Haddon Spurgeon from whom he received both inspiration and encouragement. This nineteenth century British Baptist pastor would have identified with many of the challenges Ron faced over the years. In his preface to his daily readings compiled in the *Checkbook of the Bank of Faith,* he says:

> I commenced writing these daily portions when I was wading in the surf of controversy. Since then I have been cast into "waters to swim in," which, but for God's upholding hand, would have proved waters to drown in. I have endured tribulation from many flails. Sharp bodily pain succeeded mental depression, and this was accomplished both by bereavement, and affliction in the person of one dear as life.
>
> The waters rolled in continually, wave upon wave. I do not mention this to exact sympathy, but simply to let the reader see that I am no dry-land sailor. I know the roll of the billows and the rush of the winds. Never were the promises of Jehovah so precious to me as at this hour. Some of them I never understood till now. I had not reached the date at which they matured, for I was not myself mature enough to perceive their meaning.
>
> Oh, that I might comfort some of my Master's servants! I have written out of my own heart with the view of comforting their hearts. I would say to them in their trials—My

brethren, God is good. He will not forsake you; He will bear
you through.

C. H. Spurgeon's sentiments could well have been written by Ron
who, though himself was familiar with the "roll of the billows and the
rush of the winds," was used of God to speak a word of hope and encouragement to thousands who were facing their own rough seas.

Someone has called Christian history the "Third Testament," for it
leaves us a chronicle of faithful witnesses who, for two thousand years,
have handed the gospel down to us. In every stage of the church and in
every generation, a faithful few have borne the challenges, kept the faith,
and finished the work. Their biographies are among the most helpful
books on our shelves because we learn from their lives, their faithfulness,
and even from their failures.

One of the challenges in writing Ron's story has been deciding, out
of the scores of tributes received, which ones to include. And, to those
whose "favorite" sermon is not included in this work, I direct you to the
A Continuing Legacy page at the end of the book where you'll find instructions on how to download many of Ron's messages or purchase them on
either CD or DVD from LifeStyle Ministries. A wealth of material is
available.

Needless to say, writing Ron's story has been a spiritual and emotional
ride as I've looked back over a life so powerfully used of God. Much more
could have been written as "the half has not been told." Fortunately, however, much of the other half can be found in Ron's books and messages.

I pray that this limited account of one of God's choice servants, who
kept the faith and finished the assignment God gave him, will be both an
encouragement and a challenge for each of us to press on toward the prize
of the high calling of God in Christ Jesus.

Prologue

Memorial Day Weekend, 2001

Nothing was going to deter Ron Dunn from driving those two hundred miles north on Interstate 35 to Del City, a suburb of Oklahoma City near Tinker Air Force Base. It was Memorial Day weekend, 2001, and though Kaye was too weak to accompany him, due to the lymphoma treatments she was undergoing, he persuaded her that he could make it on his own. He'd be fine. He promised to return Sunday afternoon, right after he had preached and had lunch with Tom and Jeannie Elliff.

Knowing how much it meant to Ron to be back with this family of believers who had so faithfully prayed and supported them through the years, Kaye was not going to stand in his way, in spite of the risk she knew they were taking.

As she watched him drive off in his black Mark VIII, little did she or Ron realize that this would be his last trip on Earth and that the next morning, when he struggled up the steps to stand behind the pulpit of Del City's First Southern Baptist Church, he would be preaching his last sermon.

PART ONE

Beginnings

*It pleased God, who separated me from my mother's
womb, and called me by his grace,
to reveal his Son in me, that I might preach him.*

—GALATIANS 1:15–16 KJV

[1]

From Fence Post
to Fort Smith

Poteau—French for "post," as in fence post, is an eastern Oklahoma town sitting on the Poteau River, surrounded by mountains—Sugar Loaf to the east and Cavanal Hill, the "world's highest hill," to the west. No one knows for sure why the founding fathers came up with a French name, rather than an Indian name based on the tribes that had lived in this area over the centuries, unless they went back to Bernard de la Harpe, the French explorer who passed through that region in 1719.

Where Poteau, Oklahoma, got its name, however, was the last thing on the minds of Cecil and Eunice Dunn on October 24, 1936, when their second son, Ronald Louis Dunn, was born. Nor could they ever have anticipated the impact this child was going to have on the world, and the body of Christ in particular. They did not know that the little baby they were holding in their arms was born to preach and that in just a few years preaching would become the passion of his life.

Some Early Background

Ron's early childhood was quite normal, other than an accident at age two when the Dunn family was living on Qxley Street in Poteau. Ron's mother was ironing one day when he and Barry, his older brother by three years, tipped over the ironing board. The hot iron fell on the back of Ronnie's left hand, and though many surgeries and grafting procedures followed, his fingers were maimed and webbed together for many years.

"In spite of that accident, however, those were good years," recalls Barry. "Dad was a bookkeeper at a glass plant in Poteau before we moved to Kansas during World War II. Then, after a brief time in the Sunflower State, we moved back to Poteau for a year and finally to 2818 Alabama Street in Fort Smith, Arkansas, where Dad had purchased a wholesale gasoline business. Ron was nine when we moved, and after attending Albert Pike School and Darby Junior High, he went on to graduate from Fort Smith High School."

Brothers and Best Friends

Ron and Barry, in addition to being brothers, would become best friends. Barry doesn't remember Ron taking part in any particular sport, though he did enjoy playing the trumpet, and he also enjoyed having fun, a trait that lasted throughout his adulthood. Being able to see the lighter side would eventually play a part in helping Ron navigate some heavy seas that lay ahead.

Barry remembers one particular lighter-side moment when the Dunn families were spending their annual summer weeks at the 330-acre farm their father had purchased in the Greenwood, Arkansas, area.

"Ron and I decided we needed to cut a large limb off one of the trees in front of the house in order to make a better tire swing for the kids. So Ron got the ladder, and I got the chain saw. (Anyone knowing the two of us will be tipped off that bad things were about to happen.)

"I climbed up on the limb and started sawing, neither of us noticing that the ladder was on the side of the limb that I was sawing off. The limb fell and broke the ladder in two. There I was, stuck up in the tree with Ron down on the ground, laughing his head off. He finally went and got the tractor and raised the tractor bucket high enough for me to get in it. I told Ron that I wouldn't tell anybody if he wouldn't, but of course he did. He said it was worth the embarrassment to us for the pleasure it provided to our wives, Kaye and Janet."

A Family Move

No one in the Dunn family could have anticipated how significant the thirty-five-mile move the family made from Poteau, Oklahoma, to Fort Smith, Arkansas, would be to their young son's life. This town, rich in frontier history, was where Judge Isaac Parker, nicknamed "The Hanging Judge," was its only true law from 1875 to 1896. This western military post would become the setting for the Academy-Award winning movie *True Grit*. This area was where the Cherokee and Choctaw Indian tribes settled after their forced twenty-two-hundred-mile Trail of Tears march from the southeast to "Indian territory" in the Fort Smith and Oklahoma area. This rich history made a lifelong impression on young Ronnie.

It had been but forty years since Judge Parker had been "the law" in that part of the country when young Ronnie was born, and he would always identify with the West. As already mentioned, among his favorite leisure reading were the Western tales written by Louis L'Amour. He claimed to have a touch of Cherokee blood running through his veins. His e-mail address was Cherokee40@juno.com. Learning about Ron's claimed Cherokee connection, Adrian Rogers began introducing him as Chief Yellow Horse.

Each summer, when on vacation with his family on his father's farm, Ron enjoyed riding the tractor while cutting grass. He always had a bandana tied around his head and a six-shooter on his hip. He loved to shoot snakes and other critters he felt were a nuisance. He was a good shot. He loved guns and had an enviable collection, including an Uzi, a gift from Milldale Bible Conference in Zachary, Louisiana. He prided himself in his ability to make his own ammo, and he loved to spend time target practicing, often with Kaye and the children.

An Early Call

But not only was the move to Fort Smith significant in his identifying with the Old West; it was here that young Ronnie made his profession of faith at Southside Baptist Church when he was nine. A short time later he came under the influence of J. Harold Smith when the Dunns made a providential membership move to First Baptist Church. The preaching of J. Harold Smith would have a profound impact on his life and ministry, and six years later, at the age of fifteen, he surrendered to the ministry at Siloam Springs Baptist Encampment, near Siloam Springs, Arkansas.

An Early Start

If you're called to preach, then you preach. There was no waiting around to be told how he should do it. He had seen it modeled week after week, and with the encouragement of his pastor and men of the church, Ronnie Dunn preached his first sermon in the Fort Smith City Jail, now the Sebastian County Jail. ❋

[2]

One + One = One

"I was fourteen, and a member of First Baptist, Fort Smith, Arkansas, when I watched J. Harold Smith ordain Ronnie Dunn to the ministry that Wednesday night," recalls Kaye. "I had never met him, but I thought it was so neat that they would ordain someone who looked so young.

"He had just gotten engaged, and his fiancée showed me the ring he had given her. But the engagement didn't last long. A few days later I heard that her parents had made her break off the engagement because they felt their daughter and Ronnie were much too young to be thinking of marriage."

A Go-to-Church Companion

This upset young Ronnie, so he began looking for someone else to go to church with him, just to show his ex and her parents that others would gladly accompany him. The problem was, everyone he called turned him down. He finally asked Richard Hill, a young man in the church, if he knew someone who would sit with him in church.

In God's providence Richard's response was: "Well, I know Rita Kaye Mitchell. Why don't you call her?" So Ron did, not having a clue who Rita Kaye was. He just wanted a date for church.

"But wouldn't you know it," recalls Kaye. "It was love at first sight. We were a couple from that point on."

Ron and Kaye dated for two years while he was at Oklahoma Baptist University. Since Kaye was still in high school, Ron came home every weekend he could, which wasn't all that many, because he was starting to preach a lot. Preaching was becoming his passion.

An Unconventional Proposal

When the telephone company transferred Kaye's father from Fort Smith to Little Rock, it meant an additional 180 miles of travel for Ron to see her, so, he came up with this suggestion. "When I get a church, we'll get married!"

"I guess that was the proposal," says Kaye. "Anyway, that was fine with me, and it was only a few weekends later that he called to say he had been asked to pastor a little church up in Panola, Oklahoma. He was so excited."

"I got a salary! It's about $40 a week!" (pause) "But, do you think your dad will let us get married?"

Though Kaye was only sixteen, she knew there was a good chance her dad would agree because he had always said he was going to marry her off at sixteen.

"It just was one of the things my dad would say, and though I wasn't sure whether or not he really meant it, there was a chance. Well, when Ron asked him, he said: 'Sure, she's sixteen, isn't she'?"

Kaye's parents trusted Ron. They thought he could do no wrong because he was a minister. They grew to love and respect him.

"My mother said that the real reason they let me get married so young is that she and my father had eloped and they were afraid we might do the same. They wanted to give their blessing to our union. They didn't need to be concerned that we would run off, however, because I wouldn't have done that to my parents, and anyway, I was afraid of what my dad would have done!"

The Wedding

Ron and Kaye were married on December 21, 1956, in her parent's Little Rock home. Kaye's mother made her dress and the wedding cake. Her pastor, Dr. Branscum, officiated. Her sister, Julie, was her matron of honor; and her other sister, Vickie, was a bridesmaid. Jack Edmonds, Ron's college roommate who would precede Ron at both Panola Baptist and MacArthur Boulevard Baptist Church in Irving, Texas, was his best man. Parents and grandparents attended.

High School, College, and Instant Pastor's Wife

Though Kaye still had another semester of high school to finish, she had enough credits, except for one class, to graduate, so Kaye went on with Ron to OBU. She enrolled in classes there and took the high school class by correspondence at the same time. She didn't return for her high school graduation, however, because she was pregnant at the time, and she thought it could have interfered with the ceremony in the minds of those who wouldn't know she was married and already a pastor's wife.

Speaking of a pastor's wife, Kaye not only became a student at OBU immediately following the wedding, but she was an instant pastor's wife, a role that she never ceased to love everywhere Ron pastored.

She soon observed that, as far as she could tell, she, and her friend, Fran Schoeppey, were the only students on the OBU campus who wore maternity dresses. Ronnie was born October 13, 1957, in Shawnee, Oklahoma, while Ron and Kaye were still students.

Early Adventures

Every weekend she and Ron drove three hours to Panola Baptist Church in Southeast Oklahoma's Latimer County, where he preached and where they would stay at one of the member's homes. Special recollections from those days were the homes in which they stayed that had no indoor plumbing—only outhouses. It was hard with the baby, but the love of the people more than made up for this hardship.

Kaye recalls: "We had little money, but every weekend, as we were ready to head back to OBU, we would find our car loaded down with government supplies like cheese, rice, beans, powdered milk, etc. That's what kept us alive during those student and first pastorate days."

Another special memory Kaye has was where they lived while attending OBU. They initially moved into a little apartment until they were able to rent a duplex out by the airport. Since they had no furniture, they headed for a downtown Shawnee discount store where they bought three rooms of furniture for $99.

"We just took what they had in this little cheapo place. The furniture was red and black with gold flecks. The lamps were red, black, and gold; my rocker was red and black, and the bedroom furniture was blond Danish modern. What a sight!"

"To top it off, the $99 also included an old refrigerator, a stove, and a dinette set. Now that we had our three rooms of furniture, we were set for homemaking!" recalls Kaye.

The duplex itself was something else. It was painted royal blue, the windows were trimmed in day-glow pink, and inside that trim was a little silver stripe. "Since the duplex was at the end of the runway," Kaye says, "we were sure the planes used our royal blue duplex to line up their landing."

OBU Memories

One of Ron's good friends at Oklahoma Baptist University was John Bisagno.[2] Ronnie and Johnny, as they were known back then, began doing youth revivals together. John looks back on those special days.

Ron and I were roommates for a semester at Oklahoma Baptist University before he and Kaye married. I recall how he never stopped praying; morning, noon and night. I think he walked closer to God than almost any man I've ever known. He challenged me, he inspired me, he changed me. Just one problem as roommates—Ron was a neatnik.

We lived together and ate together almost every day at a boarding house. We liked the same food—corn on the cob, fried okra, beans, and cornbread—the good ole country stuff. Perhaps my most thrilling memory, however, happened in First Baptist Church of Bowlegs, Oklahoma, a little town about twenty miles from our campus in Shawnee, Oklahoma. It was so important in my life that, to this day, I have a hand-bill from that revival hanging on my office wall.

Ron was in his last semester at OBU and commuted every day to a youth revival in Bowlegs where I was leading the singing. Ron and I worked together in college as a youth revival team in about fifteen or twenty such campaigns, and this meeting was scheduled for Sunday through Sunday. Having just graduated in December, Uldine and I were staying in the home of Pastor Self while Ron and Kaye commuted from OBU.

Sunday morning the building was packed to overflowing, and a great number of young people made decisions for Christ. The same thing happened that night as well as Monday. On Tuesday, Uldine and I were having lunch with Pastor Jake and his wife, Galela, and as we were finishing our dessert, the phone rang. It was Ron. He was calling to say that he had a 104-degree fever and would not be able to make it back that night, and he didn't even think he could finish the revival. When he hung up the phone, Pastor Self looked at me in unbelief and said, "Johnny, what are we gonna do?" "Well," I said, "I've heard Ron's sermons several times, I'll just give it a shot if you want me to. We'll see if I can preach."

The next six nights, Tuesday through Sunday, were the first six sermons of my ministry. The crowds continued to fill the auditorium with numbers of young people making decisions for Christ. That was January 1954, and now, fifty-eight years later, I'm still preaching—about seven hundred revivals and seven thousand sermons later.

I have a framed copy of the poster[3] on my study wall announcing that Bowlegs Youth Revival that God used to redirect my life. ✳

[3]

Crossing the Red River

The Texas Longhorn-Oklahoma Sooners "Red River Rivalry," named after the Red River that separates the two states, is one that dates back to 1900. This, however, was the last thing on the minds of Ron and Kaye as they crossed the river in August 1958 on their way toward Fort Worth, Texas. Little Ronnie was not yet a year old, and study at Southwestern Baptist Theological Seminary lay ahead, as did a new life of ministry, a new home state, and challenges that neither Ron nor Kaye could have anticipated at this point in their lives.

Settling In

With Ron focusing on his seminary studies, Kaye needed to find a job in order for them to keep body and soul together. So, after committing this need to the Lord, Ron dropped her off on a street corner to job hunt. (Kaye had made several interview appointments.) With her personality, giftedness, and God's leading, she found work as a lawyer's secretary, and over subsequent years she also worked for Bell Helicopter and Pan American Petroleum.

Ron would eventually be called to pastor the Valley View Baptist Church in Farmers Branch. Kaye recalls being church pianist at both Panola Baptist in Oklahoma and at Valley View, and how grateful she was "when Valley View got an organist and a pianist. I never played in church again."

During this period, on July 4, 1961, Stephen, son number two, was born in Baylor Hospital, Dallas.

Put on the Shelf

Ron had been pastoring Valley View Baptist for two years when he began observing some of his friends who were in evangelism. To Ron, they seemed to be having it a lot easier than he was having it in the pastor-ate. They didn't have any administrative responsibilities; they didn't have to make hospital visits or do all the other things a pastor has to do—all they did was travel around and preach. So, seeing the grass looking a lot greener on that side of the fence and having now completed his seminary studies, he decided he'd go into evangelism.

With a wife, two children, and one (Kim) on the way, he resigned as pastor of Valley View and announced his intentions. As Kaye recalls, "This didn't exactly turn out the way he expected. He didn't receive more than three or four meeting invitations in eighteen months. It was like God slammed the door."

But Ron was not about to give up; so he decided God must want him to do some "tent-making" to supplement his evangelist income. He got a job making mops and brooms. For two days he worked at a service station. He tried selling *Great Books of the Western World.* After eighteen months of this, he realized he was not a broom and mop maker. He didn't do well at the service stations, and he sure wasn't a salesman. He finally told Kaye, "I can't do anything but preach."

Called to Be a Preacher

God used this to confirm to Ron that he was called to be a preacher, period. If he had succeeded at what he had been trying to do, no telling where he would have ended up. God had totally thwarted every attempt Ron made to make money his way. He finally realized that he was out of God's will, so he and Kaye went to their knees. They told God they would do anything He asked them to do. That was just what God was waiting to hear.

The next Sunday two churches called him to be their pastor. One was a wonderful church in Fort Smith, Arkansas, and the other was Munger Place Baptist in Dallas. The latter, though at one time one of Dallas's leading congregations, was now an older, transient church; but Ron, sensing that God was giving him a choice, chose Munger Place. These people were just what Ron and Kaye needed at this point in their lives. The Munger Place congregation knew how to love Ron and Kaye back into fellowship with the Lord.

Kimberly was born on June 15, 1965, at Brookhaven Hospital in Dallas. ✳

[4]

Another Crossing

❄ ❄ ❄

It was now eight years since Ron, Kaye, and little Ronnie had crossed the Red River on their way to a whole new adventure of schooling, family, and ministry. Many lessons had been learned, some easier than others, some that would help Ron and Kaye understand what Joshua and the nation of Israel had faced at the Jordan River.

Sermon: *Which Side of the Jordan?*[4]

The Primacy of Preparation

As a kid I loved it when the family talked about taking a trip, but of course, like most families we talked more than we traveled. But occasionally the hoped-for opportunity would come and we'd be off! And do you know how I knew we were actually going? When Mom made preparations to leave. Getting ready to go was the sign and sometimes the best part of the trip. It was also often the hardest and most important, occasionally taking more time than the trip itself.

It's the same in the spiritual realm. Preparation is an act of faith. If we really believe God is going to do something, we get ready for it. When we pray for rain, we ought to carry an umbrella. In my own spiritual pilgrimage I'm discovering that God gives me only what I'm prepared to receive.

After God spoke to Joshua, Israel's new leader, he was convinced that God would go with them and give them the land. He was so certain of this that he ordered the people to get ready for immediate action. God had spoken and preparation was the evidence of their faith.

> Then Joshua commanded the officers of the people, saying, "Pass through the midst of the camp and command the people, saying, 'Prepare provisions for yourselves, for within three days you are to cross this Jordan, to go in to possess the land which the LORD your God is giving you.'" "Consecrate yourselves, for tomorrow the LORD will do wonders among you." (Josh. 1:10–11; 3:5 NASB)

If it is a prepared people who possess the land, we need to examine the preparations we need to make for our own trip into Canaan.

A New Diet

God said, *"Prepare provisions."* Now, that's interesting. Here are as many as three million people about to cross a flooding river, and what is the first thing God asks them to prepare? A bridge? That would seem reasonable—boats, at least. But without a bridge or a boat in sight, God tells them to prepare, of all things, bread! Bread?

During the wilderness years God had provided manna to eat. It was there every day, and if you're stranded in the desert with no other food available, manna is all right, but it has been highly overrated in sermons and songs. Manna is a coarse, dry, hard bread. It is not steak and potatoes. It could sustain but not satisfy. The lesson for us here is that the diet that was adequate to maintain life in the desert would not nourish combat troops conquering and settling a new land.

Many Christians I know exist on a desert diet—just enough to keep them alive. But if you're intending to move into the land of promise and experience daily victory, you must upgrade your diet and increase your intake.

I'm referring to your personal worship time with the Lord in prayer and the Word. The strength and stamina you have in the conflicts of life will be determined by the quality of nourishment you are receiving from the Lord. Think on that.

A New Delay

This part of the preparation is even more surprising than the first. There would be a three-day delay. "But Lord, why a three-day delay? We've already been delayed forty years, and now we're ready to go!" But God said, "Wait!"

One thing I've learned about God is that He never hurries. The toughest thing I have to do is wait. I hate it. We Americans are accustomed to instant gratification—instant credit, instant comfort, instant coffee, instant this, instant that. Our cry is, "Lord, give me patience right now!" But the Lord never wastes time, and every delay plays an important role in His plan.

The Lord used this delay to accomplish three things. First, it was a time of **observation.** They were required to camp on the banks of the Jordan and watch the swollen river surge over its banks. "We're going to cross that?" they may have whispered to each other. "But there's no bridge, no boats! It can't be done."

That was exactly the point God was wanting to make. He was letting the impossibility of the task sink into their minds.

Has God ever dealt with you in this way? He has with me. Many times He has plopped me down beside the Jordan of my life and forced me to look at it, and the longer I looked the more impossible the situation became. I'd sit there wondering how God could love me and yet refuse to remove the problem. I could see no bridges, no boats, no way out of the situation. After awhile I would know that apart from God there was no solution. When we reach the point of being convinced that only God can get it all together, then we're ready to move.

Second, the delay was a time of ***confrontation.*** Forty years earlier twelve spies were sent out from Kadesh-barnea and returned with a faithless report that they blurted out in front of all the people. The people believed what they said, turned back, and forfeited the land. But, this time, Joshua sent out two spies who spent three days scouting the land, and their report, delivered directly to Joshua, declared that the Lord was surely with them and the inhabitants of the land were terrified of them. God used the waiting period to confirm His promise. The lesson here is that, during frustrating delays, if we keep our eyes and ears attuned to God, He'll give us evidence that He is capable of handling our situation.

Third, the delay was also a time of ***separation.*** While Moses was still living, the tribes of Reuben, Gad, and the half tribe of Manasseh became enchanted with the wilderness land along the Jordan River. It was fertile land and they wanted to settle there. In other words, they preferred the wilderness. Angrily, Moses said, "So, you want your brothers to fight alone for the land God has given us. Well, you can stay here if you want, but first you must go over and fight with the rest of us." They agreed to that, and in verses 12–18 of chapter 1, we find Joshua honoring the arrangement Moses had made with those tribes.

LESSONS FOR US

That incident is packed with spiritual instruction. God lets us choose the level of our spiritual Christian experience. He forces no one to enter into victory. If the wilderness is what you want, the wilderness is what you'll get. Make your choice.

Descendents of those tribes are found in every church. They do their share of fighting along with the rest of the congregation, but they always return to their spiritual wilderness, refusing to live in the victory Christ has won for them. They will help with the budget, the building program,

Vacation Bible School. They'll attend the Sunday morning worship service, but when twelve noon strikes, they tuck their Bibles under their arms and plod wearily back to a spiritually barren and defeated life.

The tragic conclusion to this story is that these tribes were the first to be conquered and carried into captivity by the Assyrians in later years. When the real testing comes, the first to falter and fail are those who choose to live on the wrong side of Jordan.

A New Dedication

After a period of waiting, Joshua told the people to **consecrate** themselves. The last time they had heard this command was when Moses had received the law from God (Exod. 19:10ff). He told the people to consecrate themselves so they would be ready to hear God's words upon his return. A lot had happened since then—many years of unfaithfulness. Now God was about to do something new, and they needed a **new dedication.**

Consecrate means "to purify, to sanctify, to make something holy by setting it apart for a special use." There is a sense in which God sanctifies us and another sense in which we sanctify ourselves. By virtue of our salvation we are all sanctified, set apart for God's special use. Every Christian is a saint, but the Bible also commands us to purify ourselves (1 John 3:3), to set ourselves apart from the filthiness of this world. This is a must for the life of victory.

In Our Public Lives

Our activities are to be pure. In Exodus 19 the people are required to wash their garments. That which was seen by all was to be spotless. We are to present to the world a clean life.

In Our Private Lives

Our affections are to be pure. In Exodus 19:15, we find God requiring a complete dedication in the most intimate area of our lives. When we get down to business with God, our private lives will be characterized by holiness.

I suggest we pray the last two verses of Psalm 139 (vv. 23–24). "Search me, O God, and know my heart; try me and know my anxious thoughts; and see if there be any hurtful (wicked) way in me, and lead me in the everlasting way."

Does your heart cry out for the "much more" of Christ? Are you ready to let Jesus, our Joshua, lead you into the Promised Land, or will you be satisfied with staying on the desert side of the Jordan?

Heirs to the Kingdom[5]

Those who cling to temporal treasures forfeit grace that could be theirs
Occupied with earthly trivia when they could be heaven's heirs;
Heirs and joint heirs to the kingdom, the provision God has made,
Rich in all His spiritual treasure for which Jesus Christ has paid.

Lord, forgive our shortened vision, seeing only what's at hand;
Blinded to those spiritual blessings waiting in the Promised Land.
Land where milk and honey's flowing, where the giants are our bread,
While we stay camped in the desert, doubting what the Lord has said.

Those mirages of the desert that seem like the real thing,
I've discovered all end up, Lord, in a heap of broken dreams.
I am sick and tired of wandering over barren desert sand,
With your help, I'm crossing Jordan into Canaan's Promised Land!

PART TWO

MacArthur Days
(1966–1975)

❊ ❊ ❊

Pay careful attention to yourselves and to all the flock, in which the Holy Spirit has made you overseers, to care for the church of God which he obtained with his own blood.

—ACTS 20:28 (ESV)

What the church needs today is not more or better machinery, new or more novel methods, but men whom the Holy Ghost can use—men, mighty in prayer. The Holy Ghost does not flow through methods, but through men. He does not come on machinery, but on men. He does not anoint plans, but men—men of prayer.

—E. M. BOUNDS (POWER THROUGH PRAYER)

Prelude

❃ ❃ ❃

The next nine years would prove to be among the most reward-
ing and exciting of Ron's and Kaye's lives. Past experiences and lessons
learned had prepared them for what God was about to do. Those had
been years of character and ministry shaping, getting them ready for this
next chapter in God's providence.

The MacArthur Boulevard Baptist Church (MBBC) period can be
divided into two not quite equal parts.

1. The Early Years: Pre-Revival (September 1966 to April 1970). The
"early years" were good ones. They were marked by a lot of activity and
steady growth, much of it attributable to busy, hardworking church members in Irving, Texas, a city in the Dallas/Fort Worth Metroplex that was
not just growing but was bursting at the seams.

2. The Latter Years: Revival (April 1970 to August 1975). After
almost four years of seeing what would be encouraging to any pastor and
congregation, Ron, and MBBC, were to witness God do what could only
be explained as being His doing. God came! ❃

[5]

A Providential Move

Ron had been pastoring Munger Place Baptist Church in Dallas for eighteen months when he was contacted by Jack Schoeppey, associate pastor of MacArthur Boulevard Baptist Church in Irving, Texas. Their senior pastor, Jack Edmonds, had just resigned, and Schoeppey, looking for a supply preacher for the next Sunday, gave Ron a call, little realizing what God was about to set in motion.

He and Ron were friends from their college days, but in addition to that, Dr. J. P. McBeth, upon hearing of the resignation of Jack Edmunds, had already written a letter to the pulpit committee, recommending Ron.

J. P. McBeth, Ph.D.
Author, Expositor, Evangelist

July 26, 1966
Dear Brethren,

One of your good members asked me to recommend a choice pastor. The man I ask you to consider is Rev. Ronnie Dunn, who is now pastoring Munger Place Baptist in Dallas.

In the last nineteen years I have conducted more than seven hundred revivals. Bro. Dunn is one of the half dozen choice young preachers I have met. He is about twenty-eight or thirty years of age, a college and seminary graduate. He has a talented wife and three small children.

He is a strong preacher, has a delightful personality and is devoted to his work. He studies and knows things. He is my one recommendation to you for a pastor.

Yours in Him,
J. P. McBeth

When Jack Schoeppey phoned to ask Ron to fill the pulpit that next Sunday, Ron told him that he was on vacation and that he and Kaye planned to go to First Baptist Church, Dallas, to hear Dr. W. A. Criswell preach. After a bit of persuading, however, Ron agreed to change his and Kaye's plans. The rest is history because, after hearing Ron preach, the pastor search committee decided they needed to look no further, even though they had barely begun. When this was announced, a few members expressed concern about Ron's age. He seemed a bit young to them. They felt they needed someone more mature. When Dr. McBeth heard this, he told them that extending a call to Ron would mean they'd be getting a pastor who was already a great Bible teacher yet young enough to have years to mature ahead.

The Business Meeting

Jack Schoeppey recalls the special business meeting that took place to discuss extending a call to this young preacher:

"What a delight it was to moderate that meeting. It was difficult, however, to have any meaningful discussion from the floor, as people were literally yelling, 'Let's vote.' 'Call for the question.' I purposely let it go on for a while, enjoying every moment."

In the meantime, Ron and Kaye, waiting in another part of the building for the vote result, had begun to think that, since it was taking so long, there must be serious resistance to extending him the call. They had even thought of just slipping out. Not so. Ron was called, and so began a bonding between pastor and people that would take them over the highest peaks and through the lowest of valleys in the years to come.

Testimony: Shirley Calvert, MBBC Member and Church Historian

I've been a member of MBBC since 1960. When the church was discussing whether to extend a call to Ron, I remember asking, "Does he preach against specific sins?" Well, God took me from that kind of spiritual immaturity to the realization that I had been sitting by the pool, dabbing my feet in the water. Though I had been a Christian for many years, Ron led me into a deeper awareness of all that I have in Jesus. It not only impacted me personally, but my four children, twelve grandchildren, and ten great-grandchildren; all are contributing to the kingdom.

MacArthur Boulevard Baptist Church
2616 N. MacArthur Boulevard
Irving, Texas 75062

September 29, 1966
Dear Church Member:

This Sunday will be a significant day in my life, for it will be my first Sunday as your pastor. I thank God daily for allowing me to be pastor of this great church. Already the warmth and friendliness of the people have made me feel more than welcome.

I think the word which best describes a New Testament church is FELLOWSHIP—a mutual sharing of a common life. Our heavenly Father shares with us His life, and we share with one another our lives—our pain and prosperity, our trials and triumphs, our sorrows and satisfactions. In such a church joy is doubled and sorrow is halved. I pray that God will bless us with this kind of fellowship.

As I come to MacArthur Blvd., it's my prayer that God will grant me the spiritual wisdom to minister effectively to each member. I hope that you will consider me your interested friend and will call on me for any need. But more than this, I covet your prayers, for we are coworkers together with God in this ministry.

Feel free to call upon me at any time. I'm as near as your telephone. God bless you as we begin our work together this Sunday.

Your Pastor,
Ronald L. Dunn

A View from the Inside

Ron inherited Joanne Gardner as his secretary when he was called to pastor MacArthur Boulevard on October 1, 1966.

"They seemed so young at the time," recalls Joanne. "Kaye was not yet thirty. At the beginning I wasn't sure I even wanted him to be my pastor. That shows you a good bit about my spiritual condition at the time."

Joanne ended up working with Ron for thirty-five years, going from the role of church secretary to his assistant when he moved on to an itinerant ministry and formed LifeStyle Ministries. She watched him live what he preached, and it changed her life forever. Hers is a unique view from the inside.

Recollections by Joanne Gardner

When Ron came to pastor MacArthur Boulevard, one of the first things I observed was the relationship he and Kaye had with each other. It was a picture of the fifth chapter of Ephesians that talks about the relationship between husbands and wives and how husbands are to love their wives even as Christ loved the church and gave Himself for her. That was not what I had always observed in pastors.

Preacher

When you say "Ron Dunn," you think *preacher*. And what an education it was to watch him prepare sermons. The discipline of his study habits, and the way he loved to study the Word of God, was something to behold. His study time was carefully guarded. He'd lock himself in his study from 8:30 to noon every weekday morning, giving me implicit instructions that there were to be no interruptions. This endeared him to many people.

There was one exception, however, for which I could buzz him, and that was if Kaye needed to talk with him. What a beautiful picture of love that, as important as his study time was, he was always available to Kaye. And the picture became even more beautiful when she said to me one day, "I know Ron has told you to always put me through, but I don't want to interrupt him when he's studying." How I saw Ron treat Kaye taught me more about loving your wife as Christ loved the church than all the sermons he could have preached on that subject.

More than a Hired Hand

Another thing different about this new pastor that would endear him to me and my family through all the years was the way he treated those who worked for him. This became evident from the moment MBBC voted to call him as their pastor.

I was the church clerk the night we took the vote, and I wasn't sure I wanted him to come, but I didn't have to vote because I was taking notes of the meeting in shorthand. When the vote was taken and he was told of the call, he and Kaye asked me to show him his office. When we had finished and were in the process of leaving, Kim, who was just a toddler, ran back into the office. Ron went after her, and as he picked Kim up, he walked over to me and said, "Joanne, I'm looking forward to working with you."

"With me?" Did I hear correctly? *Oh my goodness,* I thought. *I don't believe this man.* I told him later what this meant to me. "Oh yes," he said with a twinkle in his eye. "I've gotten more mileage out of that over the years." At that point God began a friendship that I don't have the words to describe.

A Special Memory

When our son-in-law, Dan, and our daughter, Debra, were preparing to go as missionaries to Hong Kong, I cried for months. Ron noticed this and one day he said: "When Dan and Debra have been in Hong Kong a year, I will buy you a ticket to go to see them."

I said, "But Ron, I couldn't go without Don."

"OK, I'll buy two tickets."

"But Ron, how are we going to leave Greg behind?"

"OK. Three tickets." He bought us three round-trip tickets to Hong Kong.

Ron and Kaye drove us to the airport in the second worst ice storm in Dallas history and, of course, met us when we returned. That's the kind of people they were.

The love that he and Kaye showered on me and my family was unbelievable. I wish he had written a book on how to treat your "help." His family is as dear to me as family can be. It was, and continues to be, one of my greatest privileges to be associated with the ongoing ministry of Ron Dunn. ❋

[7]

A Divine Encounter

※ ※ ※

J. Edwin Orr described revival as "that strange and sovereign work of God in which He visits His own people, restoring, reanimating, and releasing them into the fullness of His blessing. It is a work of God in the church, and among individual believers, resulting in an unusual harvest of souls."

The MacArthur Boulevard revival of the 1970s began in its own unique way. Ron had, almost inadvertently, agreed to preach an eight-day meeting at Central Baptist Church in Aurora, Colorado, a suburb of Denver. This meant he would be out of his own pulpit for two consecutive Sundays, something he had never done before.

Unbeknown to Ron at the time, however, during those eight days he was going to have an encounter with God that would forever change his life and ministry.

Never the Same Again

He began calling the MBBC office every day. The whole staff hung on the phone listening to what he had to say. They were all so excited.

They couldn't wait for him to get back—everyone, that is, except Joanne, Ron's secretary.

"Personally," Joanne Gardner recalls, "I wasn't too sure about what he was talking about. I could tell that something was happening to him, but I didn't understand it. I had never known anyone to talk about the Lord the way he was talking, and I had been working in that church office for eleven years.

"I was hearing phrases like *'abandoning yourself to the Lordship of Christ.'* I was hearing so many things I had not heard before." But when our pastor returned, it was evident to us all that something had happened. He did not so much try to explain it as live it. I watched him lovingly lead a congregation of believers into a closer walk with the Lord—lead us to experience continuous revival from that time to when he resigned the pastorate of MBBC in 1975."

Back Home

Ron returned from that Colorado encounter with a holy boldness that those who knew him had seldom, if ever, seen. He returned exceedingly burdened over the spiritual climate of MacArthur. During the previous six to nine months he had observed a falling away from their first love.

As he stepped to the pulpit that Wednesday night in April 1970, the people who had gathered in the sanctuary were not looking at the same pastor who had flown to Denver twelve days before; they were looking at a man who had returned, literally and figuratively, from the mountaintop where he had met God.

Sermon: *From Your Pastor's Heart: A Watershed Moment*

I want to talk to you tonight about the revival at Central Baptist in Aurora, Colorado, a suburb of Denver. I feel I need to do this because I know many of you were praying for me.

As part of the revival preparation of this church that runs about five hundred on a good Sunday, I was asked to speak at a Saturday evening *Men's Victory Prayer Meeting.* One hundred men were there that night. Think of that. One hundred men in a church whose top attendance is five hundred. When I told this to one of our deacons, he said, "Here at MacArthur, we probably couldn't get a hundred men out for the Second Coming!"

The pastor told me that he was expecting one hundred to be saved and join the church that week. We ended up with ninety-one. Among the converts were narcotic users, runaway young people, folk from all walks of life. Interestingly, however, after Thursday evening we stopped keeping track of what was happening. Numbers became unimportant. We talked very little about what was happening. The important thing was that God was there. The pastor was afraid that we'd touch God's glory and think that we were doing something if we talked too much about what God was doing. It was like walking on eggs. We didn't want to say or do anything that would cause the Lord to be grieved.

We found ourselves being careful about our personal lives, what we said, how we responded to people, how we acted in the restaurants. It was an awesome feeling to be so aware that we could grieve the Holy Spirit.

I realized that I was where God was doing something that couldn't be explained. There were overflow crowds every night. We had weekday morning services and never had less than three people saved in every one of those. Morning and night they came, through sleet and freezing weather. Last Sunday morning was the most exhausting time I've ever had in my ministry because the presence of the Lord was so strong. I turned around as the choir was singing the special, and most of the choir members were weeping.

In addition to the lost being saved, all across that congregation people were getting right with one another, confessing wrong attitudes they had had toward their brothers and sisters. The altar calls sometimes lasted until 10:30 at night as folk got things right with God and one another. There were some who had been at odds with the pastor, and they came to be restored. There was no coaxing of folk to do anything other than to listen to what God was saying and to respond. There was a spirit of unquestioning obedience to whatever God was saying.

The pastor was concerned over the number of his church members who were lost. He had made a list of those he suspected were not born again, and before the week was over every one of them was saved. As we were standing together on the platform, I'd hear him say, "There's one of them. There's another. There's the head of the baptismal committee. Look, there he is, getting saved!"

It's hard for me to get across to you what happened. I've been preaching since I was fifteen, but last week I discovered that the Holy Spirit can teach you more in five seconds than what you've learned in twenty years. Now, let me get personal and tell you what happened to me.

It was Tuesday night, and I didn't feel I had really preached well, but when I got to the end of the sermon, it was like I heard God say, "You just get out of the way, and I'll show you what I can do." I then actually backed up against the choir rail and watched as twenty-eight people came to the altar to be saved. As the pastor and other staff members were talking with each one who had come forward, I heard someone behind me say: "You've never totally surrendered to the lordship of Christ. Jesus has never been your Lord." I looked around to see who was talking. I thought it must be some backslider standing next to me that someone was talking to. But there was nobody there—just me.

I bowed my head and said: "Jesus is my Lord." Then I heard the voice say, "Yes—off and on." Now, if anyone had told me in the past that I had not surrendered to the lordship of Christ, I would have told them they were nuts. That's what I mean by saying that the Holy Spirit can teach you in five seconds what a lifetime cannot.

"No," said the voice. "You have never really, honestly, once and for all surrendered everything to God—your home life, your work life, what you eat, what you drink, what you . . . everything to the constant lordship of Christ." I said: "Lord, I have to think about that."

You see, that revival did more for me, your pastor, than it did for that church. Sunday night, when they gave me the envelope with the love offering in it, I told them that I felt I should be giving them a love offering rather than them giving me one.

It's now been but a few days since I've been back home, and the only way I can explain what has happened is that it's like I've just gotten saved all over again. Besides being set free from the anxieties, inhibitions, problems, those things that we've all dealt with, the greatest thing that has happened to me is knowing that Jesus is now absolute Lord. I have experienced a liberty to do some things that I've never been able to do before, and I'm now able to overcome some things I've never been able to overcome before.

Because I Love You and This Church

One thing that God has made possible for me to do is to love some people in this church I've never been able to love before. The love that God can give is a love that loves in spite of the mistakes we see in each other. I can say tonight that there's not a member in this church that I don't love.

But then I began to be aware of some things that were happening that I'd not considered before. I realized that the reason the Lord was working like He was in Colorado was because of the hearts of the people who were responding to Him. God showed me that I had not brought the revival. The song leader had not brought the revival. The pastor had not brought the revival; it was the response in the hearts of the people. I also realized that the kind of revival I was witnessing can't happen in every church. Hearts have to be prepared.

There is a core of people in the church in Aurora who have turned everything over to the Lord, and as I stood there that Tuesday night, watching the people respond to the Spirit of God, without having been "begged" to come, I thought to myself, *This is just like MacArthur.* I had no sooner had that thought than I heard an inner voice say, "No, this is not what MacArthur is; it is what it used to be."

Never Satisfied Again

As I flew back to Texas on Monday, I knew that I could never be satisfied to return to the same old thing that we've been experiencing for the last six to nine months here at MacArthur—not with thousands and thousands of people lost out there, and nobody telling them about Jesus. Last week I was reminded of what MacArthur used to be, and because of what I saw, I want to talk to you tonight as pastor to people. I want to talk to you as friend to friend.

When I came here four years ago, I felt that this was the greatest church I'd ever been in. The spirit, the fellowship, the witness, the presence of the Lord in the services, people getting saved every week—it was uncanny. But it hasn't been that way for over half a year.

You know, when you take your eyes off the main thing, of glorifying Christ and winning souls, you begin to see all the little imperfections in each other. We've begun quarreling over little things. We've been nitpicking. The harmony, the unity, the fellowship has been missing from our services. I can tell it when I preach. I can tell it when I give the invitation. I can see in your faces that something is wrong.

Someone calls the office and says, "I hear that . . ." Someone else says, "I've heard that you've . . ." Complaining, constant sowing of doubts, and if you don't think these things won't hurt the power of God in a church, you don't know anything about my Lord. What I'm saying to you is that there is no one in this church, from the pastor on down to the newest member, who is more important than having the Lord's power and blessing in our midst. And we're not going to have that as long as there is disunity over things that do not count.

If there is anyone in this church who does not want to live in harmony with the body, and who doesn't want to get on with the assignment God has given us, then I think it's time for you to move on. I can say that to you tonight because I love you. I would not have been able to say that a week ago. I'm telling you this because it costs too much to lose the presence of God, while it costs but a six-cent stamp for us to move your letter.

The Lord is jealous for this church, and I am jealous for it. I want MacArthur to get to the place when it will not tolerate all the littleness that has been going on. And I want to remind you that it is not just wrong to be talking like some of you have, but it is just as wrong to be listening to that kind of talk. If someone complains to you about someone else, tell them to go to that person and get it straightened out. We've taken our eyes off the main thing, of winning souls to Christ, and we've suffered for it. So I invite you to get with it or find a place where you'll be happy.

God has some great people in this church, but folk, I refuse to go on in the same way we've been going. Too many people are dying tonight who have never heard the plan of salvation. God showed me something last week that He'd never shown me before. He showed me that it was a sin for me to spend my time running here and there, trying to get this and that patched up, worrying myself to sleep at night over this person being upset or that person being angry, while millions of people out yonder are without hope.

If you don't think that God can remove His candlestick from MacArthur, you don't know my Lord. I believe a main reason God allowed me to experience what I did last week in Colorado was to show me that I've been too easy and gentle. I've not wanted to confront those of you who have been sowing discord in the body. But now, I tell you, the only thing that means anything to me tonight is that Jesus be Lord of my life, and whatever He tells me to say, I'm going to say it.

The other thing that means more to me than anything is that Jesus be Lord of this church, and if you get in the way of Him being Lord of MacArthur Boulevard Baptist Church, you're unwelcome. If you're not willing to meld your heart with us and wholeheartedly get behind the mission of this church, you know what I'm asking you to do.

And, by the way—I've never asked for anyone in this church to agree with me 100 percent on everything I do. That would be ridiculous. I'm not demanding head-unity, but I am asking for heart-unity. Do you understand what I'm saying? Do you hear the spirit in which I'm saying it? I pray that you do. I want God to be able to bless this church, but we're going to have to get "blessable." That's all I want, and I'm jealous of that. I want us to be intolerant of anything or anybody that threatens the harmony and fellowship of our body. Let's pray.

Having prayed, Ron turned off his microphone. Nothing more needed to be said. He didn't know how his people would respond. He didn't have to wait long. Before the lights were extinguished two hours later, everyone, every family, with one exception, who were known by the staff to be causing dissension, made their way to the pastor to ask his forgiveness and to pledge their support. The family that didn't respond went underground and caused no further problems.

What would become known as the MacArthur Boulevard Revival was on its way. There were times over the next four plus years that people would report sensing God's presence when they drove onto the church parking lot. The people had gotten their hearts right with God and with each other; they had become blessable, and God was pleased to pour out His Spirit on a blessable people. ❋

[8]

Revival Years: A Place Shaken (1970–1975)

That Wednesday night service proved to be a turning point in the life of MacArthur Boulevard Baptist Church. They were soon to experience what Arthur Wallis described revival to be in his book, *In the Day of Thy Power*: "Revival is God revealing Himself to man in awe-full holiness and irresistible power. It is such a manifest working of God that human personalities are overshadowed and human programs abandoned. It is man retiring into the background because God has taken the field. It is the Lord making bare His holy arm and working in extraordinary power on saint and sinner."[6]

From Ron's Journal

May 6–12, 1971: One Year into the Revival

We're in the midst of our Crusade. So far, through Wednesday night, 340 people have made professions of faith. And God has met and exceeded our budget needs.

May 14

The crusade closed Sunday night with a total of 882 making professions of faith, many to whom we had been witnessing and praying for, for over a year!

September—Revival of Soul Winners

A thrilling thing happened this evening. I was working later than usual at the office when Brenda Graham, one of our teenagers, called to ask if she could bring a girl by who wanted to be saved. While shopping at Skaggs with her mother, Brenda had approached this girl, whom she had never seen before, and began witnessing to her. This nineteen-year-old turned out to be on a national scholarship at SMU and had no money. She had spent the last four nights walking the streets because she had nowhere to stay.

When they arrived in my office, this young lady, Linda Young, was obviously ready to be saved. As I was explaining that Jesus paid for her sins on the cross, she said:

"But, that's not fair!"

"I know it," I said. "That's love."

Huge tears filled her eyes as she said, "Wow!" The Grahams are going to give her a place to stay. She is coming this Sunday to make her decision public.

At our last prayer meeting, three of our members stood to share how God had used them to lead someone to Christ. David Haddon, a student at the University of Dallas, a Catholic school, brought Mr. Yoo with him, a Korean whom he had led to Christ the night before. Praise God! He is continuing to raise up soul winners at MBBC.

1972: A New Year Begins

January 3—I believe last Sunday was prophetic of what God has in store for MBBC in 1972. Echoing the feelings of many, I believe last

Sunday's services were two of the most Spirit-filled meetings I've ever been in. Praise God for His presence and power.

The Spirit of revival continues to surge among us. It's thrilling to see God working in the lives of so many MBBCers. And the great thing about it is that He has just begun to do what He wants to do in our body. Paul said it best: "Now glory be to God who by his mighty power at work within us is able to do far more than we would ever dare to ask or even dream of—infinitely beyond our highest prayers, desires, thoughts, or hopes" (Eph. 3:20 TLB).

March 6

Well, we don't usually have packed-out services until spring. January and February are not big attendance months. Normally a flu epidemic means low attendance. But the supernatural is becoming the natural around here. The crowds for our worship services have been unbelievable— no room to park, dozens standing while extra chairs are brought in, and Sunday evening services are about as large as in the morning. People are being saved in every service, and our offerings are consistently over the budget. The Spirit of God is being poured out without measure!

A leader in our denomination recently asked me, "What are you doing? What kind of program are you using?" I told him that we don't have a program. I guess if God stops blessing us we'll have to come up with one, but until then we'll just do what comes supernaturally.

I'm not being presumptuous. God is sovereign, and He can turn it off as easily as He has turned it on. Sometimes we say, "God gets the glory," while we take the credit. But to God goes both the glory and the credit. God has been gracious to us, and we humbly bow before Him in worship and praise for visiting us with power and blessing.

TESTIMONY: NELSON MCKINNEY—MBBC DEACON

God's presence was so real, not just on Sunday but in all of the services during the revival, in those days that you didn't want to miss any of them. I recall having to be in New York City for a three-day business meeting and not wanting to miss the Wednesday night service, so I flew home that afternoon, made it to the church on time, then headed back to the airport for the red-eye flight to New York in order to meet my Thursday commitment.

Eleven different ministries from as far away as California and Colorado moved their headquarters to the DFW area just to be in on what God was doing at MacArthur Boulevard. Many of the students from seminaries other than Southern Baptist schools attended regularly. The men who started the Eastern European Seminary behind the Iron Curtain grew up under Ron's preaching.

So many young men were surrendering to the ministry during those days of revival that I took it upon myself to meet with some of them to see if I could talk them out of it. I wanted to make sure they were being called by the Holy Spirit, not out of emotion or some other influence. We still had over seventy men surrender to the ministry.

People who hadn't been to church in years would be driving by the church and testified that they couldn't keep their car from turning into the parking lot. They'd come in and get saved. Service after service, for forty-eight plus months; there was no explanation for what was happening other than the sovereign work of a great God.

TESTIMONY: BARBARA (MRS. NELSON) MCKINNEY—MBBC MEMBER

I lived through the best of the Ron Dunn era. God changed my life through Ron. One time he preached a message that freed me from something that had plagued me from the time I was saved as a child. I can't get up at 5:00 a.m. to pray and read the Word. Ron assured me that God wanted to see me when I was at my best, when I could pray coherently, when I could understand what He was saying to me through His Word, and that the time of day was not what was most significant. What was most significant was that I daily spend time alone with the Lord.

I eventually became a regional representative for the Southern Baptists of Texas and have traveled all over the State. I've found that, whenever I have taught a breakout session at any of our conferences, invariably, when they've advertised that I'm from MBBC, I get the largest attendance because people want to know about my association with Ron and Kaye and how Ron's ministry impacted my life.

MacArthur Boulevard Baptist Church
2616 MacArthur Boulevard
Irving, Texas, 75062

April, 1972
Dear MacArthur Blvd. Members

A PLACE SHAKEN

That's what happened to MBBC two years ago. This Sunday is the second anniversary of revival in our church. On the last Sunday in April 1970, God moved into our midst with a power that can only be described as earthquake power—a power that transformed the countenance and composure of MBBC.

Shaken with an overwhelming awareness of God's presence: *Without a doubt the greatest thing that's happened is this: Jesus has become real; God is no longer something we pray at, but a Father we pray to. The actuality of the indwelling Spirit has become a reality. Milkshake religion has become an earthquake experience.*

Shaken with unbroken unity and harmony: *"One heart and one soul"—the fiery heart of the Holy Spirit melted differences and welded hearts together in a loving fellowship that grows sweeter each time we meet to worship.*

Shaken with supernatural power for living and witnessing: *God has consistently done "exceeding abundantly above all that we ask or think." We've seen* *things happen that two years ago we would have never believed. People who never witnessed before (who never had the course!) found themselves gossiping about Jesus wherever they were. Sinful habits and attitudes have been conquered through the power of the Holy Spirit. We've come to know that if it isn't supernatural, it's superficial.*

Shaken with overflowing liberality: *Until Revival came, MBBC had never met a budget in its history! Then the Holy Spirit revealed a fixed law of heaven: when a man's lordship is right, his stewardship will be right! The issue isn't "Will you tithe?" but "Is Jesus Lord?" With no budget drives or pledge campaigns of any sort, we have met our budget and finished the year with no unpaid bills and have tripled our giving to world missions.*

Shaken with a knowledge that is God's doing: *What has happened in the past two years, the increased growth in every single area of church life, is not, I repeat, is not the result of hard work, clever programs, keen administration, intelligent leadership, etc. It is the result of God's Spirit breathing new life into these old bones. And nobody knows this better than this pastor. God forbid that we should ever glory in any of these things.* ***To God be the glory, great things He has done!***

Your Pastor,
Ron Dunn

TESTIMONY: JACK SCHOEPPEY—MBBC STAFF MEMBER

One of the main characteristics of the revival was the conviction and confession of sin. When the invitations were extended, in both morning and evening services, the aisles would immediately be full, and the ministerial staff would be waiting at the front of each aisle to counsel people. It was not unusual to have two hundred or more decisions in each service.

Folk of other denominations told us how, when just driving by the church, they sensed something was happening. People stopped and came in to inquire what caused them to feel strangely drawn to the church. ❊

[9]

The Birth of a Ministry

June 1972 saw the launching of MBBC's Intercessory Prayer Ministry. Though the church had been involved in intercessory home groups for several years, this was the beginning of an around-the-clock work of prayer.

Ron Dunn wrote: "After last Sunday night's service over two hundred intercessors knelt at the altar as we asked God to sanctify and anoint the Intercessory Prayer Ministry. What a thrilling night—heaven rejoicing and hell trembling."

Ron alerted the church to expect two things—God's blessing and Satan's opposition. "But praise the Lord," he added, "we can overcome him by the blood of the Lamb and the word of our testimony!"

The MacArthur Boulevard Baptist Church revival was one of those memorial stones that even today sits as a measuring stick for what God can do.

MBBC Members Remember

TESTIMONY: DON AND ANITA STANCOFF—MBBC DEACON
AND WIFE

Though it's been more than thirty-five years, what remains most indelibly in my mind is the sense of God's presence during those days. It was atmospheric. God was there. In every service, whatever was happening, people came expecting to meet God. And it was not just to hear Ron preach, as great as that was.

People would testify to sensing the presence of God, even on the parking lot. Visitors would tell us that the moment they walked in the church they knew something was different. As I look back, I've wondered if that was not a little example, a glimpse of what God has in store for us in heaven.

This changed the lives of our church members. It was not unusual to see, in every service, people going to each other, to pray together, to ask forgiveness, to affirm one another. It didn't matter when in the week the service was. I recall one Saturday when we had gathered that people began to flood the altar, weeping, as a young lady sang a special. Lives were changed that day. Across the auditorium a hush fell as we bowed in God's presence.

A lasting remembrance was the emphasis Ron placed on intercessory prayer. I guess we were one of the first Southern Baptist churches to build a chapel exclusively for prayer. But in addition to this, unplanned prayer groups would spring up all over the church. Sometimes folk would have gathered for a particular purpose but before they knew it, their gathering had turned into a prayer meeting. We recall how you didn't want to walk into the church with known sin in your life for fear of quenching the Holy Spirit.

Another remembrance is how the altar calls would last for at least forty-five minutes. No one tried to make anyone do that. None of it was worked up. Folks just continued responding to the Lord.

TESTIMONY: ED AND MARIAN HARRIS, MBBC DEACON AND WIFE

Marian and I had just moved to Irving, and we were looking for a church home. We attended a city-wide crusade being held in the high school football stadium. Angel Martinez was the evangelist, and at the offering time a young man by the name of Ron Dunn was asked to pray. That was the first time we had heard or seen Ron. After hearing him pray, we both said that we needed to find out where his church was. That was the beginning of our relationship with Ron and MBBC.

Ron became a dear friend. I was ordained as a deacon during those years. Our three children were saved at MBBC, and though we knew he had made the right decision, it was a sad day when God called him to a wider ministry. He went from primarily teaching us at MBBC to preaching and impacting thousands he would never have touched if he had stayed with us.

During his itinerant days, I was privileged to occasionally help him out with his travel by flying him to some of his engagements. Those were special times of fellowship, both serious and fun.

One time I drove over to Longview to drive him home after a speaking engagement. No sooner had he gotten in the car than he took off his shoes, his coat and tie, and said, "Let's stop at What-a-Burger." We did. He got a big Coke, and was set for the ride home! On the way I said, "That was a great sermon you preached tonight, but I've heard it before." He said: "I know you did. That's why I preached it again. I thought this time it might have some effect on you." Wonderful memories.

TESTIMONY: JOANNE GARDNER—PASTOR'S SECRETARY

God was also moving in people's pocketbooks, and it wasn't just in the offerings and budget area. I had the hardest time keeping up with people bringing me cash they wanted me to give to someone in need but didn't want them to know who gave it. This went on for over four years, and I can't help believe that what the church experienced was in large part because God knew He could trust Ron, who in the midst of much heartache, still trusted and loved the Lord.

Caution

The moment God begins to do something unusual, observers want to know the "whys" and "hows." They are often not satisfied with the kind of answer Ron gave to that Baptist leader who asked what new program Ron had initiated that was resulting in the kind of growth and excitement MacArthur Boulevard was experiencing.

"We haven't made any program changes. I'm preaching the Word, we're getting our hearts right with God, we're doing a lot of praying, and we're watching God do His sovereign work."

"Yes, but . . ."

"No, that's it!"

Sovereign—Not Man-made

In Ron's study of past awakenings and in his own exposure to revival movements in his lifetime, he had observed that the Spirit of revival can be quickly quenched by man's publicity and promotion. Only God knows how many movements of His Spirit have ended up being short-lived because of this—the feeling that the work of God would benefit from man's creativity—and in so doing the focus turned from God to man.

Ron, on the other hand, talked little about what was happening. If you heard about it, it was from the testimony of someone whose life had been changed. The news spread by the word of their testimony, not by newspaper ads, nor by Ron's hitting the road as a pastor-reporter. He resisted writing articles in religious periodicals, and God honored a pastor's and a church's humility with a revival that lasted more than four years.

Ron also knew of the danger inherent in man's attempt to clone the work of God—to reduce it to the explainable, to a formula. Such efforts are always destined to fail because you cannot clone or package a sovereign work of grace.

Pattern Versus Principle

Someone has explained how often when God works in remarkable ways we try to reduce what He has done to a pattern or a formula we can reproduce. There is value in learning from movements of God, but to imitate them will be to make them a human operation. **It is always easier to copy a pattern than to learn a principle.** The question is not so much, "What is God doing?" as it is, "Why is He doing it?" The latter question is more likely to lead us to the principle, the reason, that underlies why God is blessing us in the way He is.

Jesus' ministry was not carried out according to patterns. When He healed, sometimes He spoke, sometimes He touched, and sometimes He spat! The pattern changed, but the principle remained constant. The Son could do nothing by Himself; He could do only what He saw His Father doing.

And the principle behind God's blessing for us is nothing less than a person, the Lord Jesus Christ. Just as the Son kept His eyes on the Father, so are we to keep our eyes on the Son. ✳

[10]

When the Church Prays

TESTIMONY: D. L. LOWRY—FORMER PASTOR, FIRST BAPTIST, LUBBOCK, TEXAS

Though I was not a part of the MacArthur revival, I was very much aware of it because I was pastoring another church in the Metroplex at that time. What was happening at MBBC gave encouragement to a lot of us to hope that God might do the same thing where we were.

Many things initiated at MacArthur were replicated in other churches around the country. When we decided to begin an Intercessory Prayer Ministry at First Baptist, Lubbock, Texas, where I was pastor, I told the man who was working with me on it to get in touch with the leaders at MBBC because they were doing it better than anyone else I knew. The sparks of the MacArthur revival blew across the land and impacted hundreds, if not thousands of churches.

MacArthur was a sweet, loving church before the revival, but as prayer became increasingly important, we began to see change in every area.

We had our share of fellowships. In fact there seemed to be a fellowship every time you turned around. But as God was moving, almost without exception, the fellowships turned into prayer meetings. And it wasn't long before we were seeing tangible evidence that God was hearing and answering our prayers. Specific answers to prayer were faith builders for the whole church.

But, right in the middle of all the excitement over seeing specific answers to prayer, there was an incident that showed how quick and how easy it is to lose focus right in the middle of God's activity. Ron tells the story.

What a Church! What a Pancake!

Our youth choir was invited to participate in a citywide evangelistic crusade in Salt Lake City. They were to sing in malls and parks during the day and crusade services each evening. Everyone was excited, but we had a $4,000 problem. That's what it was going to cost to send them.

Someone suggested that we raise the money, and in a moment of sublime unconsciousness, I agreed to let the young people stage a pancake breakfast. I've always hated things like that—you know, buy a pancake and lend a hand to a God who has fallen on hard times—that kind of stuff. I'll never forget the sight that greeted me that fateful Saturday morning.

Our church was located next to a Whataburger, and on our church marquee, for all to see, I read: *What-a-Church! What-a-Pancake!* And there they were, our young people, standing in the middle of the busy street, wearing Whataburger chef hats on their heads, and hanging around their necks were placards, hawking pancakes. I parked my car and, with my head down, looking neither to the right or to the left, I stepped quickly into the church. And there, standing in the foyer, wearing their own silly-looking *Whataburger* chef hats, were my deacons, men "full of faith and the Holy Ghost," cooking pancakes for people who didn't look like they especially wanted to eat them, but they were willing to help God through this crisis as they nibbled at what appeared to be some species of pancakes. I stood there as the aroma of Aunt Jemima and Log Cabin maple syrup filled the sanctuary of the Lord.

We raised $2,000 that Saturday, but for the next several days God banged me over the head until I repented of that foolishness. The Lord seemed to say, "Let me show you now what I can do. Trust me for the next $2,000—the whole $2,000 to come through one person." Wednesday night I told the church we still needed $2,000, but we were never again going to do what we had just done to raise money. Someone asked what we would do if we didn't get the money. "We won't go," I said. Then I shared with them what I felt God had led me to trust Him for. Our people agreed and committed it to God.

I began to wonder who would give the money. I could think of two or three who could do it, but none of them came forward. Then a few days later my phone rang. It was a young woman in our church who had recently married. I knew that both she and her husband had to work to make ends meet.

"Pastor," she said, "a few months ago I was in an automobile accident, and I received $3,000 from the insurance company. I still have $2,000. My husband and I want to give the $2,000 for the youth choir trip.

We raised $2,000 selling pancakes and $2,000 praying. When we sold the pancakes, we thanked the choir members for standing in the middle of the street. We thanked the deacons for giving up their Saturday to cook pancakes. We thanked Whataburger for the silly-looking hats. We thanked Aunt Jemima and Log Cabin for selling us their product at a discount. Then we were worried that we might have forgotten someone.

When we raised $2,000 by prayer, we simply thanked the Lord. He got all the glory and all the credit. After all, that's what prayer is all about.

Note: The young couple who felt led to give the $2,000 to pay the balance needed for the youth choir to make their mission trip gave out of their little, and God gave back out of His abundance. They had come out of the Jesus Movement and, along with friends, would attend MBBC, sit on the floor in front of the pulpit, with their Bibles and notepads, and soak up Ron's teaching. Their lives were profoundly impacted by Ron's ministry, as were many other young people who became missionaries, pastors, evangelists, and other church leaders. The husband became a pastor and at this writing is pastoring an inner-city church in Oklahoma City. His wife was elected to the state legislature and continues to have a strong Christian influence in the state against the sins of the day.

History shows that there has never been a mighty outpouring of the Spirit of God that did not begin with the persistent, prevailing prayer of a desperate people. Revival has never come because men "planned" it and put it on the calendar. This was evident during the years of revival blessing at MacArthur Boulevard as they witnessed God's sovereign hand at work.

Sermon: *When the Church Prays* (Acts 4:23–33)

When the Church Prays, the Presence of God Is Perceived

"The place was shaken where they were assembled together" (Acts 4:31 KJV). This symbolizes God's presence and activity. You find a similar phrase in Acts 16:26. While Paul and Silas were conducting a midnight prayer and praise service, "suddenly there was a great earthquake, so that the foundations of the prison were shaken" (KJV). This is a manifestation of the presence of God, manifesting Himself, letting His people know that He is present and has the situation under control.

But, you say, isn't God always present when two or three are gathered together in Christ's name? Yes, but God being present doesn't necessarily mean we perceive His presence. Jacob could say of Bethel: "Surely God was in this place and I knew it not." When the church goes to its knees in real prayer, the presence of God is perceived. Suddenly we know He is with us, working, moving, answering.

We Must Pray in Unison

They were all doing the same thing. It wasn't just the apostles who prayed. They all prayed. Here was a group of people who were concerned enough to gather in one place for one purpose—to pray. This is a testimony to united prayer.

We Must Pray in Unity

They prayed with one accord. Not only were they all praying, they were all praying for the same purpose. There wasn't one over here praying for his pet project and another over there praying for his. They were gathered in unity with one heart and one soul.

When the Church Prays, the Presence of God Is Received

"And they were all filled with the Holy Ghost" (4:31 KJV). Upon the conclusion of their praying, the Spirit of God filled every believer gathered in that room. "They were *all* filled," not just the apostles but every member of the church. There had been a filling on the Day of Pentecost, but the church cannot operate on past experiences. The church's experience of God must always be fresh. Every new task requires a new filling.

There is something remarkable about this incident. As a result of their praying, they were filled with the Spirit, but, looking at their prayer closely, the Holy Spirit isn't even mentioned in their petition. Though they didn't pray to be filled, they were filled. I believe, as we look at the content of their prayer, we'll discover what kind of praying results in the fullness of the Spirit.

WE MUST RECOGNIZE GOD AS SOVEREIGN

In verse 24 we read: "And when they heard that, they lifted up their voice to God with one accord and said, 'Lord, thou art God, which hast made heaven, and earth, and the sea, and all that in them is'" (KJV). The word translated "Lord" here, is rare. It is not the same word rendered Lord in verse 29. This is an extremely strong word meaning "despot," one who rules with absolute, unrestrained authority. *Omnipotence* is the word. This is where they started—not with the threats of the enemy but with the absolute sovereignty of their God. And that's where victory always begins—with the recognition that God is our sovereign Lord. His sovereignty is seen in His creation of all things. They prayed: "Thou art God, which hast made heaven, and earth, and the sea, and all that in them is."

Why did they acknowledge this? Because they were having problems with some of the "all that in them is." They recognized that the Sanhedrin were creatures and that their God was the Creator. They looked beyond the creation to the Creator. They looked beyond the visible to the invisible.

And they acknowledged God's sovereignty in His control of all things. In verse 26 they pray: "The kings of the earth stood up, and the rulers were gathered together against the Lord, and against his Christ" (KJV). What a formidable foe had gathered against Christ! And what did these enemies of Christ come together to do? Look at verse 28. "For to do whatsoever thy hand and thy counsel determined before to be done" (KJV).

These persecuted believers looked back to the darkest day of their lives—the day their hopes and dreams had disintegrated with the death of Christ—and they saw God in charge of it all, and now, how much more with the persecution of His disciples. What a display of His absolute sovereignty.

WE MUST RECOGNIZE OURSELVES AS HIS SERVANTS

In verse 29, they refer to themselves as servants, bond slaves. Their prayer was one of submission. They didn't complain about their circumstances or call down fire on the Sanhedrin. They didn't ask God to move them to a more favorable situation. They simply asked God for more of what got them in trouble in the first place—boldness.

- This is submission to God-allowed circumstances.
- This is submission to their God-appointed commission.

The point of the whole prayer is that they would have the boldness to continue speaking the Word and that Jesus would be glorified because that was what God had called them to do in the first place.

Now, putting it all together—in their prayer, which brought a fresh supply of the power of God, they acknowledged Him to be their sovereign Lord and submitted to Him and His redemptive purpose. And any Christian who recognizes and submits to His lordship will be filled with the Spirit. In other words, when the Holy Spirit finds a Christian who wants what He wants they "get together." He is interested in only one thing—glorifying Jesus as Lord and Savior, and He is ready to empower any Christian whose sole desire is to see Jesus glorified in his body.

When the Church Prays, the Purpose of God Is Achieved

"And they spake the word of God with boldness" (Acts 4:31 KJV). Here we find a chain reaction. When a church is filled with the Spirit, they will inevitably speak the word of God with boldness. You cannot divorce the fullness of the Spirit and witnessing. The power of God is given to accomplish the purpose of God; and unless we are willing to be instruments of His purpose, it is useless to pray for power. Witnesses are not made by training programs. As good as programs may be to teach us how to witness, they will not make us witnesses. Only the compelling power of the Holy Spirit can do that.

THE OBLIGATION TO WITNESS

Verse 33 says that they "gave" witness. The word translated "gave" carries the idea of repaying a debt, fulfilling an obligation. The fullness of the Spirit awakens a man to his sense of obligation; it makes an honest man of him, and an honest man always pays his debts.

THE OPERATION OF THIS WITNESS

"They spake the word of God with boldness." *Boldness* is one of the great words of the New Testament. God uses this word to characterize the lives and ministry of the New Testament Christians.

THE OBJECT OF THE WITNESS

They gave witness of "the resurrection of the Lord Jesus." The object of all our witnessing is that Jesus is living, and He is Lord.

This brings us right back to where we started. When the place is shaken and the presence of God is perceived, it is easy to convince men that Jesus is alive and that He is Lord. When the Philippian jailer stood amid the rubble of his demolished jail and heard Paul and Silas praying and praising the Lord and saw all the prisoners still there, he was convinced and cried out: "What must I do to be saved?" (Acts 16:30 KJV). He wasn't a prospect for the "God is dead" movement! He had perceived the presence of God.

The church must go to its knees. Spiritual revival and national survival demand it. I think we ought to consider what brought the church in Acts 4 to its knees. It was active opposition to the gospel. The American church has known little of this and perhaps in our complacency we feel no desperate need to pray. It may be that God will have to allow persecution and opposition in order to get us on our knees in persistent and prevailing prayer. Whatever it takes, it will be worth it.

TESTIMONY: SHIRLEY CALVERT—MBBC MEMBER AND SUNDAY SCHOOL TEACHER

I believe one of the main reasons God blessed MacArthur was the Intercessory Prayer Ministry. This had such an impact on our church. I would go, week after week, and pray for as many requests as I could that were on what we called "The Wheel." It was not long before we began to see answers to prayer. In almost every service we witnessed these answers as people we had specifically prayed for made professions of faith. I would hear names that I immediately recognized as someone I had been interceding for—women's husbands I had never laid eyes on, folk I had only known by name—now, there they were, coming to Christ. This became the norm during those days. ✳

PART THREE

The Best of Times and the Worst of Times

❊ ❊ ❊

The Lord gets His best soldiers out of the highlands of affliction.

—C. H. SPURGEON

[11]

The Best of Times

A Tribute

TESTIMONY—RICHARD BEWES, O. B. E. FORMER RECTOR OF
ALL SOULS CHURCH, LANGHAM PLACE, LONDON

I remember how we at England's Keswick Convention, or at London's
All Souls Church, always looked forward to Ron and Kaye Dunn's visits
from the other side of the Atlantic! Yet Ron, immersed in the Word and
having been to the mountaintop, saw himself as but an onlooker, as God
moved in reviving power among the thousands who were transformed
through the preaching, inspired by the books, and inwardly elevated both
by "the best of times and the worst of times."

Prelude

Charles Dickens began his 1859 novel, *A Tale of Two Cities* (London
and Paris), with these words: "It was the best of times, it was the worst of

times." He went on to say, "It was the season of light, it was the season of darkness; it was the spring of hope, it was the winter of despair."

These words could well describe the lives of Ron and Kaye Dunn. As Ron said in his sermon, "Surprise, It's God!" "Good and evil run on parallel tracks, and they often arrive at the same time."

Interestingly, there is also a parallel between the period in history in which Dickens's novel takes place and the life of Ron and Kaye. The setting of *The Tale of Two Cities* is just prior to and during the French Revolution that erupted in the mid-1800s. Historians, writing about this time in European history say that if it were not for the 1858–59 Evangelical Awakening that took place during the days of John and Charles Wesley, George Whitefield, and others, the unrest that was turning France upside down would likely have crossed the English Channel because the signs of revolution were beginning to foment in England as well. *But God!*

And so it can be said of the life and ministry of Ron and Kaye—*but God!*

A Very Good Year

The year 1972 was turning out to be one of the best Ron and Kaye had ever had, in spite of their having struggled, over a period of eight months, with the tempting invitation to follow Dr. Adrian Rogers as pastor of First Baptist Church, Merritt Island, Florida, after he had moved on to Bellevue Baptist in Memphis. God was continuing to bless MacArthur Boulevard, and the family was doing well. In fact, things had been going so well that Ron climaxed the year by giving Kaye a special gift at Christmas—a gold watch. On the back of the watch was inscribed:

To Kaye from Ron with love.

Christmas, 1972. A very good year.

It is to be expected that when God is at work in a church or in a family—when His people are enjoying His blessing—that times of testing will follow. And, not unlike Job, the testing of Ron and Kaye would begin not long after their "very good year."

In 1973, at the height of the revival, when the church was experiencing blessing upon blessing, when all seemed to be going well, the Dunn family was blindsided by a severe crisis—Ronnie Jr. began to demonstrate serious inconsistency in his behavior, which soon led to signs of rebellion.

This took Ron and Kaye by surprise. It had been less than two years since they had been so excited over the spiritual growth they were seeing in Ronnie's life, as we find recorded in Ron's journal.

Journal Entry

February 28, 1971

For months I've been praying two prayers regarding Ronnie. First, that he would get right with God, and second, that God would call him to preach. I claimed Psalm 37:4, "Delight thyself also in the LORD: and he shall give thee the desires of thine heart" (KJV). I asked God that if He never gave me any other desires, that He would grant me these two. And He did!

We were in revival meetings at MBBC last week. On Monday night the first prayer was answered. Ronnie got right with God. Then, on the closing night of the revival, Ronnie made the next step—he surrendered to the ministry. Praise God! Kaye and I have been so excited. As far as I'm concerned, this has been the greatest revival I've ever witnessed."

The remainder of 1971 went well for Ron and Kaye, as did 1972, the year that climaxed with the special Christmas gift Ron gave to Kaye. And on top of all that, God was continuing to bless the church with a wonderful spirit of unity and excitement. Many souls were being saved. Those were still *the best of times.*

Then the tide turned. Ron and Kaye could not have anticipated how quickly their fortunes were about to change. Ron and Kaye were to experience this to a depth never before encountered. ❋

[1 2]

The Worst of Times

*Character cannot be developed in ease and quiet. Only
through experience of trial and suffering can the soul be
strengthened, ambition inspired, and success achieved.*

—HELEN KELLER

As Ronnie Jr.'s rebellion increased, Ron just knew that it had to be the
devil attacking them, trying to disrupt what was happening in the revival.
So they prayed, rebuked the devil, pled the blood of Christ over the situation. They tried everything, but the problem with Ronnie only worsened.
Then one Sunday, right after church, he ran away. They didn't know where
he was for two weeks. They found out later that he had hitchhiked from
Dallas to Fort Lauderdale, Florida. When he did return, things kept getting worse until, in August, when the family was on vacation at the farm
in Greenwood, Arkansas, Ronnie attempted to take his life.

They rushed him to the hospital in Fort Smith where, to their shock,
they were told by the doctors that they would not admit Ronnie unless
Ron and Kaye gave them permission to put him in the psychiatric ward
for two weeks.

"Well now," recalls Ron, "that's another matter. You see, Christians don't go to psychiatrists. This is just the devil." And yet Ronnie was in such bad shape that they finally said, "All right, if you'll take him, we'll agree to the two weeks in the psychiatric ward."

"I'll never forget when, at the end of those two weeks, Kaye and I were to meet with the psychiatrist for his evaluation report. I was ready to be told that I was a lousy father, that Kaye was a lousy mother, and that all of Ronnie's problems stemmed from his being brought up in a preacher's home. I had never been as nervous in my life. And yet none of that happened. The doctor said, "Your son in suffering from a mood disorder caused by a chemical imbalance in the blood." Later it came to be known as manic depression, now known as bipolar disorder, but in 1975 you didn't hear much about that.

"They put Ronnie on three drugs, including lithium, which was the new miracle drug at that time, and the amazing thing was, it worked. We saw an immediate change in him. And Ronnie was so glad to know that there was something wrong with him, a reason for the way he had been acting, a reason why he would run away, then call me, weeping on the phone, "Dad, can I come home?" And he always got the same answer, "Oh yes, son. You can come home."

"When he'd return, he'd sit there and cry, 'I don't know why I'm doing what I do.' So, what a relief it was for us all to find out that there was something you could put your finger on, something you could nail down, a medical cause for what had been happening. We all rejoiced. We remembered how Ronnie had surrendered to preach several years before, and now we just knew that everything was going to be alright. God had answered our prayer."

That was in August 1975. Three months later, on Thanksgiving day, Ronnie took his life.

Why?

Kaye would periodically find doses of Ronnie's medicine in the pockets of shirts she was washing. She would remind him that he had to stay on his medication, but he would either forget or would feel so good he wouldn't bother to take it.

The family planned, as usual, to spend Thanksgiving at the farm in Arkansas, but when they were ready to leave, eighteen-year-old Ronnie couldn't be found. They finally went on without him, believing that he would be able to take care of himself, though every day at the farm Kaye journaled her concerns about their boy.

Saturday evening when they returned, Don Gardner, Joanne's husband, was waiting for them as they pulled into the drive. Kaye and Ron knew immediately what he was going to say: "Ronnie's gone."

Ronnie's gone. "It was amazing," recalls Ron, "how God gave Kaye and me the strength to bear up under this tragedy. Part of it was due to the hundreds of friends who surrounded us with love and support. I had always been a private person. I had never really felt that much need of support from others, but now I was learning how desperately you need other people and how important the family of God is in our lives."

Then there was that moment they will never forget: As family and friends gathered back at the house following Ronnie's graveside service, the phone rang. Ron and Kaye were told to each get on the line. It was eighty-three-year-old Miss Bertha Smith, former Southern Baptist missionary to China and Taiwan from 1917 to 1958. Without hardly saying another word, she sang all seven verses of "How Firm a Foundation."[7] She had previously sung this hymn to her Chinese nursing students who had been with her, huddled under a hospital bed as the Japanese bombed their city in 1941. Verse 5 says:

When through fiery trials thy pathway shall lie,
My grace, all-sufficient, shall be thy supply;
The flame shall not harm thee; I only design
Thy dross to consume and thy gold to refine.

But Why?

As time passed, what made what they were going through that much harder to handle, especially for Ron, was that the sons of several other preacher friends were also having trouble with their teenage boys, and Ronnie was the only one who didn't make it. All the others did.

"And you can't help but ask why," recalls Ron. "Why couldn't my boy, why couldn't Ronnie have made it? I admit that there was a point when I struggled with bitterness, and for a period of time I wasn't interested in hearing good news about anyone else's child.

"But God's grace was sufficient to see us through that period, which included having to face the stigma of having a son who committed suicide—the feeling of being a failure as a parent."

Be Still My Soul

Be still my soul, the Lord is on thy side;
Bear patiently the cross of grief and pain.
Leave to thy God to order and provide;
In every change He faithful will remain.
Be still my soul, thy best, thy heavenly Friend
Through thorny ways leads to a joyful end.
—Katarina von Schlegel
(Translated from German by Jane L. Borthwick)

TESTIMONY—O. S. HAWKINS: PRESIDENT/CEO, GUIDESTONE FINANCIAL RESOURCES

Over a lifetime most of us can count on one hand the people who have uniquely impacted the spiritual dynamic of our lives and set us on course to being conformed to Christ's image. Ron Dunn played this part in thousands of lives through his tapes, writings, and personal encounters. Even as I type these words, a smile is on my face as I remember this good and godly life. I was with Ron in some of his highest hours and in some of his lowest moments. I know of no single person who journeyed through as many emotional valleys as did Ron Dunn and yet always managing to stand on the mountaintop holding to the hope that "joy comes in the morning" (Ps. 30:5). ❋

[13]

Surprise, It's God
(Genesis 32:24–32)

❊ ❊ ❊

From Ron's Journal

Ronnie's death in 1975 changed the direction and disposition of my life forever. When it happened, I thought I was coping with it, but I wasn't. People told me I was handling his death so beautifully—that I was an inspiration to them. They were telling me how my ministry was giving them hope and strength.

What actually was happening, was that, in my preaching out of my own despair and discouragement, I was being an encouragement to others. They didn't know that as I was preparing and preaching those messages, such as "Surprise, It's God," the sermon about Jacob, that I was in my own pit of despair and discouragement.

Sermon: *Surprise, It's God*

It's better to learn sooner, rather than later, that God is full of surprises. I don't know about you, but for most of my Christian life God has caught me off guard because He doesn't always work in the way I expect Him to. As a matter of fact, I guess I could say that God hasn't worked at all like I expected Him to.

When I surrendered to the ministry as a fifteen-year-old teenager, I wanted to be everything God wanted me to be. I was aware, however, that I was failing in many areas, and I looked at the twenty- to twenty-five-year-old folk in the church and thought, *When I get to be older like them, I'll have conquered all these things. I'll have learned all these lessons, and everything will be all right.*

Well, when I got to be in my early twenties, I looked at the old people in the church who were in their thirties, and I said, "I know when you get to be that old and you get married and settled down, by that time you'll have learned what you need to know about how to live the Christian life, and you'll be able to overcome all the temptations of the flesh, and you won't have to fight the battles I'm fighting."

Now, when I got into my thirties, I looked at the "really old" folk in the church, those who were in their forties. I was sure that by that time I'd have conquered all those things that I was still having problems with. I'd have gotten this whole business put together.

I said that when I was fifteen. I said that when I was in my twenties. I said that when I was in my thirties. I said that when I was in my forties, but I didn't say it when I was fifty because I had decided by that time I wasn't going to learn anything. It's awful when the future catches up with you and you haven't done what you thought you would have accomplished. I began to realize that the one cataclysmic, "in the twinkling of an eye," experience that would transform me was never going to happen.

Many of us feel that there must be a secret out there that, if somehow discovered, is going to change everything. We've heard about people who say they've "found the secret," and we're hoping that one of these days

God will put a "holy zap" on us, and all of a sudden all our problems will be solved, and we'll emerge from that experience transformed into everything God wants us to be. Perhaps, we think, it will happen in the next revival meeting or in the next seminar. We just know it is out there somewhere.

Well, I've come to the conclusion that there are a lot of secrets, but there is no "one" secret, just as there are a lot of experiences but no "one" experience that will suddenly transform you into everything God wants you to be. That's like thinking that you can take one big gulp of air and not have to breathe for the rest of your life or eat one giant Big Mac and not have to eat again. It doesn't work like that.

I've come to realize, not only from my own experience but more importantly from Scripture, that the transformation God wants to work in my life doesn't happen in a single moment, but rather it takes place gradually over a period of time, usually when we are alone and in the dark. Now I've no problem with thirty-second experiences at the altar, but thirty-second experiences will not transform you.

A number of years ago things began to go awry in my life. I thought, *This is not what I planned at all.* It caused me to become increasingly interested in learning just how God works in a person's life to shape them into what He wants them to be. This led me to make a fresh study of the Word of God, and as I studied the Scriptures, I found one person whose story helped me more than anyone else to understand God's process in conforming us into the image of Jesus Christ.

This story is found in Genesis 32:24–32 and has to do with twin boys, Jacob and Esau, who began fighting each other in their mother Rebecca's womb. Esau was born first, and Jacob, the second born, followed immediately. He came out holding on to Esau's heel, an early sign that he was going to live up to his name that means deceit, trickery, and fraud. It's a word picture of someone who sneaks up on another person, grabs his heel and trips him up. It's the word found in Jeremiah 17:9 where Jeremiah talks about the heart being deceitful above all things.

"Deceitful" is the same word used for Jacob. You could say that the heart is a "Jacob" above all things.

You recall how Jacob bargained Esau out of his birthright and deceived his father, Isaac, and ended up with the inheritance that was rightfully Esau's. Not only that, but Jacob also stole Esau's blessing, and when Esau heard what had happened, he said, "I'm going to kill him." At that point, Rebecca told Jacob it was time he took a vacation, so he went to visit his Uncle Laban for about twenty years. While there he married Leah, then finally, Rachel. Now, in Genesis 32, the story picks up with Jacob heading back home after wearing out his welcome at his Uncle Laban's house.

Jacob knew he was going to have to face Esau, and remembering how Esau has vowed to kill him, we find Jacob praying that God will somehow deliver him from his brother's wrath. He is hoping he will be able to "see the face of Esau and still live" because he's heard that Esau is on his way to meet him with four hundred men.

Jacob and his entourage arrive at a little brook called Jabbok, and as evening fell, Jacob told his wives, eleven children, and the rest of his group to go ahead and cross over the brook while he stayed by himself on the near side. He told them that he would join them in the morning.

We read in Genesis 32:24–30 that, when Jacob was left alone, a man wrestled with him until daybreak. When this mysterious man saw that he couldn't overpower Jacob, he touched the socket of Jacob's hip so that the hip was injured as they wrestled together. The man told Jacob to let him go as it was daybreak, but Jacob replied that he would not let the man go until the man blessed him. Then this mysterious person asked:

> "What is your name?" And he said, "Jacob." He said, "Your name shall no longer be Jacob, but Israel; for you have striven with God and with men and have prevailed." Then Jacob asked him and said, "Please tell me your name." But he said, "Why is it that you ask my name?" And he blessed him there. So Jacob named the place Peniel, for he said, "I have seen God

face to face, yet my life has been preserved." Now the sun rose upon him just as he crossed over Penuel, and he was limping on his thigh. Therefore, to this day the sons of Israel do not eat the sinew of the hip which is on the socket of the thigh, because he touched the socket of Jacob's thigh in the sinew of the hip. (Gen. 32:27–32)

This is one of the most familiar stories in the Old Testament. Jacob, all by himself, alone in the dark, is suddenly jumped on by some mysterious person who wrestles with him until dawn. I believe this story is a model, a paradigm, of how God deals with His people, taking them from where they are to where He wants them to be. I also believe this account has significance beyond its being a historical incident.

I'm persuaded of this because in verse 32, where we find that the Jews, looking back on this event, saw a special meaning in it and placed a ritualistic ban on eating a certain portion of meat where Jacob's thigh was wounded by the angel. This tells me that God is saying more here than may meet the eye.

The second reason I believe this story has more than a historical significance is that this is when Jacob's name is changed to Israel. This is actually where we first hear the name, Israel. This is a picture of how God takes a Jacob, a deceiver, a trickster, someone who is not what they pretend to be, and turns them into a prince, a princess of God. And you know how it is done? It is accomplished through a struggle, an all-night struggle, until the breaking of the day.

That night, Jacob, who had been figuring out all the angles to save his own skin—this schemer who had sent all the others across the brook where they would be the first to face Esau—this deceiver had been praying for God to deliver him from his brother, Esau. And God answered but not in the way Jacob had expected. God had a few surprises for Jacob, and out of this story we're going to find several surprises God has for us, in making us what He wants us to be.

Surprise 1: Our toughest battles are often with God and not with the devil.

This has been one of the biggest surprises for me. I don't mean that we don't fight the devil because we do engage in spiritual warfare. In Ephesians 6, Paul talks about our wrestling against the powers of darkness. What I am saying, however, is that my toughest battles have not been with the devil; they've been with God. I find it easier to say "no" to the devil than to say "yes" to God.

Let me ask who you think Jacob thought jumped him that night? There he is, all by himself. Everyone else has crossed the creek, and he is scared to death, with no one to protect him from Esau, when suddenly a man leaps on him and throws him to the ground. Let me ask again—who do you think Jacob thought that was? I think he thought Esau had taken a page out of his own old book of tricks and had snuck up in the dark and had jumped him. Or he may have thought it was one of Esau's henchmen or perhaps just a thug who was walking by and saw an opportunity to mug a tourist.

We know from Hosea 12 that it actually was an angel who wrestled with Jacob, and some of the old rabbis who copied the Talmud had an interesting theory about this. They suggested that it was Jacob's guardian angel who jumped him. To me that is kind of funny. Here is an angel who has been sent by God to guard Jacob, who turns out to be such an obnoxious character that the angel beats up on him.

The truth of the matter is that none of us knows who Jacob thought it was that night, but I bet you this much—Jacob's first thought was not, *Oh joy! Someone's come to bless me.* Not really. This was not the act of a friend. This was not the act of a benefactor. As far as Jacob was concerned, this was the act of an aggressor; this was the act of an enemy, for only an enemy would treat you this way.

We know that sometime during the night, as they wrestled, Jacob realized that he was not fighting with Esau or an enemy, but he was wrestling with the Lord. Jacob, who had been thinking his greatest problem was with Esau, discovered it was with God.

Now this was not the first encounter Jacob had had with God. You remember twenty years earlier, when he left home, he spent the first night at Bethel where he had a dream that the heavens opened, and there was a ladder reaching from heaven to earth on which angels were going up and down. What a sight that was, and what an experience! In fact, it was such a great experience that Jacob signed a pledge card right then and there to start tithing. It takes a great experience for a fellow to make that kind of decision.

Have you ever had an experience like that? I must confess that I haven't, though I hear some people talk about visions and unbelievable experiences they've had, and I think: *Lord, that's what I need. I need some great experience. Lord, here I am fighting the devil, fighting the flesh. I'm not what I ought to be. I've got so many problems. Lord, if you'd just open heaven. Lord, if only I could see some angels around, that would solve my problem.* Well, Jacob had had that kind of experience, but now here he is, twenty years later, the same old Jacob. What scares me is, how many great experiences you and I can have and not be changed. So I ask myself again, why do I find it easier to say "no" to the devil when he tempts me than to say "yes" to God when He's wrestling with me? I'll tell you why.

What Is "Your" Name?

Here Jacob is wrestling with the angel when the angel asks, "What is your name?" Now to me that immediately sounds suspicious. You mean to tell me the angel didn't know who he was wrestling with? You mean to tell me that some angel was just strolling by and thought, *I think I'll jump that guy.* Do you think God sent an angel with an arrest warrant that said, "To whom it may concern." Do you really believe that the angel didn't know who he was wrestling with?

Oh, he knew. That angel was not asking for information. That angel was looking for a confession. He said, "What is your name?" You see, to the Hebrews, a name was not a label you slapped on someone to tell them apart from the next person. To the Hebrews a name represented the person. That's why names are so important in the Bible, such as the names of God that describe who He is. We are to call upon the *name* of the Lord. The name represented the nature, the character of that person. So, when the angel asked specifically "What is your name?" he was looking for something more than if he had just asked, "Who are you?

Jacob cried out: "My name is fraud. My name is cheat. My name is deceiver." You see, what God is after is not some little surface experience that will make us feel good for awhile. He wants to reach down into the guts of our soul and jerk the Jacob out of us. He wants to change us from the inside out. Oh, we're willing to let God change us up to a point, but few of us truly want to be honest with who we are way down inside.

"But God, I'm not really sure I even want to know. I don't want to think about it. I'd rather have another good experience that will let me think that everything is alright." Well beware, because sooner or later, though we can run from God like Jacob did, God is going to back us into a corner, and He's going to say, "Alright son, we're going to have it out, once and for all. I want to know—what is your name?"

I think it's significant that the Bible describes it as a wrestling match. You see, if you were to come up to me after the service and punch me on the nose, you know what I'd do? I'd run because I don't want to fight. But if you come up and throw your arms around me and wrestle me to the ground, I have no choice but to fight.

Now some of you have been running from God year after year. You get by on the occasional experience, but, as I said, sooner or later, God is going to get you alone, in the dark, and He is going to put a wrestling hold on you, and He'll say, "This time you're not going to escape. We're going to have it out until I shape you into the image of my Son."

"What is your name?" The most terrifying experience in life is facing yourself—what you are. And it is inevitable that you and I are eventually going to wrestle with God over that. And so Jacob discovered, as I have discovered, that our greatest battles are with God and not the devil.

Surprise 2: We often try to get rid of the very things God has sent to bless us.

I often try to throw down the blessings God sends my way. Let's look at Jacob again. What's he trying to do? He's trying to get loose from this person he is wrestling with. Finally the angel says: "Let me go." And Jacob thinks, *My, what a change.* He realizes this is no ordinary person he's been wrestling with, so he tells the angel he will not let him go until he blesses him. That which Jacob was trying to throw down and escape from, he is now clinging to. "I will not let you go until . . ."

When my wife, Kaye, travels with me, if we have some spare time, she likes to look in little shops. I trail along. Sometimes she'll go into an antique shop, and to be perfectly honest, I don't like antique shops because they depress me. You know why? I see things in antique stores that are selling for hundreds of dollars, and I know I've thrown away better stuff than that.

I started saving baseball cards in 1948. I remember I had a Hank Greenberg, a Bob Feller, and a Mickey Mantle card when they came out. I saved baseball cards from the time I was twelve, all the way through high school. My mom died, however, long before we knew baseball cards were valuable, so later, when I knew better, it was too late to ask her what she did with them. When I was in college, every time I went home I looked for them, in the closets, in the attic. I went through all the drawers, looked in the barn, all the time refusing to admit what I knew Mom had done. What happened was when I went off to college she thought, *When Ronnie was a child, he collected baseball cards as a child, but now that he has grown up . . .* Well, I still look for them. I know where they used to be. They were in my Cub Scout scrapbook.

How was I to know in 1948 that the baseball cards I was collecting would one day be worth thousands of dollars. I can't believe I sold my

1964 mustang for $400. You see, my problem is, I can't tell the difference between trash and treasure. What is junk today may well be an antique tomorrow. Our problem is, we think we can correctly evaluate or interpret everything that comes into our lives. I've convinced myself that I know a blessing when I see one, and what's happening to me right now is no blessing. And, by the way, I know a curse when I see one.

> "What's that? You mean you're trying to tell me that this is a blessing?" "No sir. I know a blessing when I see one, and this is definitely a curse, and I'm going to do everything I can to get rid of it."

The truth of the matter is, blessings sometimes come disguised as curses. Sometimes kings come dressed as paupers. Sometimes we do entertain angels unaware. Often the very thing God is sending our way in His attempt to change us is the very thing we try to get rid of.

This is one of the problems I have with the health and wealth gospel. If you think that God intends for you always to be healthy and wealthy, then the things God may be wanting to use to make you more like Christ are the things you're trying to rid yourself of. If your happiness is based on your being healthy, then you're not free. If prosperity is necessary for you to be happy, then you are a slave. You only become free when things like this cease to be a requirement for your happiness.

I used to think faith was the power to change things the way I wanted them to be. That's a lot of what is being preached these days, especially on TV by preachers I call the "Joy Boys." One of these has a tape series that, every time I hear the title, I cringe: "How to Write Your Own Ticket with God."

That's about as close to blasphemy as you can get. Folk, we don't write our own ticket with God. But that's what we hear, and frankly that's what a lot of us want to hear—whatever problem is out there, whatever heartache is out there, if you just have enough faith. Well, here's what I've come to believe.

Faith is not necessarily the power to change things to what we want them to be, but rather, faith is the courage to accept things as they are.

Some things are never going to get any better. You say: *"Preacher, that's a negative message. That's depressing."* No, I'm "positive"—some things are not going to get any better. Now, don't misunderstand me. I'm not preaching a passive message. If there is a circumstance in your life that is painful or hurtful and you can do something about it, do it. Got a headache? Take an aspirin! What I'm saying is, some things in your life will not change, no matter what you do. You can pray and praise, rebuke the devil, but nothing will change it.

Are you in a situation like that? If you are, and you believe that it is always God's will for whatever bad is happening to be taken away, you're stuck right there. Do you realize what is going to happen? You're going to continue living under a load of guilt and shame. "What's wrong with me?" And there will always be those who'll come along and say, "There must be sin in your life. You need to die to self. You need to have more faith." I'm tired of these pat, clichéd answers for our problems.

So, what are you to do? You've prayed, fasted, rebuked the devil—now what? Well, like Jacob, you might want to say, "Lord, there's a blessing somewhere in this circumstance, and I'm not going to let You go until You bless me." And as you do, you reach out your arms and draw the blessing to yourself, you embrace it and let God use it to strengthen you for the journey. It may be that the thing you are struggling against right now is the thing God wants to use to turn you into an "Israel."

Surprise 3: The biggest surprise of all is to discover that good and bad run on parallel tracks and they usually arrive about the same time.

Some of you are going to start trying to find that in our text. Well, it isn't worded exactly like that, but the lesson that good and bad run on parallel tracks and usually arrive at the same time is here. You see, Jacob got what he wanted. He received the blessing he asked for, but he also got something he didn't want. He got a limp. He hadn't bargained for that. He hadn't asked for that.

The Bible says that the angel blessed him. This is the only place in Scripture that a blessing is ever attained through a struggle. Normally blessings are conferred. You don't get them because you've been in a fight. Jacob had never had to struggle for anything in his life. He had always depended on his wits and conniving to get ahead, but this time he had to fight for what he wanted, and he got it. "Thank you Lord for the blessing." But he also got something he didn't want—he got something he hadn't counted on.

The view of life that many of us have is that right now some good things are happening, but there are also a lot of bad things happening, and we know that's not the way life is meant to be. Good stuff, fine, but all the bad stuff? That's not the way God intends it to be so I think I'll just pull over here on the side and wait for awhile because I know that eventually it's all going to work out and life will be all good. I'm going to put life on hold for a bit and then, when I finish school, when I get married, when the kids get grown, when I get past all of this, then I'll really start living.

One of these days, when I'm successful enough, when I'm rich enough, life is going to be just fine. Isn't that what we hope for? What we're going through now is just kind of a rehearsal for the good times, but the truth of the matter is that *good and bad run on parallel tracks and they usually arrive about the same time.*

One of the most fascinating parables Jesus ever told is the story of the wheat and the tares, found in Matthew 13. Jesus is not talking about lost church members here, He is talking about the mystery of good and evil in the world. When the servants discovered that someone had sown tares in the field overnight, they went to their master who told them not to pull the tares up, but to leave them growing with the wheat. He told them that an enemy had done this, and we know that wherever God sows wheat, the devil is going to try to sow tares. Has it surprised you to find tares springing up in your life?

"But Lord, I didn't plant any tares. I only planted wheat, but look, someone has planted tares." So, what do we do? Get rid of the tares? That's the most reasonable thing to do. But the Lord says, "No, let them grow along with the wheat. Let them grow together."

The literal Greek meaning here is, "Let them grow in and out among each other." In other words the wheat and the tares are intertwined. You can't separate them. If you try to pull the tares up, you are also going to pull up some of the wheat, and it's not yet time for the harvest, so for the sake of the wheat, let them grow together. When harvest time does come, it won't matter because then you'll be able to separate them.

Jesus is saying that in the world where we find ourselves, good and evil grow together, and we're going to have to wait until the end time when God will settle it all. The only reason the master won't let the servants in this parable pull up the tares is that it would damage the wheat. The tares are left in the field for the sake of the wheat. Sometimes we may wonder why God doesn't just kill the devil and put a stop to evil. I don't really know, but I believe this parable hints that it wouldn't be good for us.

Let me try to illustrate what we've been talking about. Kaye and I have two good friends who have a daughter who, some years ago, started dating a boy who had serious character flaws. The parents did what all good parents would do: they began warning their daughter about the dangers of getting serious with this boy. But in spite of the warnings, the daughter went on to marry this young man.

A few years and two babies later, the parents evaluation of this person proved true, and he walked out on her. I've never seen anyone so hurt as those parents were. They were devastated, as was their daughter. She'd been abandoned. Kaye and I prayed with them; we cried with them; we did everything we could to help them. Then, one night while we were driving home, I began to fantasize.

Now one of my favorite fantasies is playing God. You know, I'd just like to be God for a day. Kind of like that program my mother used to listen to on the radio, *Queen for a Day*. Yes, if only I could be "God for a day," I'd straighten a lot of things out. From my viewpoint it seems like God is wasting a lot of good power.

As I drove, I got to thinking about our dear friends. What if I could tell them that God has given me a special dispensation, that He has fixed it so that I'm now able to reverse this whole tragedy with their daughter. I can turn back the calendar so that she never meets that boy, she never marries him, she never has to go through all the heartache she's been experiencing, she'll never have to shed any tears over being abandoned.

"Isn't that great?" I'd tell them. "God has given me the power to fix it all right now. Do you want me to do it?

"Oh, before you answer, there's one thing that I ought to mention. You do realize, of course, that if I turn back the clock so this tragedy will have never happened, you'll have to give up those two grandbabies.

"What's that you say?

"Oh, I'm sure you love them, but, you see, you can't have it both ways. You sure don't want the pain, do you?

"No, I didn't think so. And you don't want the heartbreak, so . . . What's that? You don't want to give up the babies? But, you see, if I turn the clock back, you can't keep the babies. To undo this tragedy, you're going to have to give up those babies. I need your answer."

Well, what would your answer be? If you had to make a choice like that, what would you say?

Recently, after a service in Louisiana, I saw an older man standing near the book table with a little baby wrapped up in a pink blanket. I walked over to him and asked, "What do you have there?" Tears welled up in that ole boy's eyes as he said, "Oh preacher, this is my grand-daughter." He said, "The day our daughter came home pregnant was the darkest day of my life. I thought I'd die. But, oh preacher, this precious girl is the joy of my life."

Let me ask you a question. "How can you say that what happened to the daughter of my friend was all evil when out of it came two precious lives that you would die for?" *Good and evil run on parallel tracks and arrive about the same time.* Jacob got what he wanted, but he also got what he didn't want.

The Morning After

As the sun gently nudges its way into the eastern sky, Jacob's wives, Rachel and Leah, gather their children and servants at the edge of the Jabbok stream. The long night of waiting is over. Suddenly someone shouts, "There he is!"

Sure enough, it's Jacob crossing the brook. But wait—something's not right. He's limping.

"It looks like a bad limp," someone calls out. "Do you suppose he stumbled in the dark and twisted his leg?"

As Jacob draws closer, it's obvious more is wrong than just a limp. His clothes are dirty and torn. His face is bruised and his hair is disheveled. Jacob looks like he's been in a dogfight, and the dog won.

They rush over to him. "Jacob, Jacob! What happened?"

"Oh," he says, smiling, his eyes bright. "I got blessed last night."

Shaking their heads, they watch him as he limps away.

Someone whispers: "Doesn't look like any victorious Christian I've ever seen." ※

PART FOUR

The Dark Night of the Soul[8]

Perfect people may condemn you for having it; but what know they of God's servants? You and I have to suffer much for the sake of the people of our charge.

—C. H. Spurgeon

[14]

Another Giant

❋ ❋ ❋

*Suffering has been stronger than all other teaching, and has
taught me to understand what my heart used to be. I have
been bent and broken, but, I hope, into a better shape.*

—CHARLES DICKENS

From the beginning of their relationship, Ron and Kaye had determined that they wanted everything God had for them—they would not
be satisfied with anything less. Little did they know, however, that this
was going to mean that, rather than their being carried along on "flowery
beds of ease," the kind of life they had observed some of their peers enjoying, they were going to experience a life more akin to Job than they could
have ever anticipated.

Not only had they physically crossed the Red River into Texas, but
spiritually, their commitment to cross the Jordan River into Canaan
meant facing "giants" that, if the Lord had not been with them, and if
they had not been buoyed by His promises, they may have made a hasty
retreat.

Having already faced one of these giants in watching Ronnie, their first born, battle depression for three years before taking his life, Ron and Kaye could not have anticipated what they would soon be facing—an even more formidable giant in a battle that was to last ten long years.

Depression

Try to exclude the possibility of suffering which the order of nature and the existence of free-wills involve, and you find that you have excluded life itself. —C. S. Lewis[9]

In researching the subject of depression, I was surprised to find how many of the world's most creative and famous people suffered from this illness. For years, however, and still in some circles today, depression is not thought of as being in the same category as physical illnesses such as cancer, heart disease, or other bodily sicknesses. Many think of it as having to do only with the mind, thus, one ought to be able to overcome it by sheer willpower, or at least prayer and faith, not that these don't play an important role in our lives.

What makes clinical (chemical) depression confusing for people, the kind Ron was dealing with, is that traumatic events, such as the death of a loved one, can trigger a chemical reaction in the brain that cannot be treated through counseling or self-help techniques as normal or reactive depression can. Chemical or clinical depression requires medication.

What many also do not understand is that sometimes clinical depression is caused by hormonal imbalances in the blood. At this point, whether caused by a hormonal imbalance or a traumatic event, that person finds himself, or herself, unable to overcome the depression through normal therapy. Such was the effect of Ronnie's suicide on Ron.

Those of us who have never been there may wonder why a person who looks so normal, who has everything going for him, can't just snap out of it. "Have faith; trust God; rebuke the devil, and he will flee from you; refuse to accept it," and on and on we go.

What would Charles Haddon Spurgeon say to that when he was experiencing his own dark night of the soul?

C. H. Spurgeon

One Sabbath morning, I preached from the text, "My God, My God, why has Thou forsaken Me?" (Matt. 27:46 KJV) and though I did not say so, yet I preached my own experience. I heard my own chains clank while I tried to preach to my fellow-prisoners in the dark; but I could not tell why I was brought into such an awful horror of darkness, for which I condemned myself.

On the following Monday evening, a man came to see me who bore all the marks of despair upon his countenance. His hair seemed to stand up right, and his eyes were ready to start from their sockets. He said to me, after a little parleying, "I never before, in my life, heard any man speak who seemed to know my heart. Mine is a terrible case; but on Sunday morning you painted me to the life, and preached as if you had been inside my soul."

By God's grace I saved that man from suicide, and led him into gospel light and liberty; but I know I could not have done it if I had not myself been confined in the dungeon in which he lay. I tell you the story, brethren, because you sometimes may not understand your own experience, and the perfect people may condemn you for having it; but what know they of God's servants? You and I have to suffer much for the sake of the people of our charge.

You may be in Egyptian darkness, and you may won-der why such a horror chills your marrow; but you may be altogether in the pursuit of your calling, and be led of the Spirit to a position of sympathy with desponding minds.[10]

Abraham Lincoln

Abraham Lincoln wasn't able to snap out of it. Depression afflicted the president throughout his entire life. We know that he was often sorrowful, but not many know that he suffered suicidal impulses so strong he didn't dare carry a knife in his pocket. This was clearly an illness that modern psychiatry would attempt to treat and cure. And yet, as author, Joshua Shenk, argues in his book *Lincoln's Melancholy,* Lincoln's depression "fueled his greatness." From black despair grew identification with the sufferings of others. From self-alienation grew commitment to a cause greater than himself.

Oswald Chambers

Oswald Chambers, the author of *My Utmost for His Highest,* describes the four years of his own dark night of the soul.

> I was at Dunoon College as tutor of Philosophy when Dr. F. B. Meyer came and spoke on the Holy Spirit. I determined to have all that was going and asked God simply and definitely for the baptism of the Holy Spirit, whatever that meant.
>
> From that day on for four years, nothing but the overruling grace of God and the kindness of friends kept me out of an asylum. God used me during those years for the conversion of souls, but I had no conscious communion with Him.[11]

William Cowper

William Cowper was considered to be one of England's greatest poets. He changed the direction of eighteenth-century English poetry by writing of everyday life and scenes of the English countryside. His association with John Newton, author of *Amazing Grace* and five hundred other hymn poems, led to much of the poetry for which he is best remembered.

But how many today are aware when they sing, "There Is a Fountain Filled with Blood," or "Oh, for a Closer Walk with God," or "God works in a mysterious way, His wonders to perform. He plants His footsteps in the sea and rides upon the storm," that he battled bipolar disorder for most of his life, survived several bouts of insanity, and attempted to commit suicide?

Others

Tolstoy, Beethoven, Rachmaninoff, and Churchill suffered long bouts of depression. Some believe Churchill had a condition that today is known as bipolar disorder. He went from extreme highs to extreme lows, periods he called his "black dog." This all led to the misuse of alcohol, for which he became famous. It was the only escape he could find as, in his day, there was no effective medical help for his condition. His doctor had to give him a shot of "speed" to get him through his last address to parliament.

Though the medical world knew much more about depression by the 1970s, other mitigating factors made Ron's situation even more challenging to him. He was to discover that the way God eventually led him to deal with it was itself "pioneer" territory. ❈

[15]

An Answer:
Strangely Clothed

※ ※ ※

God's faithfulness is not proved by the absence of trouble,
tension, calamity, disaster, or personal pain. Indeed, His
faithfulness is seen most clearly in those times when we
question His plan and feel the pain of our circumstances.
—David Jeremiah[12]

As effective as Ron's ministry had already been, a whole new world was
to open up to him when he reached the point of being able to talk about
his journey through his own dark night of the soul. As he began to share
where he had been for ten years, and what God was using to bring him into
the light, he was surprised to discover how many others, in and out of the
ministry, were experiencing similar issues in their lives—issues they were
afraid to admit to themselves, let alone to others, afraid to seek help.

But this had not come easily. Having for years impacted thousands
of people in many parts of the world through his preaching, writing, and
monthly cassette ministry, few knew what he had been battling for ten of
those years that only God's grace saw him through.

The resolution to Ron's own dark night of the soul came packaged in a way neither he nor Kaye could have ever anticipated. Clichéd answers and advice from well-meaning "comforters" were not working when the phone rang at the Dunn residence on Vancouver Street, Irving, Texas, that night. What Kaye heard on the other end of the line would soon lead to the first glimpse of light at the end of the tunnel. It was to lead them on an unconventional path, unconventional that is, to the thinking of most of the evangelical world they were part of.

"Kaye, get me help. I can't go on anymore. I'm going crazy."

Watch now how God had already begun the orchestrating of what He was going to use to meet Ron's need. The day before Ron called Kaye from Tulsa, Oklahoma, one of Kaye's friends had matter-of-factly told her that if she knew anyone who would need a Christian psychiatrist, she had just became acquainted with Dr. Gary Etter,[13] a psychiatrist who worked at the Rapha Christian Counseling headquarters located in Irving, Texas. Irving! Right where they lived.

Kaye phoned, an appointment was scheduled, and as soon as Ron returned home, they found themselves walking through the door of the Rapha Counseling Center to see Dr. Etter. Ron's inclination was to pull his jacket collar up around his ears, hoping no one would recognize him. But God does have a sense of humor, and in His way He was saying, "It's OK Ron. Trust me. I'm in this with you." The receptionist who greeted them at the clinic was a former member of their church!

The cat was out of the bag before it had even been put in. Ron knew his ministry was ruined because he had been one of those, as were most of his peers, who had a prejudiced view of that arm of the medical world.

But rather than ruin, this step would prove to be the beginning of a ministry that would eventually touch thousands of people around the world, many of whom were embarrassed to admit they had a problem. It was their own dark secret.

To many, even to this day, the mention of seeking psychiatric help triggers responses, both negative and positive—negative, from those who have never faced the darkness of depression, and positive, from those who have found help for the chemical imbalances in their bodies that many times are at the root of this illness. But why would a good God allow such things to happen to His children?

The most challenging part of knowing truth is in its being worked out in life. Knowledge, revelation, to become experience, is a process that takes time—sometimes longer than we would wish. And the process often hurts.

The Process[14]

Without the boiling process a teabag's of no use,
but when immersed its flavor is released.
That's how it is with our lives, should God increase the heat,
our usefulness to Him will be increased.

The beauty of a diamond, we know will not be seen
until some skillful cutting has been done.
An athlete knows that sacrifice and pain must be endured
before the victor's trophy can be won.

The breaking of its leg to help a lamb learn to obey
is sometimes what the shepherd has to do.
Without birth pangs and labor new life cannot be born,
nor until seeds will die can flowers bloom.

Lord, though I do not understand just what You have in mind,
I trust You for the grace to live this hour.
I trust that through the process the world I touch will know
the fragrance of Your beauty, love and power.

TESTIMONY: WARREN WIERSBE—AUTHOR AND FORMER
PASTOR OF MOODY CHURCH AND DIRECTOR OF THE BACK
TO THE BIBLE BROADCAST

Ron Dunn lived, preached, and taught what I call "muscular Christianity." He had been in the trenches and fought the battles, and he knew what it meant to meet the enemy head-on and live by faith. He offered no "three easy steps" to victory, nor did he peddle simplistic prescriptions for joy and peace.   ❋

[16]

Strange Ministers

❈ ❈ ❈

The will of God is never exactly what you expect it to be.
It may seem to be much worse, but in the end it's going to
be a lot better and a lot bigger.

—Elisabeth Elliot

From Ron's Journal

I'm not sure how it's going to end. This is when I was supposed to start the actual writing, but my family has entered into another great crisis, and I've got to admit that it is hard for me to see this as any kind of "minister from God." If it is, I'm tired of these "strange ministers." Personally, I think my family has suffered enough. I keep waiting for the all clear signal that it's safe for me to go back out into the world again.

Most of Ron's preaching from 1976 to 1986 was in self-defense. During those years he preached more for himself than for anybody else because he was trying to make sense out of the traumatic emotional ride he was on.

When there are two equally "true truths," as Ron explains, and yet they are in absolute conflict with each other; when the Bible says, on the one hand, that you have this kind of life, but in reality you don't have it; when there is a great gap between the ideal life you think you ought to be having and the reality of what you are experiencing, you have what in music is called dissonance.

Dissonance is when two notes struck simultaneously do not blend but rather cause a jarring discord. Psychologists have a term for it, they call it *cognitive dissonance*, which is when you have dissonance and you know it. For years Ron was up to his ears in cognitive dissonance, while all the time searching for some kind of resolution.

In music the resolution happens when the dissonant notes resolve into a harmonious chord. Ron sought that chord for many years. He recalls when the dark night began.

Sermon: *Strange Ministers*[15]

The Dark Night Begins

I was sitting on the front row of the First Baptist Church of Enid, Oklahoma, when I suddenly realized I could not preach. I could not preach. I was overcome with fear. I went out to the hallway where I paced back and forth saying: "God, you've got to help me, or I'm not going to be able to preach." I rebuked the devil, I praised the Lord, I quoted Scripture—I did everything you're supposed to do. Finally, when it came time, God enabled me to preach. But then this began to occur more regularly. I would go back to my motel room and fall across the bed, crying. I felt I was such a failure and that I ought to quit the ministry. I asked, "God, why are You doing this to me?"

All through this period Kaye was suffering for and with me, and I tell you, it is ten times harder on your wife and loved ones than it is on you. Then on top of all that, I began having serious stomach problems for which I would end up in the hospital. I felt totally beaten down. So many of my thoughts were about darkness. Finally, after years of this, I said, "Lord, I'm willing to do anything."

I found out something during this dark night period—I found out that contemporary, popular spirituality doesn't have much to say to people like me. Why don't we ever sing Psalm 13? We say the psalms are the hymnbook of the church.

> "How long, O Lord? Will you forget me forever? How long will You hide Your face from me? (Psalm 13:1 NASB)

> "Your wrath has swept over me; your dreadful assaults destroy me. They surround me like a flood all day long." (Ps. 88:16–17 ESV)

> "I am poor and needy, and my heart is stricken within me. I am gone like a shadow at evening." (Ps. 109:22–23 ESV)

You know what those psalms are about? They are psalms of lament, of protest, of complaint, in which nothing is resolved. There are as many psalms like that as there are happy ones. But we just go on, acting as though they aren't there.

I read books by popular spirituality authors but found nothing there to help me. Sadly, now listen carefully, I found more understanding for what I was going through from the world than from the church. Some told me it was sin—there's something wrong with you. When you take that kind of attitude, you lose all compassion. Then there are those who, when you share that you are hurting, say, "Well, you just need to cheer up. You need to have faith. Trust God." When you do that, you are trivializing my suffering.

Some were there for me, however, such as my wife and some friends without whom I would never have made it through those ten years. But, in spite of all that I was going through, I never lost my faith in God. Oh, I did lose one kind of faith. I lost the zippity-do-dah kind of faith that says, "Just pray, and your problem will be gone."

Up until 1976 I believed I could rise above all the problems of life, just because I knew how to pray and believe God. But I discovered that I could no longer do that, and the answer God gave to my cry for help came in the form of two doctors—a medical doctor in Little Rock, Arkansas, who came to me one day and said, "You need help." Dr. Harden was used to help me with a serious stomach ailment.

And then there was Dr. Etter, a Christian psychiatrist. I called Kaye from Oklahoma, where I was in a meeting. I told her I couldn't take it anymore. I told her I felt as though I was going crazy.

I went to Dr. Etter, and I still go to him. He gave me medication that I still take. God chose to use him to lead me out of my dark night of the soul. Some of you may be thinking this is a long way from the victorious life we all have preached about. Well, whatever you may be thinking, I do know that some of us need a good old dose of reality. We don't hesitate to seek medical help for every illness under the sun except the kind I'm talking about. And I do know this—help is available.

I had no idea Ronnie's suicide would trigger traumatic repercussions in my life, in Kaye's life, and in the life of our two remaining children. Nobody talked about it. Christians wouldn't talk about it, and we sure didn't dare go to anyone else. There was no help for what we were going through. Today, when I know of someone who is going through what we did, with the kind of loss we had when Ronnie died, I tell them: "Go and get some help. Get some help because this has created a trauma in your life that is going to express itself one way or the other. You can count on it."

After Ron had shared the process through which God had taken him, a process that eventually led him out of the ten years of his dark night of the soul, he turned to the ninth chapter of John. In the following message he points out an often overlooked truth. ❋

[17]

What Now?

❄ ❄ ❄

And as He passed by, He saw a man blind from birth. And His disciples asked Him, saying, "Rabbi, who sinned, this man or his parents, that he should be born blind?" Jesus answered, "It was neither that this man sinned, nor his parents; but it was in order that the works of God might be displayed in him. We must work the works of him who sent Me, as long as it is day; night is coming, when no man can work."

—JOHN 9:1–4

Sermon: *What Now?*

I want first to point out that the word "saw" here means "to look with rapt attention." Jesus fastened His eyes on that man so much so that the disciples followed His gaze and they asked the question, "Master, who did sin, this man, or his parents, that he was born blind?" (KJV).

The prevailing theology of that day was, as it is in many circles today, that blessings mean God's favor, and lack of blessings means God's "unfavor." If you are doing well, if you are healthy and everything is going well financially, then you must be on track with God, and He is blessing you. But suffering has a stigma. If things are not going well, if you are losing your money, if life is serving up one reversal after another then, "Aha! Sin somewhere brother. Yes sir. Sin somewhere."

So, when the disciples saw Jesus looking at this blind man on the side of the road, they asked the most stupid question that has ever been asked. "Master, who sinned, this man or his parents that he should be born blind?" This man? Who was born blind? Did he sin? How in the world could a man who was born blind be made blind because of his sin?

Many today think the same way the disciples were thinking back then. *Oh, you are sick, you are having problems. There must be sin in your life.* Well, what do you do with all the children in the world who are starving? What do you do with the thousands of little babies we see on TV, dying in the arms of mothers who have no more tears to cry? Is the reason those little ones are starving because they, or their parents, sinned? What are you going to do with all the children who are living in war-ravaged areas of the world who are having their arms and legs blown off? Are you going to go over there and preach a health-and-wealth message?

Those disciples were so absolutely certain that sin had to be the cause that they were stupidly oblivious to the absurdity of the question they were asking, that is, until Jesus answered: "Neither this man nor his parents sinned, but that the works of God should be made manifest in him."

Now that sounds as though God had that man be born blind just so He could work a miracle. But that's not what Jesus is saying. I checked this out with leading biblical scholars, including F. F. Bruce and Leon Morris, and they agreed that in the Greek construction of that sentence it does not mean it happened for this "reason," but rather, for what "purpose."

The reading should go as follows. Notice that we're going to place a period at the end of verse 3, which is as the Greek reads: "Neither this man sinned nor his parents." Period!

Jesus gave no explanation. Have you ever thought about how much Jesus did not tell us? Do you realize that Lazarus was never interviewed? We would have had him written up in all the papers. "What was it like to be dead back there? How'd you like it down there in that tomb?"

So many of the things you and I crave to know are not issues with Jesus. They're not important. Jesus made it clear that He had not come to answer the riddles of life but to do the Father's will. "Neither this man nor his parents sinned." Period! No explanation.

Now watch what happens. Jesus continues: "But, now that we can work the works of God, let's get on with it. Let's do it." That's what He is saying. "But now that the works of God should be manifest, let us work the works of Him who sent us" (v. 4, author paraphrase).

The question to be asked was not, "Why did this happen?" Jesus never answers that. But rather, now that this blind man is here before us, what are we going to do about it? To what end can this situation be used to get God glory? So often the reason we ask the question, "why?" is because we feel that an explanation would satisfy us.

I have a friend whose teenage son went into the bathroom three years ago and shot himself. I talked to him recently. He said: "You know, Ron, I can see God doing a lot of things. I can see how God is using this. A number of our relatives have been saved." And then he said, "But that's not enough. That's not enough."

Well, am I going to question that man? If God tells me why our own son committed suicide, Ronnie's still gone. He's still gone. The life he could have had is gone. The children he could have fathered are gone. Comfort does not come from explanation; comfort comes from the promises of God. We do not live by explanation; we live by promise. So, in light of this, I'd like to suggest something.

Instead of asking the question "why?" let's change it to, "Alright Lord, what now? What now? To what end, for what purpose has this happened?" This helps us in three areas.

It Saves Us from Self-Pity

I confess I wallowed in my own pity. I have felt sorry for myself to the extent that I wouldn't want to get out of bed in the morning. I'd hear myself saying, "What's the use?" An egocentric person is the most miserable person on the face of the earth. Why? Because what we want to do more than anything else is to control our lives, not realizing we cannot control our lives.

In asking, "why, why, why," we're really asking, "why me? why me? It wouldn't bother me as much if it were happening to you, but, why me?" We don't often ask, "Why did that happen to him?" It's usually, "Why me?" and so, we turn inward and focus on ourselves.

It Saves Us from the Moment

When we ask, "What now?" it saves us from the moment, the immediate, and gives us a future to look forward to. "Now that we've encountered this man who was born blind, let's get to work," Jesus was saying. There is something to do."

I went through a period when I thought, *No matter how good life was in the past, it can never be as good again. All the good times are gone.* I even thought, *How terrible it is to have outlived your good times.* That's a terrible way to live. But when you begin asking, "What now?" you begin to realize that there is a future, and the future belongs to God.

At the end of a meeting some time ago, a couple approached me, and as we talked, the wife said: "It was sure good to see you smile tonight." I replied, as I chuckled, "Well, thank you." "No," she said, "I was so glad to see you smile tonight." "Well, that's great. I'll take any compliment that comes my way." She said: *"You don't know why I'm saying that, do you?" "No ma'am, I don't."*

Then she continued, "Six months ago my seventeen-year-old daughter was killed in a car wreck, and I knew my life was over. I saw in the paper that you were in town, and knowing about some of the things you have been through, I came tonight to see how you were doing. And as I sat there and saw you smile, I said to myself, 'One day I'll smile again. One day I'll smile again.'"

Folks, that's all anybody wants to know. Am I going to make it? Am I going to survive? Will I smile again? In Psalm 42:11, the psalm Ray Stedman called the King David Blues, David says: "I will yet praise the Lord." He couldn't praise the Lord right then, but he knew that one day he would. "I will not drink the bitter cup forever, I will yet praise the Lord."

I was met at an airport by a pastor who had been going through one of the hardest family situations you could imagine. At the end of his story, he turned to me and said: "Bro. Dunn, I just want you to know that when you get up to preach tonight to all those pastors there will be a lot of guys sitting out there, just like me, wanting to know, 'Are we going to make it? Are we going to make it?'"

God Can Use Us to Display His Glory

When we get to the point of being able to ask the question, "What now?" instead of "Why?" it makes us, it makes you, it makes me, a part of God's work.

As I studied this John 9 passage, I began to realize that a "whole man" would have been of no use to Jesus that day. There would not have been any opportunity for God to manifest Himself if that man had been whole. This has led me to ask myself the question many times, "Lord, am I willing to be less than whole if that's what You need to manifest Your power through me?" I've come to see my ministry as a vehicle for caring for others and not as an arena for ambition or success. My life has been changed.

Some of the most profound revelations that come to me don't happen in my study but when I'm out mowing the lawn or weed-eating. That's what I was doing a few years back on my father's farm in Arkansas. I began thinking about how often people had come up at the end of meetings to tell me what an encouragement I had been to them. More and more churches that were going through difficult times were contacting me to come and encourage them. As I looked back, I realized that this was happening at the exact time when I was going through the darkest days of my life. Those sermons I had prepared and preached out of my own despair and depression, seeking an answer for myself, turned out to be encouragement to others.

The Lord has been good to us, but I wish I could stand here today and tell you folk that everything is alright. It isn't. The last three years have been the toughest three years Kaye and I have ever spent, and yet, in the midst of it all, God has blessed more than He ever has.

Now I haven't told you all this to whip up sympathy. Everybody has their own story. I've been telling you part of mine with the prayer that maybe it will help you, that it may help somebody open up and begin letting their own dark night be exposed to the light. It may well save your marriage, and it could even save your ministry.

Let me say again—**Jesus could not have done what He did that day with a whole man.**

TESTIMONY: A PASTOR'S WIFE

Now that Ron is gone, what I'm going to miss most is having someone like him who understands what it is like to deal with the roller-coaster ride of chemical depression. He knew how difficult it is for those of us in the ministry who are supposed to be immune to things like that.

I never admired him more than when he stood before hundreds of pastors and wives at the Rapha Luncheon at the Southern Baptist Convention and openly and honestly shared his own testimony. I sat there and wept.

I pray that, because of Ron's genuine faith and transparency, many people will continue to be better informed and, as they think of Ron, that they will realize it isn't unspiritual to seek help that will enable them to live a more normal life. ✳

[INTERLUDE]

Family

❋ ❋ ❋

Family is a place where principles are hammered and honed on the anvil of everyday living.

—Chuck Swindoll[16]

Prelude

The importance of family to Ron cannot be overstated. His parents and grandparents, brother, Kaye, his own children, in-laws, occupied a very special place in his heart. Family gatherings, especially times at the farm, other events, whether good or bad, every illness, every death, impacted Ron, some more profoundly than others, some leading him into periods of deep introspection. This was particularly true of the illnesses and deaths of his mother and father—and most deeply, Ronnie Jr.

From Ron's Journal

The older I grow, the more I find myself returning to the days when I was young, remembering the house on Fortieth Street in Fort Smith that represents a time when everything was all right. But no matter how hard I try to replicate it, there always seems to be a sense of something missing because the real home we long for is the one that has been called our "long home." Paul put it this way: "For indeed in this house we groan, longing to be clothed with our dwelling from heaven" (2 Cor. 5:2).

We'll never have to move away from this home because we'll be where all things are made new, and the tears of this life will be permanently wiped away. Our longing for this home is because God has put eternity in our hearts.

Journal Entry

Ronnie Jr. came in the house straddling his stick horse. He was all out of breath, panting and puffing and covered with sweat. I asked him what he had been doing. He said: "I've been riding my stick horse, playing cowboy." I teasingly said, "Cowboys don't get out of breath just riding their horses." "But Dad," Ronnie replied. "I have to do my own gallopin'." I thought, How many of us are doing our own galloping?

The following letter was written by Ronnie Jr. to his parents when he was visiting his grandparents in Arkansas.

> *Dear Mom and Dad,*
>
> *I've been having a lot of fun since I've been here. Two days ago I was watching TV when Grandma noticed two boys out in the alley smoking cigarettes. She said, "Ronnie, why don't you go out there and just for fun tell them that you took their picture." So I did. One of the boys said, "You got a HERE COME DA JUDGE shirt," trying to make me forget about the smoking. Then I said, "You shouldn't be smoking." Then one of them said, "We don't smoke like most people do. We don't inhale the smoke." "Then I said, "Where do you live?" They said, "We don't*

*know," and they walked off. Grandma and I thought that
was the funniest thing! Now they are my friends, and now
I must go.*

Journal Entry

*But now he's gone, and I know I can't bring him back. I still wish I
could. I saw a teenager the other day walking along the highway, smoking
a cigarette. He looked just like Ronnie. I wished it could have been him.*

*One of the questions my doctor once asked me was, "What would be the
first thing you would say to Ronnie if you could talk to him?"*

"Doc, the first thing I'd say to my son is, 'I love you, Ronnie.'"

*Now, some people may have a hard time understanding what I'm going
to say, but that's OK. The way I feel now is when I get to heaven the first
person I'm going to look for is Ronnie, so I can tell him again how much
I love him.*

Journal Entry

*Last night Kaye and I watched the tape of the old home movies of
Ronnie, Mom, and Dad. I had forgotten how beautiful a child Ronnie was
and how much we lost when we lost him. It caused me to miss him again,
as though for the first time.*

*Later, in bed, Kaye said she still had some grieving to do about
Ronnie. She didn't say exactly what it was, just that she realized there were
some things she had not been able to close the door on.*

*In spite of all Ronnie's death has put us through, I still agree with
what Frederick Buechner says in his book* Now *and* Then*:*

> What man and woman, if they gave serious thought to what
> having children inevitably involves would ever have them? Yet,
> what man and woman, once having had them and loved them,
> would ever have it otherwise? If by some magic you could
> eliminate the pain you are caused by the pain of someone you

love, I for one cannot imagine working such magic because the pain is so much a part of the love that the love would be vastly diminished, unrecognizable without it. To suffer in love for another's suffering is to live life, not only at the fullest, but at its holiest.[17]

Journal Entry

It's raining, and Dad is dying. But I'm not outraged. I was when Mom died. I was indignant. She was only sixty and so beautiful and full of life. Another ten years was all I asked the Lord for. Just until seventy, the number the Lord Himself had picked. I wasn't asking for more—just what He had promised. I wasn't asking Him to violate the rules of the universe.

I never doubted He could do it. He who set the stars on their course could change the course of the cancer rolling through her body. Whether or not He could do it was not the question. He chose not to—ten years short of the three-score and ten. I felt she had been cheated. God said, "no."

I remember when my paternal grandfather died. He was in the hospital, an old converted frame house. He just lay there in bed, the bluish bruises on his arms, needle tracks from the shots they had given him. The sweet smell like someone had sprayed perfume over the death in that room. I know dad prayed for his healing, but God said, "no."

Did Dad feel what I am feeling right now? Back then, was I totally unaware of the grief in his heart when his father was dying—a child's unconcern? Thomas Wolfe, in his novel You Can't Go Home Again, *says: "Every man and woman is filled with his own journey." What he is saying is that every individual makes sense of life in his own way.*

Each person has to discover for himself. We're still wrestling with the same questions Job and Habakkuk dealt with, and we haven't advanced beyond their conclusions, yet we keep writing on the subject. Just because a question can't be answered doesn't mean it can be ignored.

Midnight Run

Ron took Highway 59 out of Houston where he had been in a meet-ing. It was raining. In Texarkana he picked up Highway 71 toward Fort Smith, and when he got to De Queen, Arkansas, he tanked up on gas and caffeine—unleaded gas and leaded coffee. De Queen was where his dad was born. As he headed north on 71, passing through little towns that brought back a lot of family memories—Wilkes, Hatfield, Waldron, Abbott. He found himself writing a letter in his mind, a letter to his dad. It was a letter telling him that he loved him, that he was proud to be his son, things like that.

"Maybe when I get there I can whisper some of these things in his ear, things I've wanted to say but never really did. Maybe he'll be able to hear and understand."

It was still raining when he turned off of Highway 71 on to FM 10 and headed east toward the farm. Kaye flew into Fort Smith the next morning. Ron picked her up at 10:50 and on their way back to Greenwood they went by the hospital to see his dad. It was a very emo-tional time. He tried to tell his dad the things he had on his heart—the letter he had written in his mind.

> *Dad, I'm so proud of you. You worked hard six days*
> *a week, sunup to sundown all your life, and you became*
> *more than a successful businessman in spite of never*
> *having finished high school. Thank you for the home you*
> *provided us and for giving us a Christian upbringing. I'm*
> *so proud to be your son. I love you.*

When Ron finished, his dad opened his eyes. There were tears. This experience caused Ron to begin wondering how many parents, how many children, and how many friends there are who have not adequately expressed themselves to each other before one of them dies and leaves an aching sense of a door never opened. "What counts," as Max Lerner says, "is that we reach into ourselves and have come up with griefs, failures, satisfactions, anxieties, triumphs and have shared them."[18]

The Farm

Barry and Janet were living at the farm during this period, and while Ron was getting ready for the next engagement at First Baptist Church, Elk City, Oklahoma, he and Barry had time to reminisce.

Journal Entry

We talked about the simple life we had as children and how "nonquality" time is as important as "quality" time. We played in the backyard or in our rooms by ourselves, secure in the knowledge that our parents were there if we needed them. This was before all the books were written and the "enlightenment" age arrived that manufactured artificial time periods rather than the natural, spontaneous life kids used to have. Back then children didn't know that they were supposed to feel insecure if their parents weren't doing all the things they have to do these days to keep their children engaged and happy.

Journal Entry

Elk City, Oklahoma—I wish it were not such a beautiful day, but it is. And that makes it all the harder to accept what is happening in Room 5518 at Saint Edwards Mercy Hospital in Fort Smith. If it were a blistery cold, grey, rainy day, it would make it easier. The contrast is too great.

I can't help but think back on the many summer evenings we spent together, cooking suppers (and what great food), playing games . . . laughter, joking. I guess we'll never sit at that farm table again, just like that, but we will sit at another table in heaven.

The contrast is always there. Johan Christiaan Beker in his book, Suffering and Hope, *says: "The tension between suffering and hope is basic to the Christian life. It is so basic that for many of us the tension itself has become a contradiction. It suffocates hope and compels resignation and despair. Life between hope and hopelessness . . . is that really where we find ourselves today?"*[19]

So life goes on as if nothing bad were to happen. Makes me wonder how many times someone has hated me for having a good time in the mall when their dearest has just died.

At the noon meetings I'm speaking on prayer. Before the meeting today I went into the darkened auditorium where the only light was the soft red glow of the exit light. I sat down, leaned forward, and rested my head in my hands on the back of the pew in front. I prayed, "Lord, can I pray for Dad to be healed? He was a little better yesterday, they said, but doctors also said for us not to get our hopes up because he is only going to get worse. Can I pray for Dad to be healed?"

So far my response in prayer has been to thank God for giving Dad to us for so long, but I'm still asking God if I can pray for his healing. No answer yet.

Journal Entry

Dad's dying is bringing about the closure to my decade-long struggle with life, death, and faith. When Mom died, I was starry-eyed and believed prayer and faith could change anything. I felt they were a way of rising above the groanings of this life.

Then Ronnie's death shattered this illusion. At that point I dipped into a ten-year battle, starting in 1976, and that didn't begin to end until 1986 while Kaye and I were in Cape Cod.

But now, with Dad's illness, right from the beginning I have been at peace, knowing that I am able to face anything through Christ (Phil. 4:13). There is an incredible sense of peace and well-being, knowing that this is the taste of life. These things are what give life its fullness and richness.

I'm not sure how to say it, but, dealing with Dad and his illness has somehow settled many issues and laid questions to rest. I feel bitterness melting away; resentment and outrage of life, dissipating.

With Dad's illness and death I felt that we were experiencing a vital part of the life process—death as a part of life, rather than an interruption. I've once again been struck with the cold, hard fact that life doesn't skip a beat; the world doesn't stop for one moment to mourn a loss—life goes on and you can either go on with it or . . . ?

Max Lerner's observation in his book Wrestling with the Angel, *is noteworthy:* "The ways in which we experience the death of others defines how we will face our own death."[20]

Journal Entry

Dad's gone. It doesn't seem possible, and it sure doesn't seem real. It's been a month since he died. I don't think it will sink in until we go to the farm for our family vacation in August. Kaye and I had to leave right after the funeral to start another meeting, then on to the New Orleans Convention and on and on.

But there are the good memories. We used to laugh at Dad because he was so predictable. He had a routine. He would call us at the same time every day, phrase what he said in exactly the same way. He'd close the garage door at exactly the same time every night. We'd laugh about it, but now that's exactly what I miss. Those are the kind of things that make a life solid, real, and tangible.

I miss him very much, and I don't know if this is normal, but I seem to grow closer to him every day; the sense of him grows stronger. My love for him is growing. Can this be?

I have a good feeling about it all, a sense of satisfaction. I have no regrets. We were close. He was a great dad and granddad. He was loved and respected not just by his own family but by others. He was a good man who made something of himself and left this life with honor and dignity. I'm proud to be his son.

He has left an indelible mark on us. A lot of him is in us. It's strange, but as I write this, he seems more real than when he was alive. I find myself wanting to stand on a soapbox in the mall and tell everybody: "Hey, this was my dad! Isn't he great?"

Journal Entry

Christmas Eve, 1991—tonight I phoned my brother, Barry, at the farm in Arkansas.

"Have you sung it yet?"

"Sung what?"

"White Christmas!"

Years ago, during the Second World War, we lived in Kansas while Dad worked in one of the war plants. It was the first white Christmas I had ever seen. On Christmas Eve night, Barry and I were lying in bed when he said to me, "If we don't sing 'White Christmas,' we won't enjoy Christmas."

And so we did. Back then I believed everything my older brother told me, after all, he was ten and I was only seven.

Every Christmas since then I've remembered that night. It always fills me with a melancholy joy. And it is that little snatch of memory that makes that Christmas one of those that I remember best and hold dearest. Funny how little simple things make an inerasable impression on the mind, and it is usually something that is shared with someone you love.

Saying Good-night

Barry started this practice when we were teenagers. After being out for the evening, when we got home, we would go into Mom and Dad's bedroom to say good-night. I remember how afraid I was to smoke or drink with friends because I knew that when I got home I was going to have to say good-night to my parents, and Mom, who had the nose of a bloodhound, would know. Amazing how little things often wield the greatest power.

Mom

We usually arrived pretty late at the farm, and on each visit, as we drove up the hill before the turnoff onto Milltown Road, Kaye would wake the kids up to comb their hair so they would look nice for Mom and Dad. I remember how, on one particular night when we arrived, Mom was so turned on that she had us sit up late, listening to a *Blood, Sweat and Tears* album she had just bought. Who would have thought . . . ? Mom loved music. She had rhythm in her bones. Many times I would walk in on her and catch her dancing to music on the radio. She loved the Charleston when she was young. There was a lot of play in her. She would sometimes sneak up on me and pour cold water down my back or rub hot peppers on my lips. But she also had her mood swings. She was a worrywart and would often become moody and depressed. This was long before we knew anything about stuff like that.

Journal Entry

The note: I found the note several years after Mom died. Evidently, during one of her visits she had gone to my desk and half way through a notepad had written: Ronald Dunn, I love you. October 1972.

A Cemetery Visit

On the way to the cemetery in Monroe, Oklahoma, we drove by the old sawmill where I used to play when I visited my grandparents. Their house had a potbellied stove in the middle of the room—the smells of the fire, the kerosene lamps, and pipe tobacco are to me still among the best smells ever. Ma made banana pudding and introduced me to peanut butter-laced cereal. Pa had a razor strap hanging on the back porch near the water bucket and the dipper he used to get cold water out of the well. He had been a barber, farmer, a carpenter, and, according to Mom, had once played a mean fiddle.

I used to climb the mountain of sawdust at the sawmill, getting it in my hair, mouth, clothes; and I can smell it even now.

As we crossed the railroad tracks, I remembered when I was a little boy how I would stand on the tracks with a nickel in my hand. Someone had told me that if you placed a nickel on the track, it would wreck the train. I would place the coin on the gleaming rail and stand there imaging a great wreck. Then I'd quickly retrieve the nickel and walk away with a sense of pride that I had overcome a great temptation and had prevented a train wreck.

We drove around the old white church with its rotting steeple to the cemetery behind. This was my fourth visit to the graves of Mom and her parents—my Big Ma and Pa.

I remember . . . I remember each time hearing the birds sing.

Journal Entry

I'm about to leave on a three-week trip to churches in Chattanooga, Tennessee; Corinth, Mississippi; and Savannah, Tennessee. I'm so glad Kaye is going with me on this trip. We treasure the times we can travel together, to explore, see new sites, meet new people. She has not been able to travel much this past year because of Dad's illness.

Losing Dad has been a potent reminder that we don't have forever to savor and cherish our times together. We need to squeeze everything we can out of life—suck it dry so as not to have to face the stiff judgment of an unused life, opportunities not taken, blessings not realized, experiences not tasted.

Family Memories

Barry Dunn—Brother

I miss my brother more than I ever thought I would. We were always close, but it wasn't until after he died that I realized how close we were. He was a sentimental cuss. We'd sit around and talk . . . "Do you remember this, or do you remember that?" Then when Ron was gone, there was no one to remember with because there were just the two of us. Ron was one of the most thoughtful guys you'd ever meet. Out of the blue he'd surprise you with some gift. He was always thinking about doing something for you. He was a loving and mischievous kid, and I guess you could say he never grew out of either.

I noticed a change in Ron after Ronnie's death. As much as he loved humanity, it did not always translate into the one-on-one kind of relationships, other than with his own family and close friends. But after Ronnie Jr.'s death, it was different. He began to sense the pain in others. God used Ronnie's death to open up a whole new ministry to the hurting in this world.

Janet Dunn—Sister-in-Law

We got a phone call from Ron when Kaye was going through her chemo treatments for lymphoma, when he himself was so sick. She had been such a stabilizing force and strength to him for so many years, and he was afraid that the Lord was going to take her. He told us that if Kaye died we would have to "adopt" him. We understood what he meant. Family always meant so much to Ron. He couldn't imagine life without her.

Stephen Dunn—Son

Having a father like I did was a blessing that can't be put into words. He had a way of teaching me life lessons I've never forgotten. One time, when I was in elementary school, we were driving under Stemmons Freeway in Dallas when we saw a couple street people begging for money. I don't recall if I asked my dad a question, but I do remember what he said. "If you walked up to one of those folk and gave him $100, and you did that every day for a week, then the next week you walked on past him and gave the $100 to the other fellow, as you walked away, the first guy you gave money to is going to yell, 'Hey, where's my $100?' Just remember that, Stephen." I waited for Dad to say something more, to tell me what he meant, but he just left it at that. He left me to figure it out for myself.

Years later, when a situation came up in college, I suddenly remembered what Dad had said back then, and I immediately understood what was happening. That's the way he was. He would put something out there, knowing that when I needed to apply it, I would understand what he meant.

That's how it is to this day. In almost every decision I make, I remember the little things he would say like, "If you don't get what you really want, you're not getting a deal." I heard him saying that in my mind the other day when I was shopping. When I'm doing something wrong, I remember a statement he made years ago. You can't get that kind of thing anywhere else. That's the way he taught me about God, about life in general, little nuggets of wisdom I'll never forget. He was so gifted in communicating truth. He saw things in a way you'd always remember.

MORE THAN JUST MY DAD

I was in the seventh grade when I suddenly realized what kind of person he was to everyone else. One Sunday morning we were on our way to a church in Richardson where Dad was going to preach. I was sitting in the backseat when I heard Mom say that a number of pastors from other churches in the area were going to be there to hear him preach. I didn't say anything, though I wondered why pastors would leave their own church to hear my dad speak. I was confused. But then, after the service all these people started coming up to talk to him. As I stood by his side, I was hearing things about him I'd never heard before. I thought to myself, *I think my Dad is great, but these people think he's wonderful.*

That night, as I sat in the second row, I could see how excited people were that they were going to get to hear my father preach. I was real proud that he was my Dad. Well, when he got up and said that he was going to preach on the Prodigal Son, I was so disappointed. My reaction was, "Oh no. Everyone knows everything there is to know about that story. How is he going to preach anything they haven't already heard? They've heard a hundred sermons on it."

Well, to this day I remember that sermon more than any other sermon in my life. My dad pointed out that this story has more to say about the father than it does the son. This is the sermon I fall back on for the problems I have to deal with. No matter what you do, you're still your Father's son.

After the service, on our way home, I asked Dad how he did that—how he could preach like that, how he saw that the story was about the father. He said: "It's simple. When you're studying and exegeting a passage, you have to zero in on one specific point. You can embellish it, but you need to be careful that you don't chase a lot of rabbits. You want the people to leave remembering the one message you're trying to communicate. As I studied that passage, I began to realize that the main character in the story was the father."

Back then I remember it was faddish for preachers to see how many things they could pull out of a verse, and the people would end up not remembering any of it. Dad had a way of communicating truth in such a simple way that you wouldn't forget it. But what people didn't realize is how many hours and even months he would spend in not only preparing the sermon but in processing it in his own life.

My Dad—a Family Man

I think you could say that Dad's favorite place was home. Though he had to do a lot of traveling in his ministry, he was always looking forward to getting back home. He liked to drive at night, as I do, so it was not unusual for him to drive all night to get home. At home he could have his privacy. At home he could study. And when he was at home, he didn't look like a preacher. Most people who only knew him in the pulpit would be surprised how down-to-earth he could be when he was able to let down.

Among the most favorite memories I have is of my time with Dad on the family farm in Arkansas. He loved guns, and he had a large collection of them that he'd bring to the farm every summer. Sometimes he and I would sit up most of the night making ammunition and loading as many as eight to nine hundred rounds for the guns we'd use the next day for target practice and shooting all kinds of critters. During the night, while we were working on the ammunition, we'd make several trips to the lake to check out the trout lines. He was the best father. He liked being with family.

DEALING WITH DAD'S PAIN

Dad loved to read, and though he had his favorite authors, he also read authors he did not agree with. He said he did that in order to see why they thought the way they did.

One of his favorite authors was C. S. Lewis. He started giving me Lewis books to read in the fifth grade. I have entries in my diaries when Dad was showing me how, in Lewis's book, *The Problem of Pain,* he seemed to have all the answers, even for pets dying, but when his own wife, Joy, died, he wrote how different it is when "the beast is at your own door." My dad related to a lot of what C. S. Lewis went through, and he helped me face a lot of issues that I had as I watched my own father struggle with what he did. I had a hard time dealing with why God would allow this to happen to my dad when I knew how faithfully he was serving God. I couldn't get that question out of my head, and even to this day I struggle with Dad's sermon about Job. I watch it, I know it's true, but I still struggle with it.

It's interesting, but I had a harder time dealing with what Dad went through than I did with Ronnie's death. Though the last three years of Ronnie's life were terrible, I could remember all the good years we had together and what a wonderful older brother he had been to me. Though Ronnie could get violent, it really didn't scare me; but I was so scared as I watched Dad go through those long years of depression, when I saw him crash, when I saw him struggle, while at the same time I saw him keep going. Few people knew what he was going through.

At one point I told him that I trusted him more than I trusted God, which I know was really stupid, but that's just how I felt. But as I've gotten older, I realize that what my dad went through made him who he was. It made him the person who could identify with those who were hurting. If he had not gone through the pain he did, he would not have had the ministry he had.

DAD, THE SALESMAN?

Dad told me about why he had failed as a salesman. He said he had decided to do some tent-making during the period he had entered evangelism and that he only got three invitations in an eighteen-month period. He tried selling World Book Encyclopedias and ended up not selling a single set. He told me how he was in somebody's home where he could clearly see by the condition of the place that they had no business spending money on World Books. Dad could see by the look on the wife's face that she was concerned about going into debt, even though her husband loved books. When the man decided to buy the set, Dad told me that he actually talked him out of buying it.

DAD'S FIRST BOOK

A special memory I have of one of our summers at the farm was the year Dad was trying to finish the manuscript of his first book, *Any Christian Can*. Dad was in the living room typing away, and Mom was in the dining room editing what Dad was writing. To me, they looked like two college students frantically trying to finish a term paper.

HIS HUMOR

Dad's humor seemed always to be just below the surface. He told us that he was now thinking of turning this book into a trilogy: First, *Any Christian Can;* then, *Every Christian Should;* and the third one, *Most*

Christians Don't. Dad always had something about titles. He felt that titles could make or break a book, and he was concerned when publishers changed the titles of any of the books he wrote.

MY FATHER'S SON

Because my Dad was so well known and loved by so many people, everywhere I went I was known as Ron Dunn's son; but when I went on an archeological dig in Israel, I figured that I would just be Stephen Dunn. I was assigned a section in the Beth-Shean area and was given a group of archeological student volunteers from Australia to assist me. They met me in the upper area of the mound, and the first thing I did · was introduce myself.

Now, here I was, half a world away from home where no one would know who my father was. I was just Stephen Dunn, archeologist. Well, I had no sooner introduced myself than one of the girl students raised her hand and said: "Are you any relation to Ron Dunn?" I couldn't believe it. Here was someone from even farther away, from another part of the world, Australia, who had been impacted by my dad's ministry.

I have so many good memories, some so personal that I've never shared them. I've kept them to myself, conversations I had with Dad that still run through my head—advice he gave about different things. They're always there. And many of these memory conversations took place on the farm where Dad would give me 100 percent of his attention. The farm was where I really got to know him; that's where he could totally relax and just be Dad—target shooting together, fishing, popping corn every night after Mom had gone to bed. He was like a kid, the two of us, up half the night.

Then there was the movie that was perhaps Dad's favorite. I'll never forget when he took me to see it. Mom was upset because she thought I was a bit young. Through the years, whenever it was going to be shown on TV, he would call me. He even called me one time when I was in seminary: "Stephen, it's on tonight." That was my dad—memories that I can't ever lose.

Kimberly Dunn—Daughter

Kimberly was her dad's girl. He would do anything for her, and she thought he had hung the moon. Regrettably, at the writing of this biography, Kim suffered a stroke that has affected her speech and arm movement, but even with this handicap, she has put forth a heroic effort to communicate with Kaye about her dad. Her eyes light up the moment you begin talking about him. Kaye shares some of these memories that she and Kim have of those years that are forever etched in their hearts.

EARLY DAYS

During her middle-school years Kimberly played on the Irving Basketball Team. She looked so cute in her red and navy uniform. We still have wonderful memories of those days. Though Ron was pastoring MacArthur Boulevard Baptist Church, unless it was Prayer Meeting night, he never missed a game.

Kimberly loved sports, and George Brett, third baseman with the Kansas City Royals, was her idol. Ron bought her an official George Brett shirt, which we still have, with his number 5 emblazoned on it, along with a KC Royals jacket. Through the years he continued to buy a lot of other baseball memorabilia for her. She later became an avid Cowboys, Rangers, and Mavericks fan; and as her dad traveled he would bring her banners, baseballs, and T-shirts to add to her collection. When he was home, they enjoyed watching the games together.

DAD AND DAUGHTER FUN

Her dad was mischievous, even as a pastor. Kim loves to remember the time she convinced him to take her out to "toilet paper" the trees of someone's home, much to my chagrin. It was in retaliation for one of her friends having done it to our house. Yes, Ron did it!

Mexican food was a family favorite, and after eating at El Chico's, she and Ron loved to take the leftover tortillas out to the parking lot and toss them like frisbees.

THE HORSE

Kimberly had always wanted a horse. When she was fourteen years old, a friend gave her one that we boarded in Irving where Ron could teach her to ride and how to take care of him. We began renting a horse trailer soon after that and took him to our farm in Arkansas each summer where we spent several weeks with our extended family. While at the farm her dad also taught her to ride the three wheelers, as well as how to fish in the lake and run a trout line.

TRAVELING TOGETHER

Kimberly would accompany us on many of our overseas trips. At the Keswick Convention in England, she would be so proud of him as the newspapers on every corner of the convention streets would be filled with pictures and articles of her dad.

SNIFFLES AND AN ILLUSTRATION

Kimberly loved it when her dad would use her as an illustration. One of the incidents she liked to hear her dad tell concerning her was about a family visit to Six Flags Over Texas when she was quite young. As our family entered the Six Flags park, a man was selling balloons at the front gate, and, of course, Kimberly wanted one. Ron convinced her that riding all the rides would not be feasible, trying to hold on to a balloon, but that we would get one as we left the park. We spent the whole day doing everything the children wanted to do until finally, near midnight, when the park was closing, we headed home.

As we were driving along, Ron heard a sniffle coming from the backseat. He assumed it was one of the many hot dogs they'd eaten, hitting bottom. The sniffling continued, however, so he jerked the car to the side of the road and asked what the problem was. Kimberly, in her little childish voice, said: "I didn't get a balloon. You promised you'd get me a balloon!"

Of course, we didn't think about the balloon man when we were leaving. He probably had gone home. But that answer really hit Ron the wrong way, after having spent his whole Saturday and a whole lot of money to see that we had had a wonderful time. But Kimberly was just a little girl, and in spite of all you might do for little children, the one thing they are going to remember is the one thing they didn't get.

Ron likened this experience to Nathan's telling David that God wasn't going to permit him to build the temple, and God then reminding David of where he was when God had found him—in a pasture, tending sheep. God was saying, "David, before you complain about the one thing you can't have, remember all that you do have. Before you lament over what I haven't given you, remember all that I have given to you." And now, looking back, we remember that David did leave something behind, called the Psalms, and the seed of David, and the house of David.

Kimberly also remembers how her dad would talk to her about marrying a godly man. He would list all the qualities she should look for, and then, he'd say: "Be sure he's a Baptist!"

Note: There are several cards and letters from Kimberly to her Dad in the scrapbooks Kaye provided for this biography. And almost, without exception, Kim is telling him how much she loves him, while affirming her conviction that he is both the world's greatest father and the world's greatest preacher! Following Ron's home-going she wrote:

> Here are a few things, Dad, that I didn't get to say
> before you died, but you probably already knew. I love
> you more than any daughter could. You were a great role
> model for fathers. A girl could never have asked for a
> better father than you. My only regret is that you didn't
> get to see me walk again, but someday you will. I love you
> and I can't wait till we see each other again. Your loving
> daughter, Kimberly

Julie Blevins—Kaye's Sister

Ron married Ken and me in 1967 at Lifeline Baptist Church. Kaye was my maid of honor, and Stephen was the ring bearer. Interestingly, it turned out that Ron wasn't licensed to perform marriages in Arkansas and hadn't realized that until *after* the wedding. The family, however, made it a point to wait until we returned from our honeymoon to tell us that our wedding wasn't quite official yet! They didn't want us to spend our honeymoon thinking we were living in sin. In any case Ron filled out the right paperwork, and our wedding became legal!

Ron's series on the Holy Spirit transformed my relationship with Jesus. His tapes ministered directly to me and helped me grow. I felt so honored to be his sister-in-law.

Ron was full of fun. I remember a family reunion at a state lodge where we played charades. No one was more into it than Ron. Then there was that family reunion at Kaye and Ron's home when we played a word game which had us in hysterics.

I went and stayed with Kaye when Ron had to be away after Ronnie's death. I remember suffering with her. I remember as the years passed how she still suffered. That is why Kaye is wonderful to the core, in weeping with those who weep and rejoicing with those who rejoice. And she has always been so good at celebrating the accomplishments of my own children and bragging on them—even when she is in the midst of problems or disappointments in her own life.

Vickie Mitchell—Kaye's Sister

I was very shy around Ron when I was eleven years old, the year he and Kaye married. I remember hiding when he drove up to our house to pick Kaye up. I was in awe of this older, handsome man my sister was going to marry!

I have early memories of playing chess with Ron. He used to accuse me of cheating (in jest), and I was horrified. He had a great sense of humor, which I grew to appreciate as I matured.

I admired Ron in many ways. I was so impressed with his wide range of reading interests, which included fiction and nonfiction. We were both reading Tolstoy's *War and Peace* around the same time; I'm not sure who started reading it first. Anyway, it impressed me that Ron was expanding his own knowledge base through nonreligious material from which one can find many truths. He was very intelligent and quick-witted.

I heard Ron preach many times, and though my religious views, that evolved over time, differed from his, I always enjoyed hearing what he had to say. He was very charismatic in the pulpit, and he spoke with integrity and simplicity. I miss Ron a lot! I have a section of a bookshelf organized with his books, with a picture of him nearby.

Regarding my sister, Kaye, she had her hands full in her role of being the supportive wife, a partner in Ron's ministry, and having the huge job of managing their children, especially when Ron was traveling away from home. Kaye has had an enormous responsibility and has carried it out well.

The loss of Ronnie Jr. was devastating, but I think they both grew through this loss and became more dedicated to their parenting responsibilities and to their faith. I admire her and Ron's strengths, and I know they have been an inspiration to many people. I have feelings of love and respect for them both.

Pat Grossman—Family Friend

I met Ron in 1982 while visiting the family with Vickie. I was immediately impressed with Ron's warmth, intelligence, charm, and sense of humor. We all had so much fun whenever he was part of the group.

I come from a Jewish background, and I consider myself a cultural Jew. Ron was always respectful of that and never tried to proselytize me. I remember one visit Vicki and I made to Dallas during Hanukkah. I decided to bring my menorah and light candles while we were there. I'll never forget Ron's interest and enthusiasm when I performed that simple ritual. It was such a small thing, but he embraced what I was doing and made me feel that much more included in the family.

I loved Ron. I loved how smart he was, his openness to learning, his interest in everyone, including me. I continue to miss having him in our family. ✳

PART FIVE

Going International: Switzerland, the United Kingdom, and Beyond

We must be global Christians with a global vision because our God is a global God.

—John R. W. Stott

[18]

And Beyond

Prelude

Ron's life and ministry had as great an impact beyond the shores of North America as they did at home. When Ron and Kaye boarded that Braniff plane in Dallas in January 1974, headed for the revival conference in Switzerland, they could not have anticipated what the future was going to hold. This was their first trip beyond the shores of North America, and Ron's "traveling pastor" ministry, that would begin the following year, was destined to extend farther than they could ever have dreamed— Europe, Australia, South Africa, Central America, the Caribbean Islands, and closer to home, Canada. Yet, as far as Ron's preaching ministry was destined to reach, his monthly cassette ministry would reach even farther around the world, into many countries he himself would never visit.

Switzerland

Château d'Oex (pron, "day")

January 1974, was the first of three years of consecutive ministry for Ron at the annual Swiss Revival Seminar held at the International

Christian Center (Hotel Rosat) in Château d'Oex, Switzerland. These seminars were a result of Ron Owens's assuming the leadership of the ICC ministry in 1970, and at his invitation the following year, Ralph Neighbor Jr., Jack Taylor, and Ron Dunn's mentor, Manley Beasley, formed the first Swiss Revival Seminar ministry team.

During this period God began to lay a burden on Manley Beasley for Europe. It had been twenty-five years since, in 1947, the Merchant Marine ship he was working on docked in Hanover, Germany. He was but a young teenager who was running away from God. Now, back on the European continent, a vision was stirring in his heart that eventually culminated in the establishing of the International Congress on Revival, an annual gathering at which Ron would regularly preach, well into the 80s.

From Ron's Journal

March 1975—Hotel Rosat (International Christian Center), Château d'Oex, Switzerland

This is our second trip to Switzerland, and today Kaye went skiing for the first time. I hope she doesn't break her leg. Last night Ron Owens took us down to the village Anglican church where the vicar, Richard Thompson, preached. He was saved years ago in a Billy Graham meeting. It was a precious time of fellowship and worship.

This week has been marvelously blessed of the Lord. What a privilege to share in ministry with Bro. Manley. Without a doubt this has been one of the sweetest and most profitable of my ministry. It was the right place at the right time with the right people, and God met us. Among the messages I shared was "Why We Fail to Grow," from Joshua 17. When I finished, no one moved. We all sat bowed before the Lord for over thirty minutes as He dealt with us. We came as close to genuine revival that week as I've ever experienced in a conference like this.

But so much had changed between the time Ron preached, "Why We Fail to Grow," at the 1975 Swiss Seminar and the following year when he and Kaye returned to Switzerland. Now, as they boarded their flight, just five weeks after Ronnie Jr.'s death, though surrounded by a large Texas delegation, they were feeling very much alone. This was the year Ronnie Jr. was to have joined them.

January 1, 1976—Hotel Rosat, Château d'Oex, Switzerland

A new year and, I pray, a new beginning. The year 1975 was the culmination of three years of turmoil, dealing with what Ronnie was going through that finally ended with his death. We had his ticket and passport ready for this trip. We were planning to bring him with us to show him how beautiful Switzerland is. But God had different plans and a different ticket and passport for him. One day Ronnie is going to show us around a lot more beautiful place than here.

Life Goes On

When Ron returned home from Europe, he again found himself struggling with his dark night of the soul, and when he and Kaye went to the post office on Friday, February, 18, 1977, it had been a week that had not gone well. Ron had not even wanted to answer the phone.

Kaye waited in the car as he checked the mail. When he returned he was holding a blue, international "Via Airmail" letter form which he handed to Kaye; and as he did, he began to weep. Kaye turned the form over, and when she read the return address, she began to cry. They didn't have to read the message inside. They knew it was the answer to one of Ron's heart desires. It was the realization of a dream that had all but died since Ronnie's death.

Ron carefully tore open the airmail form and through his tears read the invitation that the Reverend George Duncan, one of English Keswick's council members, had said might one day be extended to him. ✻

[19]

The UK Calls

The Keswick Convention:
All One in Christ Jesus

✳ ❈ ✳

Chairman: Canon A. Neech
157 Waterloo Road
London, SEI 8XN

12 February, 1977
The Rev'd Ronald Dunn
P. O. 3087
Irving, Texas, 75061
USA
Dear Mr. Dunn,

*At the suggestion of the Rev'd George Duncan, I write
on behalf of the Council to ask whether you would be free
to accept an invitation to come and share in the ministry
of the Convention in 1978. There are two weeks, July
8/14 and 15/21. The second is called "The Holiday Week"*

*since it is a lighter programme and attracts a growing
number of families.*

*If you can come for both or either one of these weeks,
we would be very pleased. If you can manage only one
week, we would prefer you come to the first. The council
will, of course, pay all your expenses.*

*Yours sincerely,
Alan Neech
Chairman
Keswick Convention Council*

It had been fifteen months since Ron had first met George Duncan at
the Gulf Coast Keswick in Houston, Texas. Fifteen months of wondering
if God would someday grant him one of the desires of his heart—to be
invited to speak at the famous English Keswick.

Journal Entry

November 14, 1975, Houston, Texas

*This has been a tremendous week for me. I spoke at the Gulf Coast
Keswick back in 1973, but this year has been extra special. It's been a time
of real refreshing, and I've been preaching with a greater liberty and joy
than I've had in months. I've been absolutely free of depression, and I sense
a new beginning of obedience with God.*

*I'm so excited that George B. Duncan, pastor of St. George's Tron
Church in Glasgow, Scotland, is one of the speakers. This is a thrill for
me because for years I have read his messages in the Keswick Week pub-
lication. It means more than I can say to meet him, to fellowship, and to
preach with him. Also here are Gerald Griffiths, pastor of Calvary Church
in Toronto, and Dr. Sam Cannata, medical missionary to Ethiopia. My
friends Ron and Pat Owens are again blessing us with their music. I can't*

believe the goodness of God to this sinful wretch. It shames me that God is so good to me.

Never the Same Again

There is no way Ron could have known that within two weeks of his writing the above journal entry, his and Kaye's world would be turned upside down by the death of their first-born, Ronnie Jr. Nor could he have anticipated that, by the time the "blue" air-mail form arrived, he would have already entered the darkness of clinical depression that would shadow him for the next ten years. With all he was going through, the dream of one day preaching at English Keswick had become but a distant mirage until resurrected, in a moment, sitting in his car in the Irving, Texas, post office parking lot.

Keswick?

The Keswick Convention, named after the beautiful Lake District town where it was founded in 1875, has impacted millions of believers over the years. World renowned evangelical leaders such as Hudson Taylor, F. B. Meyer, John R. W. Stott, Stephen Olford, Billy Graham, Major Ian Thomas, to name a few, have preached from its platform. For Ron, following in the footsteps of such giants of the faith was more than he could have dreamed because he had for years been collecting and reading the *Keswick Week* journals.

Keswick has spawned many other similar conventions throughout the world, including several in the United States, Canada, Japan, Australia, New Zealand, India, and numerous African countries. The Keswick "message," when adhered to, is a series of five sequential emphasizes: (1) the exceeding sinfulness of sin, (2) cleansing and renewal, (3) full surrender/the lordship of Christ, (4) fullness of the Holy Spirit, climaxing with (5) sacrifice and service, or missions. Thousands have surrendered to missions over the years, including Amy Carmichael, who, hearing Hudson Taylor speak, sensed God calling her to go to India where she spent the remainder of her life.

Keswick, 1978

Few Americans have ever been invited to speak at the English Keswick, so the invitation from the Keswick Council was based solely on their trust in George Duncan and a recording of one of Ron's messages. And this was definitely the first time they had a speaker quite like "Mr. Dunn," as we see in the following article in the *Keswick Daily Express*.

The Daily Express
Wednesday, July 12, 1978

The man from Arkansas and his folksy preaching
delights the Keswick Convention.

The Arkansas Traveler, now from Texas, carries a Bible and wears a smile instead of a six-shooter. The Reverend Ronald Dunn has come 4700 miles to give Britain a taste of his pulpit patter, and the Keswick crowds love it. They've not heard or seen anything like it since Billy Graham pulled in full houses three years ago.

Keswick's newcomer, sharply dressed Ronald Dunn, 41, told the Conventioners the good news that there was nothing wrong with them that a miracle couldn't cure. This was his way of drawing attention to the "fantastic promise" of Mark 11:23—Christ's own words to the effect that faith can remove mountains.

Mr. Dunn said that the trouble with Christians is that they have ceased to believe in miracles—if one happened they'd be amazed and expect God to be amazed. "But how should a miracle be defined?" asked Mr. Dunn. "A miracle," he said, "is God doing something that only God can do . . . building what only God can build . . . tearing down what only God can tear down. And what is a mountain? In the Bible mountains are symbols, obstacles, anything that stands in the way of a believer doing the will of God."

Mr. Dunn went on to tell his hearers not to worry about the size of their faith. Though many of those who came to Jesus for a miracle had very little faith, they were never sent away unsatisfied because the strength of their faith resided in the object of their faith. It was not their faith that saved, it was Christ.

Keswick Affirmations

From the many letters of affirmation received from Keswick leadership, and those "in the pew," there could be no doubt in Ron's mind that his ministry had impacted thousands of lives.

"Thank you, Ron, for the privilege of ministering alongside you at the recent Keswick. I found your messages to be the most helpful of all. That is the reason I am writing to say it would be great if you could come and speak to us at All Souls. Let me know in due course what would be the best Sunday for you to be with us the next time you are in the UK . . ."

Richard Bewes, O. B. E., Rector of All Souls Church,
Langham Place, London

Thank you, Ron, for your ministry at Keswick. My wife and I especially remember the message you preached on Jacob and Esau. You said, "'He who has faced God need not fear facing Esau." At that moment, my wife and I joined hands because we knew you were speaking to us. We went home to face an Esau in our church and God blessed our ministry.

B. T., Pastor, Bonnyrigg, Midlothian, UK

Dear Ron and Kaye. We all in the Harvey family so appreciated the ministry of you two. Your statement, "A good idea is not necessarily God's idea," is often with us. It is marvelous to have a team at work. It makes the occasion much more significant in many ways.

Col. Peter Harvey, Keswick Development Director

Dear Ronald, I bring you the warm greeting of the Council and their unanimous request that you visit us again if at all possible.

Phillip Hacking, Chairman of the Keswick Convention

LifeLine, Fall 1978 (LifeStyle's monthly newsletter)

"It's difficult to say which experiences are the most memorable for a Christian, but for me, preaching at the Keswick Convention ranks at the top. It was the most spiritual-enriching meeting I've ever been a part of. Two things especially impressed me.

"First—the spirit of unity. The theme of the Keswick Convention is All One in Christ Jesus and this was powerfully demonstrated in every session. Imagine five thousand believers from a score of different denominations, gathered from all over the world to hear the Word of God. And I'll never forget the closing session on Friday evening when those thousands lined the streets of the village of Keswick singing hymns while waiting for the tent to open for the Communion service.

"Second—the Convention's missionary zeal. Each night, after the main meeting, an evangelistic meeting is held in the town square with people being saved in every service. Then, the final day is given over entirely to a mission emphasis. Every message deals with the missionary responsibility of Christians. I attended the youth meetings that day where over one hundred young people committed their lives to world missions." ✻

[2 0]

LifeStyle Ministries—UK

Speaking at the 1978 Keswick Convention would prove to be but the beginning of Ron's UK ministry. Four times at the Keswick Convention and four times as a speaker at the Filey Conference would prove to be the launching pad for not only an extended preaching ministry in England, Ireland, Scotland, and Wales but would greatly expand his monthly sermons-on-cassette ministry. Joanne Gardner would send the tape masters to Phil South, director of World Action Ministries, to be copied and distributed throughout the UK. Phil and WAM would become LifeStyle's UK representative, lining up preaching tours and making publishing contacts for some of Ron's books that would soon become best sellers.

Phil South, executive director and joint founder of World Action Ministries with his wife, Betty, moved from secular business in 1969 to use his administrative skills for Christian organizations. Though he has effectively represented a number of worldwide ministries over the years, something special about his relationship with Ron and Kaye developed into a close friendship, as Phil recalls.

"In the early 80s we invited Ron to speak at the Filey Christian Holiday Conference, the largest of its kind in the UK. Seven thousand believers gathered annually to hear some of the greatest preachers of our generation. The day Ron and Kaye first walked through the entrance to our office I knew that they were to be our new American friends. Ron had the great gift of making you feel special, as if meeting you was one of the most important things that had happened to him.

"Ron made an immediate impression on the British Christian public. To us, his preaching style was unusual, but after his first visit to Filey, letters poured into our office pleading that we invite him back. And of course we did.

"In 1986, due to the response to his ministry, he and Kaye began to pray about whether they should find someone to represent them in the UK, and since I had just formed World Action Ministries to meet such needs, having us do this for him was an option.

"Unbeknown to us, one evening after a service, Ron and Kaye returned to their accommodations to pray specifically for God to show them if they were to invite WAM to represent LifeStyle Ministries in the UK. They told God that they needed £500 ($750) to help enable them to set up their ministry. Even while they were praying, Ron fell asleep (one of his famous power naps), and while Kaye was praying and Ron was sleeping, there was a knock on the door. Kaye answered the door to find a stranger standing there with an envelope in his hand. 'Someone asked me to pass this on to you,' he said, and without another word turned and promptly left.

"At this point Ron awoke, and they opened the envelope. In it they found £500, in cash, with no cover letter. They had not mentioned that figure to anyone but the Lord, and He had answered their prayer, even while Ron was asleep!"

Preaching Tours

Ron and Kaye began visiting the UK on a regular basis, and in addition to speaking periodically at the Keswick Convention and Filey, they traveled the length and breadth of the UK with Phil South and his colleague, Jenny Beardsmore, who took care of the nuts and bolts of those trips.

Phil recalls Ron's regaling them with spiritual nuggets and funny stories along the way. And there are also those unforgettable moments that will be forever etched in the memory—those times when, due to unforeseen travel delays or other disruptive events, Ron would be physically and emotionally wiped out, but God would use him to speak deeply to many hearts.

An Unwelcomed Message

Phil had been listening to one of Ron's sermons in his car when he arrived at his office late afternoon on June 29, 2001. Checking his e-mail messages he found the one from Kaye, announcing Ron's home-going.

"The emotion of the moment was overwhelming," recalls Phil. "I found that I couldn't talk without tears flowing and my heart aching. I hadn't realized how much of a friend Ron had become. I couldn't grasp that he had been taken from us. Jenny and I had just visited him and Kaye in February, and though he was bedridden, we talked about his planned trip to the UK in the fall. He was to have spoken at the WAM's fifteenth anniversary celebration. Kaye had said that getting to be with us in the fall was their goal for that year.

"Before we left, Ron found enough strength to get out of bed, and putting his arms around us, he prayed for us all. He then was able to make it to the front door to wave us off for the last time. The 'last time'? I like to think that when we get to glory that we'll see that same figure, this time, waving us a welcome greeting from his heavenly mansion."

The Impact of Ron's Preaching on the UK

There were hundreds of letters and e-mails received over the years, expressing gratitude for Ron's preaching ministry in the United Kingdom.

"I have never heard anyone more sincere than Ron Dunn, down to earth, with his dry sense of humour, explaining God's Word so clearly. His words, when preaching, kept me 'locked on to,' drinking in EVERY WORD he said, all in the anointing power of the Holy Spirit, putting it into simple language that I could understand. He certainly was an extraordinary preacher that I could sit and listen to for hours."

J. D. Melton, Suffolk

"We have benefited from Ron's ministry for many years. His ministry at Filey has been a great encouragement to us, and his tapes have been a source of blessing and encouragement to us while we have been working and ministering in China. He seemed to have the right message at the right time for us."

R. W. Larch Hill, Bradford

"There are two things in particular that Ron said that have remained in our minds. When talking about obedience to God, he said: 'The most important thing you can do for God is the next thing God tells you to do.' As for the sovereignty of God, he said: 'God is able to do as He pleases, and He does it right well.' Ron was able to help our understanding through simple but true statements, with a touch of humor to help us remember the truth."

A. C. Oadby, Leicester

Special Honor

Though all of Ron's books published in the UK were best sellers, something unexpected happened in 1993. The following letter from the president of Scripture Press advised Ron of a special recognition one of Ron's books was given at the 1993 Christian Booksellers Convention.

Scripture Press

Dear Dr. Dunn,

Great news! Scripture Press was presented with a beautiful tray at the Christian Booksellers Convention with the following inscription:

Christian Booksellers Convention, 1993
Special Award presented to Scripture Press
for "Don't Just Stand There, Pray Something"
by Ronald Dunn

This is significant as the CBC have a strict policy that awards be given only to British authors. The only time this policy was rescinded was for an award presented to Hodder and Stoughton for the New International Version *(NIV) of the Bible. Here is the award speech, for your book, given by the Norman Nibloe, the CBC President.*

From time to time we find ourselves in the situation on the CBC committee where our criteria for an award is too limiting. Most of you know that our present criteria is that the book should be a British-published book written by a British author. From time to time the situation arises where a book has been so significant that we feel it deserves an award, but it can't be given. That situation has arisen this year. There was a book that the committee felt made a very significant contribution to the Christian publishing scene in this country but was excluded because it was by an American author. We felt so strongly that it needed to be marked as significant and important. And so, I'm delighted to hand this award, this special award, to Scripture Press for *Don't Just Stand There, Pray Something"* by Ronald Dunn.

The Impact of Ron's Writing on UK Believers

"I discovered Ron Dunn a few years ago when going through a very difficult time. I happened upon his book *When Heaven Is Silent* and read and reread it several times. It spoke to my deepest need just when I needed it and I keep the book handy so I can dip into it when I need to be reminded that God is working in spite of my circumstances."

H. W. Portadown, N. Ireland

"Both Ron's friendship and his humour will live long in our memories. My wife, Marilyn, says that without his books, her study of the Scriptures and her leadership as teaching director of the Community Bible Study Class would have been infinitely poorer."

Maurice Rowlandson, former director of the Keswick Convention

"We used Ron's book, *Don't Just Stand There, Pray Something* in our church, and it was such a blessing and encouragement to us all. It is one of those rare books you can read and reread and always glean something new to stimulate your soul. We thank our Lord for all that Ron has meant to so many."

Pastor, Fressingfield, Suffolk.

[2 1]

Don't Just Stand There,
Pray Something²¹

❄ ❄ ❄

Ron's book on prayer did not come easily, as seen from the following journal entry.

From Ron's Journal

I've tried to write but can't. Sometimes I feel like I'll never be able to write this book. Today I'm not sure of much of anything. Lord help me. . . .

One hour later: I tried to sleep to get away from the depression when suddenly, lying wide awake in bed, I got the opening words for my first chapter of the book on prayer. I've now just written five good pages and believe I've made a real breakthrough.

Sermon: *Just Do It*

Prayer is . . .
No, no. Start over.

Prayer is . . .

Come on, concentrate!

Prayer is . . .

Excuse me—I'm having a hard time keeping a proper image of prayer in my mind . . .

Let's face it. In spite of all the reverence that surrounds prayer, it suffers from a poor image. Some just dismiss it as a weak alternative to practical action—something for the more delicate saints to engage in while those who get the job done are out there getting the job done.

I remember addressing a group of church leaders on how to develop an intercessory prayer ministry. At the end of one of the sessions, the director of a denominational evangelism department drew me aside and said: "You know, I think this prayer thing is a great idea, but I'm afraid it might get out of hand."

"What do you mean?" I said.

"Well, people could get so caught up in praying that they wouldn't do anything."

I assured him that I had yet to come across a church that was praying so much that they had to be told to slack off. Prayer is not a substitute for work, or merely preparation for work—it *is* work.

The other side of prayer's bad image is the picture of ancient saints kneeling on hard cold floors in the dark hours of winter mornings crying long to the Lord. Well, prayer is serious business, and what these ancients are saying to us is that there is no room for foolishness. To do it right demands rigorous discipline.

Ron calls prayer "the Christian's secret weapon." "Prayer means," he points out, "that no one has to say, 'There's nothing I can do,' because there is! You don't have to just stand there, you can pray something."

Prayer is like a missile that can be fired toward any spot on Earth. It can travel undetected at the speed of thought and hit its target every time. It can even be armed with a delayed detonation device. In His prayer of

John 17, Jesus said, "I do not pray for these alone, but also for those who will believe in Me through their word" (John 17:20 NKJV). His prayer spans the centuries and embraces all who have and will yet believe. And Satan has no defense against this weapon. He doesn't have an anti-prayer missile.

We do not pray by default—because there's nothing else to do. We pray because it is the best thing to do. Whatever the need or situation, we don't have to just stand there—we can pray something.

People Just Like Us

When God created prayer, He did not intend it to be just for some select group, He created it for *people just like us*, people who are weakened by sin, at times overcome by doubt, sometimes discouraged and bewildered.

With not many days left before His departure, the Lord made this extraordinary promise to His disciples, who themselves were discouraged and bewildered.

"Most assuredly, I say to you, he who believes in Me, the works that I do he will do also; and *greater works* than these he will do, because I go to the Father" (John 14:12 NKJV, emphasis added).

Greater works! Just fifty days after Jesus made that promise, in the very city where He was crucified, the disciples emerged from an upper room with the power of the Holy Spirit within them; and after a short ten-minute sermon by Peter, three thousand people were added to the fledgling church. Today we pray ten minutes, preach ten days, and are excited if anybody is saved.

Greater works! This refers not so much to the independent and specific acts of the disciples but rather to the fact that everything they would now do would actually be done by Jesus through them.

How did Jesus intend for us to realize the fulfillment of this promise of "greater works"? We see it in the verse that follows.

"And whatever you ask in My name, that I will do, that the Father may be glorified in the Son" (John 14:13 NKJV).

The greater works of verse 12 are accomplished by the praying of verse 13.

Jesus' Secret

Prayer was a conspicuous part of Jesus' life. If He could only say and do what He heard and saw the Father do, He had to spend a lot of time listening and watching. And He did. Prayer is the secret Jesus has passed on to people just like us.

I remember when we initiated the Intercessory Prayer Ministry at MacArthur, following a fourteen-week blitzkrieg of preaching on inter- • cessory prayer. The beautiful prayer chapel was ready and we were in business. The phone rang, signaling the inaugural petition. It was one of our mothers calling from the hospital. Her two-year-old son had swallowed a can of automotive engine cleaner. He was screaming and convulsing and the emergency room doctor gave him little chance of living, and if he did he would probably be blind.

I hate to admit it, but among my first thoughts was this sorry one: I'm going to give this request to our intercessors and they're going to pray, believing that this child will be healed and he is going to die (that's what the doctor said and he ought to know), and then they'll be discouraged.

After all my preaching on the power of intercession, the folk were all hyped-up, chomping at the bit, ready to charge hell with nothing but prayer. I had hoped we could start with something easy and work our way up to the hard stuff. I just knew this was going to be a big let-down.

Well, these rookies entered the prayer chapel and besieged the throne of God. Then, twenty-four hours later, the phone shattered the hush of the chapel once more. It was the mother. She was crying, laughing, praising God. The doctor didn't understand it, but her baby was going to recover without any damage to his eyes or any vital organs. It had been a miracle!

"And whatever you ask . . ."

For Official Use Only

As though in response to the incredulity Jesus saw flash across the faces of His disciples when He told them they would do greater works than He, Jesus said it again.

"Yes, I repeat it, anything you ask for as bearers of my name I will do it for you" (John 14:14 Williams).

What Jesus said was so important, He actually repeated those words no fewer than six times: "If you ask . . . I will do."

If I were to pick one verse in the Bible that most concisely defines prayer it would be John 14:13. "Whatever you ask in My name, that will I do."

In My Name

To pray in Jesus' name is to pray according to His will, consistent with His nature, character, and purpose. That is our authority.

This reminds me of a visit to the County Fair in Greenwood, Arkansas. All the rides cost ten cents and I had bought a roll of tickets, enough to take care of my own three children and Rebecca, my brother's daughter. I positioned myself at the entrance to each ride, and as the kids came by, holding out their hands, I'd tear off a red ten cent ticket and give it to them.

I was standing at the entrance to the Tilt-A-Whirl, handing out tickets—first to Rebecca, then Ron Jr., Kimberly, and last of all to Stephen. Right behind Stephen came a little boy I'd never seen in my life, holding out his hand for a ticket.

What's this kid trying to pull? I thought. *These tickets cost ten cents a piece—I'm not going to give them away to every kid who holds his hand out.* But there he stood, waiting for a ticket. Just then Stephen turned around, pointed at this little beggar and said, "Dad, this is my friend. I told him you'd give him a ticket."

Friend? We hadn't been there twenty minutes. I looked down at that little boy, still standing there with his hand out. You know what I did? I tore off a red ten cent ticket and gave it to him, not because I wanted to, but because my son had told him that his dad would give him a ticket. Though he didn't know it, that little boy was asking for a ticket "in Stephen's name," and I gave him the ticket "in Stephen's name."

Then I saw it. That's it! I go to the Father and say, "Your Son said that if I ask for a red ten cent ticket You will give me one." I ask in Jesus' name and the Father gives in Jesus' name. The Father makes good the word of His Son.

Why God Answers Prayer

If we wait until we understand everything about prayer, we'll never pray. Vance Havner used to say, "I don't understand all about electricity, but I'm not going to sit around in the dark until I do."

How important is prayer? All I know is that there are some things that God will do if we ask Him, that He will not do if we don't ask. We sometimes carelessly say, "Well, whatever happens is God's will." That is only partially true. The words of Jesus, "If you ask, I will do," carry the obvious implication that if I do not ask, Jesus will not act. James says it plainly enough, "You do not have because you do not ask" (James 4:2).

The supreme motive is not that we get what we ask for, but that God is glorified in our getting it. This is the third qualifier of what I call *The Big Three.* Every petition is formed within the context of: (1) the will of God, (2) the name of Jesus, (3) the glory of God.

Nothing prayed in the name of Jesus will be contrary to God's will or inconsistent with His glory. When my motive for asking is the same as His motive for answering, I'm on praying ground. When I want what God wants, when we both want the same thing, we're in business.

The Secret Kingdom's Secret Weapon

The Christian life is a life of conflict. We are at war. Six times in the warfare passage of Ephesians 6:10–18, Paul uses the word *against,* a word referring to hand-to-hand combat emphasizing both the intensity of the battle and the personal nature of the fight. Prayer is not a spectator sport viewed from a safe distance. We are in the thick of it.

The Christian is against something and something is *against* the Christian. Believers are objects of organized assaults by unseen forces, a hierarchy of invisible powers in rebellion *against* God. Paul identifies these as "principalities," "powers," "rulers," and "spiritual darkness."

In a sense, the primary target in intercession is not the person or the problem; rather it is the power behind it. We are engaged in spiritual warfare and we must meet the devil on his own ground. The apostle Paul says in 2 Corinthians 10:3–4 that we do not fight this war with weapons of the flesh but with the mighty weapons of God.

The Triangle of Prayer

Here Ron looks at Jesus' intercession, the Holy Spirit's intercession and our intercession.

On our part, this involves *bold, stubborn,* and *desperate* praying. Vance Havner used to say, "The situation is desperate, but we're not."

In Luke 11 Jesus tells His disciples about the man who went to the house of his friend at midnight to borrow three loaves of bread to feed a surprise guest who had just arrived. He himself wasn't hungry, as he had already eaten, but his guest was obviously in need of food.

Ron lists three stages, or positions, in this story.

1. **Identification with the needs of others.** Those in need, often hurt ones, listen for a cry like their own, a cry that tells them they are not alone. When God set out to redeem mankind, He identified Himself with man and walked where man walked. He came so close to us that John said "our hands have handled" the very Word of Life (1 John 1:1 KJV).

2. **Sacrifice to meet those needs.** Intercession is a ministry of sacrifice. This man was willing to go out in the middle of the night in search for food. He was willing to be inconvenienced.

3. **Authority to obtain what is needed.** From the host's identification and sacrifice came authority to obtain all he needed from his reluctant friend. The Bible says of this reluctant neighbor that "he will rise and give him as many (loaves) as he needs" (Luke 11:8 NKJV).

Moses identified with his people so deeply that he was willing to have his name blotted out of God's book of records. Jesus *identified* with man by taking on the form of a servant. He *sacrificed* Himself by carrying our sins in His own body on the cross. Then, with all *authority* in heaven and on earth, He loosed man from his sins, stripped Satan of his armor, tore the stinger out of death, and flung open the gates of glory!

Praying for Others

One summer I took my family to the south coast of Texas thinking that the gentle rhythm of the waves might wash a little calm into our souls because it had not been a good year and it was only half over. A few days before we left, our youngest son broke his leg, and now he was in a cast from his toes to his hip.

So, there we were, soaking up the sun and surf at in-season rates, and every morning when I woke, standing beside my bed, was my gloomy companion—depression. The waves had not washed him away. I couldn't shake him. We went everywhere together—me and my shadow.

That is, until Thursday morning when I woke up and he wasn't there. I was suspicious, and all day long I expected him to leap out from some dark alley. I still relaxed from the inside out.

When we got home a few days later, a letter was waiting for me that bore an unfamiliar hotel logo but was written in familiar handwriting. It was from a friend who knew everything about my situation and next to the date was written, 3:00 a.m.

Dear Ron,
I am praying for you that God will make this time you're
going through a new door to the mystery of truth. God must
love you so much to watch you go through this trying time . . .
I have asked Him to put on my heart as much burden as He
can to lighten yours. I want to bear it with you.

I was not surprised to see that the date on the letter was the Thursday
I awoke without my sepulchral companion waiting for me. Is this what
Paul had in mind when he told us to bear one another's burdens? Is this
what Martin Luther meant, when feeling unusually strong and happy he
would say: "I feel as if I'm being prayed for." This is surely what T. DeWitt
Talmadge had in mind when he said, "The mightiest thing you can do
for a man is to pray for him."

Chapters 9 and 10 deal with the *who, what,* and *how* of prayer.
Chapter 9 concludes with Ron's listing of specific supplications that we
can use in our own praying, "scooped," as he says, out of Ephesians 3:14–
19. These supplications remind us that God works through our prayers to
bring the supply of the Spirit into others lives. We can say with Paul that
we are "confident of this very thing, that He who has begun a good work
in [these] will complete it until the day of Jesus Christ" (Phil. 1:6 NKJV).

The Life That Prays

Ron looks at two things that determine whether or not our prayers
will be answered.

First, the prayer must be according to the will of God. Regardless
how earnestly we cry out to God, any petition that lies outside the will of
God is doomed to fail.

Prayer doesn't get man's will done in heaven; it gets God's will done
on Earth.

Second, the prayer must be according to the will of God. By this I
mean, it is the life that prays. If the pray-er's life is weak, the entire struc-
ture of his or her prayer-life will collapse.

The Life That Abides

> "I am the vine, you are the branches. He who abides in Me, and I in him, will bear much fruit; for without Me you can do nothing . . . If you abide in Me, and my words abide in you, you will ask what you desire and it shall be done for you. By this is my Father glorified." (John 15:5, 7–8a NKJV)

Simply put, "abide" speaks of the union and communion between vine and branches. The branch must accept the vine's purpose for its very existence. And what is that? To bear fruit. The branch itself has no other purpose or value than that.

A Water Faucet Conversation

Ron Dunn: There was a period in my Christian life when, at the end of the day, I would wonder if I had done enough for Christ. The Accuser would add fuel to my self-condemnation by reminding me of the many things I had left undone. I would end up asking the Lord to forgive me and to help me do better the next day, that is, until I had a talk with the water faucet.

Walking through the kitchen one evening I noticed that the water faucet seemed to be down in the dumps. I went up to it and said, "Hey faucet, what's wrong? You look depressed."

"Yes, Master, I am."

"Why so?"

Looking down, the faucet said: "I failed you. I'm sorry."

"Failed me? How?"

"Well, sir, I've seen you pass by a dozen times and I haven't done anything for you. I haven't washed your hands and I haven't quenched your thirst. Oh, a few times I tried to turn myself on but I was only able to squeeze out a few drops."

I patted his shiny chrome handle and looked him straight in the nozzle and said: "You silly water faucet. Listen to me. Every time I walked by you today I knew you were here. I knew that if I'd wanted to use you, all I had to do was touch you and you would have responded. I don't measure your faithfulness by how much water you dispense in a day, I judge you by your *availability*."

This conversation reminds me that God does not judge me by the achievement of my hand, but by the ambition of my heart.

The God Who Hears

Ron recalls a conversation he had with a missionary friend of his who told him about a letter he had received from a little girl whose Sunday school class had been writing missionaries. Evidently their teacher had told them that real live missionaries were very busy and might not have time to answer their letters, so the one he received said simply:

> *Dear Rev. Smith.*
> *We are praying for you.*
> *We are not expecting an answer.*

Without realizing it, that little girl summed up the prayer life of many Christians: "We're praying for you, but we're not expecting an answer." The truth is, most of us aren't surprised when our prayers aren't answered; we're surprised when they are.

Ron turns to four ingredients in a prayer that God always answers. These are found in the Matthew 6:1–13 portion of the Sermon on the Mount; (1) sincerity (v. 5), (2) secrecy (v. 6), (3) simplicity (vv. 7–8), and (4) specificity (v. 9).

Ron pointed out that prayer is both an act—"When you pray, say . . ." (Luke 11:2)—and it is a petition.

It is asking. Our private worship should, of course, include praise; and during times of prayer, we should praise God, but *prayer and praise* are not the same thing. Of the various words in Scripture to denote prayer, the vast majority are, almost without exception, unashamedly words of petition.

Almost all of Jesus' prayers, and the prayers of the apostle Paul were petitions. Christ and Paul admonished us to ask, and keep on asking. The Model Prayer is 100 percent petition. Even the phrase, "Hallowed be Thy name," is a petition. This prayer is made up of six petitions, and in each case we are asking God to do something specific.

The first part of the prayer concerns the glory of God (Matt. 6:9–10). The prayer God always answers gives priority to the glory of the Father, putting His interests before ours. This implies an emptying of self and an occupation with the things of God.

A Silence in Heaven

God didn't answer the two biggest prayers of my life. I wanted those more than all the other answers put together, and I would have gladly forfeited them all for those two. I was hurt (angry?) because I felt like God had betrayed me. He had strung me along, tantalizing me with big answers to small prayers, but when the Big One came along—nothing. And there was no explanation. Nothing! Heaven was silent. My prayer life shriveled. My prayers died in my throat.

But God didn't let it end like that. He pursued this rebel, loving him, tutoring him, until he understood that he would never understand. I learned that my feelings were a result of ignorance on my part, not indifference on His. God is bigger than our theology. God makes no promises that paralyze His sovereignty. My expectations do not bind Him. My wish is not His command.

Ron continued by looking at God's ground rules and at His mysterious freedom as witnessed in Ezekiel 22:30 and Isaiah 59:16. He then concluded the chapter by looking at Zacharias, John the Baptist's father, whose prayer for a son, after years of waiting, was well nigh, in his eyes, past all possibility of being answered.

How, and How Long?

When God hears an "answerable" prayer, He always answers immediately, but sometimes later, such as was Daniel's experience (Dan. 10:12–13). The granting of the answer to a prayer is immediate, but the giving of it into our hands may be delayed. Oh, the mystery of God's sovereignty! God always takes the route that brings Him the greatest glory.

A Praying Church in a Pagan World

Whether we call the prevailing culture "paganism," "neo-paganism," or "secular humanism," one thing is clear: Our generation has witnessed what may be the final death blows to the Judeo-Christian foundation upon which most of the Western world was established.

Today's prevailing climate, however, is nothing new to the church. It was born in the midst of paganism, and it conquered it. Three hundred years after the beginning of Christ's ministry, God, through the church, had brought the Roman Empire to its knees in worship of the Redeemer. How did that little band of eager disciples accomplish what no military power had been able to do?

Ron traced the part prayer played, and plays, in God's involvement and intervention in the affairs of man.

Instead of casting prayer as a polite nod to tradition, or a piece of pietistic irrelevance, we must see it as the true power of the church. The early church didn't have enough power or prestige to get Peter out of prison, but they had enough power to pray him out. The church has far more power than it knows.

Ron Dunn continues: For most of my ministry, I have been a student of revival and awakening, and I have constantly run into one stubborn fact: In the recorded history of the church, there has never been a mighty outpouring of the Spirit in revival that did not begin in the persistent, prevailing prayers of a desperate people. Revival has never come because men put it on the calendar. It has come because God placed it in their hearts.

When the Church Prays

Taking a brief look at some common characteristics of spiritual awakenings that have taken place during the last centuries, Ron goes on to ask what we could expect if the church were to return to its "kneeling posture" and recovered its prayer power as we have pictured in Acts 4 and Acts 12."

He pointed out that in every true revival the presence of God is both perceived (earthquakes in Acts 4 and 16), and received (Acts 4:31). They were *all* filled with the Holy Spirit.

There was something remarkable about this incident that is often overlooked—they didn't pray to be filled. They didn't ask to be filled, but when they prayed, they were filled.

There are two things of significance here. First, they were not seeking an experience. Second, there is more to being filled with the Holy Spirit than merely asking for Him. If we examine the content of the early church's prayer, we may discover the kind of praying that results in the filling of the Spirit.

1. They recognized God as sovereign. "Lord, You are God, who made heaven and earth" (Acts 4:24 NKJV).

2. They recognized themselves as God's servants (bond-slaves). "Now, Lord, look on their threats, and grant to Your servants that with all boldness they may speak Your word" (v. 29 NKJV).

This is a prayer of submission. They didn't complain about their circumstances, nor did they beg God to be delivered from them. They simply asked God for more of what had gotten them into trouble in the first place—*boldness*. When the Holy Spirit finds a believer who wants what He wants, they "get together," because the Spirit is interested in one thing—glorifying Jesus as Lord and Savior. In this, a two-fold purpose of God is achieved.

1. "And they spoke the word of God with boldness" (v. 31 NKJV). When a church is filled with the Holy Spirit of God, it will inevitably speak the word of God with boldness because you cannot divorce the fullness of the Spirit from witnessing.

2. "And great grace was upon them all" (v. 33 NKJV), as is described by the phrase, "one heart and one soul" (v. 32 NKJV).

This is what happens to a praying church. The Holy Spirit baptizes it with a new concept, with a changed viewpoint. The members have a sense of responsibility toward one another, and they see their possessions as a trust given by God to be used as needed among the family. Hands joined hearts as the church cared for both the spiritual and social needs of each other.

This is the New Testament picture of a praying church in a pagan world. The church today must learn to live on its knees.

TESTIMONY: DON MOORE, RETIRED PASTOR AND EXECUTIVE DIRECTOR OF THE ARKANSAS BAPTIST CONVENTION

Soon after Ron Dunn came to minister to our church family at Grand Avenue Baptist Church in Fort Smith, Arkansas, I learned about the Twenty-Four-Hour Intercessory Prayer Ministry that had been established at MacArthur Boulevard Baptist Church. Our church happily adopted that prayer ministry model that proved to be a great blessing. The most fruitful years of the church coincided with this emphasis.

Each year when Ron, Kaye, and the family were at the farm in Greenwood, he would give us one night of that special time. The annual meeting of the Prayer Warriors was scheduled so that he could come and encourage us. Those were tremendous times of inspiration. God used him to keep the fires of revival and intercession burning brightly.

It was only natural, after moving into denominational work, that I would ask Ron to be a part of conventions, pastor's conferences and retreats. He was always used of God to bless others. ❋

[INTERLUDE]

Mentored and Mentoring

Iron sharpens iron, so one man sharpens another.
—Proverbs 27:17

Mentored

Someone has said that "every Timothy needs a Paul, and every Ruth needs a Naomi." How blessed we are when God places in our lives those who, by their example and counsel, help shape us into what we've been created to be.

Early in Ron's ministry, as a young pastor still attending Oklahoma Baptist University, Jake Self was very influential in his life. Then God used four others over the years to shape Ron's life and ministry—three in the area of study habits and preaching, and the other who shaped Ron's understanding of faith and the purpose God has for adversity in the Christian's life.

Jake Self

Ron considered Jake to be one of his mentors during his college years and early pastoring days. He was the pastor of First Baptist, Bowlegs, Oklahoma, where "Ronnie" and "Johnny" held one of their youth revivals.

Jake spent time with Ron, as he did with other young preachers, teaching him some of the basics of ministry that were a great help in getting Ron headed on the right track.

"Jake was a country philosopher kind of person," recalls Jimmy Draper. "One time, when I was getting a lot of criticism from some church members, he told me: 'Brother Jim, the higher up the flag pole you get, the windier and lonelier it gets.'"

J. Harold Smith

Dr. Smith was pastor of First Baptist Church, Fort Smith, Arkansas, in 1952 when Ron surrendered to the ministry. His influence on young Ronnie's life cannot be overestimated. His enthusiasm for preaching and his commitment to rightly dividing the word of truth was contagious. He was a pioneer in Christian radio and television, and it is estimated that more than nine hundred young men went into the ministry due to his influence.

"I had grown up in the church," recalls Ron, "but I'd never heard anyone like J. Harold Smith. He was very different from the pastor under whose ministry I was saved. This pastor had the reputation of spending a lot of his free time going to the horse races in Hot Springs, and he was not what you would call a dynamic preacher. But J. Harold Smith was totally different. He was an evangelist through and through, and he didn't fear anyone but God. He was bold and strong in and out of the pulpit. Some considered him to be a bit legalistic, but he had a zeal and a fervor you seldom see.

"Dr. Smith was the first of three preachers who truly impacted me. He put in me a sense of mission that leads you to preach whatever God lays on your heart, without fearing man. I've always had a heavy sense of that in my own ministry, and I've never been concerned that a church would fire me. The call to preach is a serious matter, and when you stand to deliver God's Word, you don't consider whether or not the people are going to like it. I owe that fervor and evangelistic zeal to J. Harold Smith. His boldness and courage made a big mark on me.

Vance Havner

During the years Ron was a member of First Baptist, Fort Smith, J. Harold Smith had some of the finest expositors of God's Word preach for him, including Donald Grey Barnhouse, J. P McBeth, and Vance Havner. Ron first heard Dr. Havner in 1952, the year he surrendered to preach. Ron recalls how Vance was another of those preachers unlike any other. Back then they called him "The Will Rogers of the Pulpit."

"He was humorous, while really able to drive home the knife of the Word," Ron recalls. "It has always been difficult for me to describe my relationship to him. Through the years I've listened constantly to his tapes. His messages have always struck a chord in me like no other preacher has done. His messages have always made me want to pray. They have always made me want to humble myself before God. They give me a longing for God. His preaching does to you what some music does, it reaches deep into your soul and makes you ache—a good kind of ache, like 'deep calling unto deep.' I wanted to have that kind of ministry. His preaching on revival and his longing to see revival in the church also had a profound influence on me.

"I was impacted by the simplicity of his ministry. He never had a secretary. He never sent out a brochure. He never raised a finger to get himself recognized or invited anywhere to preach, yet he received enough invitations to keep three men busy. It was just Vance and God, and he trusted God to put him wherever he needed to be. The last book he wrote, *Threescore and Ten,* also had a tremendous impact on my life as I could actually see some parallels in my own ministry with his. Through the years I've tried to depend totally on God to open doors. I've had offers from well-meaning folk who thought they could be a help in promoting my ministry, but I've resisted that temptation and trusted God to take care of us, and He has opened doors that I couldn't have blasted open with dynamite."

Kaye recalls how, as teenagers at First Baptist Church in Fort Smith, Arkansas, when they heard Dr. Vance Havner preach several times, they never would have dreamed that one day they would have the privilege of being counted among his friends. Ron looked to him as one of his mentors. He preached for us at MBBC while Ron was pastor, and he and Ron ministered together in a number of Bible conferences over the years.

Kaye remembers how Dr. Havner was at least forty years old when he married for the first time. His bride was a lovely lady named Sarah. And how he loved her. She had become such an integral part of his life that he never got over the pain of losing her to Cushing's disease. "Of course," he said, "you haven't really lost someone when you know where they are."

"Dr. Havner was very honest with Ron about the void left in his life when she went to heaven. When our oldest son Ronnie Jr. died soon after Sarah's home-going, Ron and I listened to Dr. Havner's tape about her death at least twenty times to gain strength and comfort. That made for an even closer bonding in our lives.

Kaye also remembers how thrilled Ron was when Dr. Havner wrote the Foreword to his book, *Faith Crisis.* In it he said: "If I have been helpful in any way to Ron Dunn, as he graciously assures me, I am amply repaid by the example and message of this young prophet—not a *coming* preacher, whatever that means. Ron Dunn is not *coming.* . . . He is here!"

J. P. McBeth

Dr. J. P. McBeth, PhD, was a brilliant biblical scholar. He wrote a commentary on the book of Romans when he was still a seminary student, and he was a genius in both Greek and Hebrew. Ron felt he never received the recognition he deserved, but again, he was not one who sought the limelight.

Ron first heard Dr. MacBeth in 1953 at First Baptist, Fort Smith, and was captivated, as he was with Vance Havner, by the uniqueness of this Texan.

"Dr. McBeth had a way of preaching I'd never seen in anyone else," Ron recalls. "He had developed preaching almost to a science. But more than being a great communicator, he was a thinker, and it was in this area that he most influenced me. He taught me how to think. He taught me how to study. He said you don't quit studying a passage of Scripture until you find something you've not seen before. He wasn't recommending reading something into a passage, but he taught me to stay with it until I found something fresh because you can never exhaust the Word of God. Because of Dr. McBeth's influence, I developed a habit that would not let me preach in a predicable way—I keep praying and searching, even if it's a passage as well known as John 3:16.

"He taught me how to think in images, drawing from his own life rather than using books of others' illustrations. He taught me to indent my paragraphs in the pulpit by moving from one side of the pulpit to the other. At the time he was writing a book on preaching, and Mrs. McBeth passed his notes on to me after her husband went to heaven. He was a wonderful mentor for a young pastor eager to learn."

A PERSONAL TOUCH

The McBeths lived on the outskirts of Irving, and when he and his wife were not traveling in Bible conference ministry, in addition to answering mail and spending time in study when they were home, Dr. McBeth loved to work in his own little organic garden. Kaye recalls how, when he and his wife would visit them for a teaching session, they'd bring melons, all kinds of veggies, grape and apple juice, all from their little farm. And he'd always pull something out of his pocket for the children—some little trick or other surprise.

Dr. McBeth had written a manuscript on preaching from which he taught when he got together with Ron and Kaye. He'd open his notes,

"Outlines on Preaching," and Kaye remembers how he'd say, "Now, tonight we are going to learn about. . . ." "And he would begin teaching us like we were sitting in a classroom. We all just sat around, the children too, drinking his apple or grape juice, listening to him teach. Then, before they left, we'd eat some goodie, like cheesecake, that Mrs. McBeth had made. Those were wonderful times, especially for Ron, as he drank in the counsel and wisdom of this very special servant of God."

Manley Beasley[22]

Brother Manley, as he was affectionately known by the thousands of lives that were impacted by his life and message, was more than a mentor to Ron; he was a "soul mate." Ron always knew he could trust Brother Manley with his deepest struggles and count on him for godly counsel. Manley's death took Ron by surprise, even though he had been at death's door many times over the prior twenty years. Ron and Kaye had visited him in ICU six times themselves to say their final good-byes, only to hear that God had again raised him up to continue living and preaching the life of faith and revival.

Journal Entry: July 10, 1990—Chattanooga, Tennessee

Joanne called to say that brother Manley died today. When I phoned Marthé, she said, "Manley's enjoying his coronation right now." My thoughts went to 2 Peter 1:11, "For so an entrance shall be ministered unto you abundantly into the everlasting kingdom of our Lord and Savior, Jesus Christ" (KJV).

Dr. Stephen Olford said that God kept Manley alive as a witness to this generation that there is a ministry of suffering in which God's grace is sufficient.

In light of brother Manley's life and ministry I'm thinking of 2 Corinthians 4–5 that:

1. It takes a "cracked pot" to truly minister (4:7–12).

2. What you don't see is more real than what you do see (4:18).

3. Living and dying is not the issue—pleasing Christ is (5:8–10).

Journal Entry: One Week Later—Corinth, Mississippi

During the early part of this morning's service, I had a sinking spell thinking of Manley. He's gone! Every day I'm realizing more and more what a void he has left. We shared so many things—he was a soul mate. I am diminished by his death. There is a blank spot. I drew strength from him.

Mentoring

The things that you have heard from me among many witnesses, commit these to faithful men, who will be able to teach others also.

—2 TIMOTHY 2:2 (NKJV)

"What you leave behind is not what is engraved in stone monuments, but what is woven into the lives of others.

—PERICLES

While Ron had his mentors, he himself was mentoring, though more often than not he was unaware of the profound impact he was having on lives and ministries. Since tributes and testimonials to Ron's influence are found throughout the book, only several will be briefly included here.

TESTIMONY: MANLEY BEASLEY JR.—SENIOR PASTOR, HOT SPRINGS BAPTIST CHURCH, HOT SPRINGS, ARKANSAS

Ron was always an encourager to me while Dad was alive, but after my father's death, Ron got in touch with me and offered to fill the role in my life that had been left vacant by my dad's death. So we started getting together. The first time we met was for breakfast and as we were leaving the restaurant, he said: "OK, this is the last time we're going to meet for breakfast. From here on out it's going to be lunch." Ron was not an early morning person.

As busy as Ron was, he was a master at discipling and mentoring young preachers. Often it had to be done by phone, but however he did it, there was a genuine commitment to developing young men around him, a commitment to instill in their hearts a love for the Word of God and for expository preaching, a willingness to take the time to study and rightly divide God's Word. No other man has influenced me more in this area than Ron Dunn.

TESTIMONY: BILL STAFFORD—EVANGELIST, CHATTANOOGA, TENNESSEE

Two men have had a life-changing impact on my life. They are Manley Beasley and Ron Dunn. From them I have drawn practical truth on how to respond to adversity and life's storms both by what they taught and by watching them live out the truth.

So much of Ron Dunn's life could only be explained by the sufficiency of Christ. He taught me that to be a victor you must be a victim. To be a conqueror you must be conquered. To be full of Jesus you must be empty of yourself so that the only explanation for your life is Christ in you.

I always felt safe under Ron's preaching. You never had to wonder whether or not what he said was the truth. Ron helped keep me from running down dead-end alleys and following after extrabiblical truth. Whenever I heard Ron preach, I knew I could take it to the bank.

TESTIMONY: KEN WHITTEN—SENIOR PASTOR, IDLEWILD BAPTIST CHURCH, TAMPA, FLORIDA

In the life of every pastor, every minister of the gospel, there are certain men of God who mark your life. Ron Dunn permanently marked mine. He was one of my heroes. He marked me with biblical truths. When he preached, I saw Jesus, and I wanted to be just like him.

Ron taught me what to say when I didn't know what to say, and when I heard about his home-going, I felt like King David did when his hero Saul, and his best friend Jonathan, died: "How the mighty have fallen, and the weapons of war perished" (2 Sam. 1:27).

TESTIMONY: MICHAEL CATT—SENIOR PASTOR, SHERWOOD BAPTIST CHURCH, ALBANY, GEORGIA

Ron and I really got to know each other through our love for a mutual mentor, Vance Havner. Dr. Havner said: "If a man cannot turn to God in the hour of his deepest need and come boldly to the throne of grace for help, then the gospel means nothing and the Christian experience is a delusion." I saw in Ron Dunn a man who continually turned to God. I saw in Ron a man who learned that trials are not our enemies but opportunities for God to prove His sufficiency in the darkest night.

Ron taught me to live with a "what now?" mentality. "Lord, what do You want me to do with this for Your glory?" Ron taught us that great hearts can only be made through great trouble.

TESTIMONY: RON PROCTOR—MACARTHUR BOULEVARD'S YOUTH PASTOR DURING THE SEVENTIES

At the beginning of my ministry at MacArthur Boulevard, I asked Ron about the possibility of doing the youth ministry a little differently. With fear and trembling I told him that my vision was to mentor the students in such a way that they would have a love for God and a love for sharing with others, wondering how he would respond because this was not the typical Southern Baptist approach to a youth program. As I shared my vision, Ron asked me two questions: "How soon can you start?" and "What can I do to help?"

Little did I know at the time the impact this was going to have on my own life. At the heart of almost every message Ron preached was, "What does it mean to live the crucified life?

Those years with Ron laid the foundation for the ministry my wife, Della, and I would have over the years that has included managing the Mentoring Ministry for Campus Crusade for Christ. Not a day goes by that I do not remember, talk about, or emphasize something from my time with Ron that impacted me as to what it means to live the crucified life. Whether in the Spiritual Formation class I teach at a university, or when I'm mentoring a young pastor, Ron continues to be used of God in my life. ❈

PART SIX

Ron Dunn—Author

Fill your paper with the breathings of your heart.
—William Wordsworth

*Hello book. Yes, it's been awhile. What's that? Am I back
to stay? Yes, you're right. I lost that last battle.*
—Ron Dunn, Journal

Prelude

Benjamin Franklin, speaking to the matter of being an author, is credited with saying: "Either write something worth reading, or live something worth writing."

Both these could be said of Ron Dunn—what he wrote was a reflection of life experiences he had already had or what he was presently fleshing out. His were not "ivory tower pontifications," assembled to advise others how they should live. Ron's writings were the expression of one who, having been to the bottom, found it to be rock solid.

Anton Checkov, the Russian medical doctor and author, once said: "Don't tell me the moon is shining; show me the glint of light on broken glass." This could well describe Ron's journey, his preaching, and his writing. Though the moon never ceased to shine, the glint of its light was often reflected, perhaps even more beautifully, through the broken glass in his life.

Ron wrote six books—all best sellers in North America, while two were at the top of the religious books charts in the United Kingdom. In this section, "Author," you'll find a synopsis of five of the books. Ron's third book, *Don't Just Stand There, Pray Something,* is found in chapter 21. ✷

[2 2]

Any Christian Can[22]

❈ ❈ ❈

TESTIMONY: JOHN L. YEATS, SBC RECORDING SECRETARY
AND EXECUTIVE DIRECTOR OF THE MISSOURI BAPTIST
CONVENTION

Millions of believers are encumbered by the junk of life. Tragically, they have convinced themselves there is no victory until the Lord Himself splits the sky. Ron Dunn was not only acquainted with the depths of defeat, but he experienced the mountains of incredible success. His journey teaches believers powerful biblical principles that deliver the hope of victory practically attained.

In the 1976 fall issue of Ron's ministry newsletter, *LifeLines*, he wrote: "This past summer I finally wrote a book. And I did it in two weeks. Please keep that in mind when you read it! *Any Christian Can* is a study of victory based on the book of Joshua."

Ron opens *Any Christian Can* with a quote from Stuart Briscoe in which Stuart compares the life of the average Christian to an old iron bedstead—firm on both ends and sagging in the middle. This statement intrigued Ron, not because it was catchy but because it described his own life at the time. He knew he was saved—firm on that end. He knew he was going to heaven when he died—firm on that end. "But boy, was I ever sagging in the middle."

He knew, however, that he was in good company, as many of his preacher peers were in the same boat. But that provided little comfort, and Ron found himself crying out to the Lord: "I don't know what I need, but I know there has to be more than this." And as always happens, when we get desperate enough, the Lord answers our prayer.

In subsequent chapters Ron divided the Christian life into stages— the Red Sea Stage and the Jordan Stage, with a wilderness in between. Ron writes:

> What the cross is to us, the Red Sea was to Israel. It was the symbol of their redemption from the bondage of Egypt. But it wasn't enough to get them out of Egypt, as Moses reminded them. "He brought us out from there [Egypt] in order to bring us in, to give us the land [Canaan] which He has sworn to our fathers." (Deut. 6:23 NKJV)

Canaan represents the fullness of salvation and blessing. Canaan was what God redeemed Israel for, just as victory is what God has saved us for. Victory is to be the goal of every Christian. In this victory we enter into God's promises. They become experiential instead of merely theological. In the life of victory we experience God's presence—"I will go with you." And, in the life of victory we experience God's power—"No man will be able to stand before you all the days of your life." But, have you noticed the disturbing difference between what the Bible says we are and what we really are?"

Here Ron challenges readers to check their photograph against Scripture's portrayal of a victorious Christian. Might an observer say, "I saw a picture of you in the Bible, but you don't look anything like it. I see your name on the picture, but is that really you?"

Many Christians are like the man who comes home to find his house is flooded because he forgot to turn off the bathtub faucet. Frantically he grabs a mop and begins sweeping out the water, but the bathtub faucet is still running wide open. After a few frenzied swipes, he sees he's not making any headway against the water, so he gets a bigger mop. Still no success.

Weary and waterlogged, he finally concludes that God never intended him to live in a dry house, so he buys a pair of galoshes and a waterbed and settles down to live in a flooded house.

Now, I'm not against mopping, but if the faucet is still running, it is a waste of time. The solution is ridiculously simple—stop the flow at its source. Turn the faucet off.

Application: The water on the floor is our daily sins. The open faucet is our sin nature—self—the source of the sins. The secret of victory over sins is victory over self. We've been mopping sins when we should have been mortifying self.

What spiritual significance does the crossing of the Jordan have for us today? It marks the end of the self-life and the beginning of the Christ-life. As the Red Sea was a judgment on sin, so the Jordan River is a judgment on self.

But we die hard. It is often easier to get a sinner out of Egypt than to get a Christian into Canaan. We want a Canaan without a Jordan, but every Canaan has its Jordan, and there is no following Jesus into His fullness without taking up our cross and saying "no" to self.

Plugging into the Power

Ron Dunn wrote: It was going to be a great Christmas. I could hardly wait until the children saw all the neat toys under the tree—games that lit up and buzzed, tanks that fired plastic missiles, cars that raced on a winding track. But as they began opening the packages, I noticed for the first time something printed on the cartons: *Batteries not included.* It was exciting all right, staring at immobile tanks and stalled race cars while trying to ignore the little voices that kept repeating, "Daddy, this won't work."

Spiritually, that has been the frustrating experience of many Christians—they have everything but power. And you might as well try to swim without water as to live the Christian life without God's power. If the account of entering Canaan teaches us anything, it is that victory demands the release of God's power on our behalf.

God's power always flows in the stream of His purpose. It is never released simply to indulge our carnal cravings or to bail us out of a spot He didn't lead us into.

God's power flows in the stream of His timing. Understanding the principle of God's timing is indispensable if God's power is to be released. You can do the right thing at the wrong time. Moses missed God's timing when he killed an Egyptian bully. Abraham missed God's timing and nothing but disaster has resulted from his effort to help God out.

It's the Follow-Through that Counts

Ron Dunn wrote: I love to play tennis, but I have a big problem with my follow-through. When I hit the ball, instead of bringing the racket on through to complete the swing, I stop, and the ball sails out of bounds. I don't follow through. That's why I gave up golf. In every sport, following through seems to be necessary. I keep hoping to find a sport that doesn't require it.

For many, the Christian life is like a soapbox derby—someone gives you a big push down a steep hill and you're sailing. The wind is whistling in your ears and everything is great, then suddenly you begin to slow down—slower and slower until finally you stop. There you sit, stalled until you find another hill and someone else to give you a push. The roadside is littered with Christians who used to be really turned on for the Lord. Most of them are there because they didn't follow through.

This aspect of the Christian experience is a major thrust of the New Testament. Paul warned the Corinthians that any religious experience that did not result in holy living was receiving the grace of God in vain (2 Cor. 6:1–4). The Galatians were in danger of returning to their former religious rut. Paul told them that staying free was as much a part of their salvation as being set free in the first place (Gal. 3:1–3; 5:1).

Dunamis

Ron Dunn wrote: The gospel is frequently described as dynamite because we get the word *gospel* from the Greek word *dunamis,* translated "power" in Romans 1:16. Unfortunately, some of our experiences are exactly like a stick of dynamite—a loud noise, a lot of dust, over in a second and not a trace left! But there is another word from *dunamis* which I think better describes salvation. It is *dynamo*, a continual source of energy. When God saved us, He placed in us a dynamo, the Holy Spirit, who provides an unceasing flow of divine energy, a permanent power supply that enables us to become all God saved us to be—a power that enables us to *follow through.*

So you ask, Will it last? I've made the discovery that the real thing does last. I no longer lug buckets of water from the wells of others. Jesus has given me an artesian well that requires neither rope nor bucket. I have trudged through a desert where no water was, where no flowers grew, where cherished voices no longer greeted me—but the well was there.

Two hippies were on an ocean voyage. Standing at the rail, staring out at the expanse of endless sea, one of them said: "Man, dig all that crazy water." The other, mesmerized by the view, said: "Yeah, and that's only the top." And in the Christian life, this life of victory, we've only touched the top. ❈

[23]

Faith Crisis[24]

Manley Beasley, one of Ron's mentors in the faith, and thought by many to be one of the greatest men of faith of his generation, said of Ron's book, *Faith Crisis:* "This is the best book on faith I have ever read."

Ron begins his treatise on faith by reminding us that some words are like drapes that have faded from long exposure to the sun. He goes on to say that frequent use and misuse have drained the color from their meaning until they are no longer recognizable. Such words need, from time to time, to be reexamined to ensure their use is consistent with their meaning. *Faith* is a word that is dangerously close to fading. The word itself must be healed before it can bring healing to others.

Ron Dunn wrote: Many Christians confuse the key of faith with counterfeit keys—keys that bear a remarkable resemblance to faith but are actually look-alike replicas. Often what they judge to be faith is in fact presumption, or wishful thinking, selfish desire, or a denial of reality, or some form of positive thinking. And, when these bogus keys fail to open the doors of God's promises, some conclude that they are not of the "chosen few," and abandon any hope of living the life of faith. But real faith never fails to open the door. It achieves its goal. The question then is—what is true faith, and how do we tell the difference?

The Object of Our Faith

Ron Dunn wrote: True faith is authenticated by its object. "Faith in what?" is the question. *Believe* is a transition verb requiring an object. When I hear someone say, "Just have faith," or, "Only believe," I want to ask, "Faith in what?" "Only believe what?" You must believe something or someone. Faith must have an object. To many people, the important thing is to believe—what you believe is secondary.

How many times have we lamented over the weakness of our faith, using it as an example for failure—"If only I had more faith. My faith is so small. Pray for me that I'll have more faith," while the fact of the matter is that almost everyone who came to Jesus for help brought along a faith that was weak and imperfect. I agree with Spurgeon who said: "Never make a Christ out of your faith. . . . Our life is found in *looking unto Jesus* (Heb. 12:2), not looking to our faith. . . . By faith all things are possible to us, yet the power is not in the faith but in the God upon whom faith relies."

Faith in faith is really faith in yourself, in your ability to think positively, which means that our attention is concentrated upon ourselves, rather than on Christ. The writer to the Hebrews, after parading before our eyes the mighty heroes of faith says, "Fixing our eyes on Jesus, the author and perfecter of our faith" (Heb. 12:2).

A Vacation with a Lesson

Ron Dunn wrote: We were on vacation in Colorado with some friends. It was in March, and winter still had its icy grip on everything. Not far from where we were staying were twelve little trout lakes, covered with ice. One day, one of my friends suggested I walk across one of those lakes, assuring me it was perfectly safe since they skated on it all winter. Now, I had lived in the South and Southwest all my life, and the lakes there don't freeze enough (if they freeze at all) to support the weight of a child, let alone an adult. I promptly relayed these critical facts to my friend and respectfully declined his invitation.

He laughed and said, "Come on, pastor, this may be your only chance to walk on water." I wasn't crazy about the idea but finally began to venture out. Perhaps venture "out" is stretching it. I inched my way out, no more than a couple yards from the shore because, unlike Peter, I doubted Jesus would reach out and save me if I began to sink. I kept a nervous eye on the shore, watching for cracks, as I tiptoed across the ice because, if you didn't know it, you weigh less when you tiptoe. After a nervous "walk on the water," I scrambled back to the shore because I had little faith in the ice.

Later, as we drove back to our lodge, we passed another of those trout lakes where I saw a man sitting on a wooden crate in the middle of it, hunched over a hole in the ice, fishing! I did a double take, feeling foolish as I recalled my timid excursion earlier in the day.

Now to the point: The man sitting in the middle of that lake had great faith in the ice—right? I had had almost no faith in the ice. Question: Which one of us was the safest? He with his great faith, or me with my little faith? Surely the man with the great faith was more secure, but actually, the man with the great faith was no safer than I was with my little faith. Why? Because it wasn't our faith that held us up. It was the ice.

As I watched that man out there in the middle of the lake, I said out loud: "I wonder where that man gets enough nerve to do that?" Our driver immediately said, "Oh, he lives around here. He knows the ice."

"He knows the ice!" And that's the difference between faith and no faith, weak faith and strong faith. The psalmist said: "And they who know thy name will put their trust in thee" (Psalm 9:10 KJV). True faith is authenticated by its object, and the only valid object is God. The greater our knowledge of Him, the greater will be our faith.

Promises

C. H. Spurgeon, in talking about Bible promises, says that they are like checks drawn on heaven's bank that we endorse by faith and present to God for payment.

This is true, but sometimes the checks are postdated. One of the most disturbing discoveries we make in the life of faith is that God does not always operate by our time schedule. We assume God will respond immediately, and we rise from our knees expecting the answer to be standing right before us. But, more often than not, there is a waiting period between asking and receiving. This, in the age of instant everything, is a major problem because we have developed a low tolerance for delay.

But the delays are as much a part of God's purpose as are the fulfillments. In fact, the delays will usually prove a greater blessing than the fulfillments. The full story as to why God delays His answers is buried in the mystery of His infinite wisdom.

Waiting for the Promise

Waiting requires *confidence* based on God's past faithfulness. Waiting for the fulfillment of a promise involves *obedience* to God's present will. Hebrews 10:36 says, "For you have need of endurance, so that when you have done the will of God, you may receive what was promised." Faith is not idle; it works while it waits. Receiving what God has promised requires obedience. The psalmist said, "Trust in the LORD and do good" (37:3).

Waiting for the promise demands *patience* for God's future work. Patience is the bridge between doing the will of God and receiving the promise.

Resignation Versus Anticipation

Perhaps one of the most important qualities found in biblical patience is *expectation*. Biblical patience is not waiting with resignation but waiting in anticipation. The psalmist tells us that waiting for the Lord is like waiting for the sunrise (Ps. 130:6). In waiting for the sunrise, you can always count on two things—you can't rush it, and it will rise.

The writer to the Hebrews takes up this theme and applies it to the present situation when he says: "He who is coming will come, and will not delay" (Heb. 10:37). It may look like delay to those waiting, but the Lord is right on schedule.

It's in the Air

Ron Dunn wrote: I was scheduled to arrive home at midnight from a ministry engagement up north. My flight, American 214, was scheduled to arrive at DFW (Dallas-Fort Worth)) at midnight. Kaye arrived at the gate to meet me (back then you could go directly to gates) several minutes before twelve o'clock. Midnight came, but no plane. Nothing unusual about that, so she waited. But after awhile, she went to the ticket counter and asked when they expected Flight 214. "In about thirty minutes," the agent said.

Kaye went to her car to wait before returning to the gate thirty minutes later. The flight still hadn't arrived. "Looks like another thirty minutes," the agent said.

Another thirty minutes passed. Still no plane. Puzzled, Kaye wandered around the airport for a decent interval then, returning to the counter, said: "Excuse me, but you must have some idea when the plane is going to be here."

Again the agent stopped what he was doing and looked at her without smiling. "I'm sorry, ma'am, but we do not have that information." "Well," she said, "At least you can tell me what time it left." "I'm sorry, but we do not have that information. Check back with me in a few minutes."

By now, Kaye was beginning to think the worst. With visions of crashed and burning planes in her head, she rushed back to the agent.

"Sir, I don't want to know when Flight 214 left. I don't want to know when it's going to get here. I just want to know one thing, is it in the air?" The agent smiled and said. "Yes, it's in the air." "Thank you," Kaye said. "That's all I need to know."

There have been times in my life, times of unexplained trials and unrelieved heartaches, when I have gone to the Lord and asked, "Lord, why?" And the answer has been, "I'm sorry, but I can't give you that information."

"Lord," I've cried. "How long? When will You deliver me from this?"

"I'm sorry, but I can't give you that information."

And in desperation, I have cried. "Lord, can you tell me this much— not when You will end this or how You will end it; I just want to know this—Is it in the air?" And the Lord has said: "Yes, child, it's in the air." That has been enough. I can wait patiently for the Lord because I know He is coming. He is always coming. He is on the way. It is in the air.

A Final Word—How Faith Grows

That faith can, and should grow, is evident from the use of such phrases in Scripture as *little faith* and *great faith.* Paul looked forward to the increase of the Corinthians' faith (2 Cor. 10:15). In Romans 1:17, Paul employs the phrase, "from faith to faith." He describes Abraham as growing strong in faith (Rom. 4:20). We are strong in faith when our first and natural response to crisis or need is to trust—to trust God by choice. There are basically two cooperating methods to increase our faith.

1. Our faith increases with our knowledge of God Himself, and His Word. In Romans 10:17 we read, "Faith comes from hearing, and hearing by the word of Christ."

2. Our faith also increases through experience. We learn to trust God by trusting Him. As we exercise the faith we have, it grows and develops into a stronger and healthier faith. But often, we will not trust God until we have to. We find it difficult to "lean not unto [our] own understanding" (Prov. 3:5 KJV).

Having read the biography of George Mueller, that great man of faith, I longed to be able to trust God like that. I remember one day kneeling in my study and earnestly praying that God would teach me to really live by faith. I guess I expected God to wave a wand over my head and put a holy *faith zap* on me, but instead, everything came unglued. Financial, ministerial, family crises, one thing after the other. I went to my knees, begging God to help me, asking what was happening, and why?

"I'm just answering your prayer," He seemed to say.

"Prayer? What prayer? I don't remember praying for disaster."

"Your prayer for faith," He said.

God's greatest and toughest task is teaching us to trust Him,
for without faith it is impossible to please Him.

And He will do whatever is necessary to enroll us in that school from which there is no graduation.

TESTIMONY: HAYES WICKER, SENIOR PASTOR, FIRST BAPTIST CHURCH, NAPLES, FLORIDA

I was discipled long-distance by Ron through his tapes. He was so biblical and expository, and he molded my ministry as a young preacher. I recall how, during seminary days, my wife, Janet, and I were facing a financial crisis. We were newlyweds and didn't have enough money for even the basics, like food. I was expressing how upset I was with God when Janet said: "Why don't you practice what you preach?" Well, I had just preached Ron's message, "In Everything Give Thanks." I took it to heart, and it totally changed my attitude. I have remembered the impact that message made, and it continues to impact our lives to this day. ※

[24]

When Heaven Is Silent[25]

*Let us learn to appreciate that there will
be times when the trees will be bare, and look
forward to the time when we may pick the fruit.*

—ANTON CHECKOV

TESTIMONY: DANNY GREIG—PASTOR, MILLDALE
BAPTIST CHURCH AND CO-DIRECTOR OF MILLDALE BIBLE
CONFERENCE

June 20, 2006, will be forever etched in my mind. Our thirty-six-year-old son, Eddie, suddenly died from an aorta aneurysm. My wife Nancy and I were devastated. He had a wonderful Christian wife, four beautiful children, and was growing in his walk with the Lord, and all we could think of was, "Why our son? Why? Why?"

We began reading books and articles on coping with grief, and some were helpful, but it wasn't until we began reading *When Heaven Is Silent,* by my longtime friend and mentor, Ron Dunn, that we realized *why* was the wrong question to be asking. Ron pointed out how we needed to move beyond asking ourselves and God, Why? to asking the question, "What now?"

The Holy Spirit shone light and strength into our hurting souls as we became willing to ask the right question and move forward. Thank you, Brother Ron. Although you are presently in heaven, you continue to minister to Nancy and me.

Prelude

In *When Heaven Is Silent* Ron looks back at his "dark night of the soul" days, during which time he was preaching, by faith, much of what he shares in this book that he divides into two sections—book 1, "Traveling in the Silence" and book 2, "Naming the Silences."

In book 1, "Traveling in the Silence," he shares how we often don't recognize special "ministers" God sends our way because they are not clothed as we would expect them to be. He recalls how, one day, after hours of cleaning out their garage, Kaye asked him to get her something at an all-night supermarket. He was dressed in a "soiled T-shirt, faded jeans with portholes in the knees, and tennis shoes that were in their final stages of leprosy." But that shouldn't matter since it was midnight and no one would be shopping that late who would see him. So he thought.

Ron Dunn wrote: Standing in line at the checkout the one person in front of me was a woman from my church. The devil made her turn around and look at me, then turn back, then turn around again, screwing up her eyes, giving me the once over. And then the recognition. "Brother Dunn!" she gasped. "I didn't recognize you without a suit and tie."

I had been her pastor for seven years. She was present every week, and I calculated she probably had heard me preach at least seven hundred times—and she didn't recognize me without a suit and tie. I thought about that. What had she been looking at for those years—me or my clothes?

Ron went on to share how he and Kaye were waiting for a plane at Gatwick Airport in London when a man across from them asked,

Ron Dunn continued: "Are you from Irving, Texas?' "Uh, well, yes, I am." He grinned and offered his hand. "I'm your postman."

I didn't recognize my own postman because he was out of uniform. The thought pounded at me. How many ministers had I missed? How many blessings had I forfeited because they looked like curses? How many kings had I turned away because they were clad in the rags of a beggar.

As I thought about this, I realized that some of the greatest ministers God had sent me were "strange ministers" that were out of uniform and I didn't recognize them because they didn't look like ministers are supposed to look.

The Strangest Minister

In the remainder of book 1, Ron developed the story of Jacob and his encounter with his "strange minister" at Peniel. (For a complete account of this encounter see chapter 13, *Surprise! It's God!*) He shared this in the context of a visit from the strangest minister he and Kaye had ever faced—Ronnie Jr.'s suicide.

In book 2, "Naming the Silences," Ron worked through the trauma this caused in his and the family's life. He began by asking three questions—"Why?" "Why me?" and "What now?"

Why?

Ron Dunn said: When the hoped for, prayed for miracle doesn't come, when we are not delivered—this is the question that hounds us, making sleepless nights endless—"Why?"

At first, of course, I tried to be "spiritual." I refused to question God. I gave thanks in everything, voiced my "praise the Lords," like a good catholic doing his "Hail Marys," but as the days became weeks and the weeks months, and I knew Ronnie was never coming home, I felt cheated and betrayed. As the anesthesia of shock wore off, the reality of death settled in like a black fog until finally the suppressed anger and hurt erupted with, "Why, God?" which was more an accusation than a question.

The Hebrew word for *why*, used most frequently in the Psalms, is both a cry of lament and protest. It means "to what end" and "for what reason" does God remain silent?

Let's face it. Injustice inhabits our world. Sufferers of every age have struggled with this dark enemy. In Psalm 73 the psalmist airs his frustration. "I have envied the arrogant when I saw the prosperity of the wicked." We simply aren't prepared for the unannounced sharp curves in the road that life throws at us. Just when we get a grip on life, our hands go numb and our exclamation points turn into question marks.

Why Me?

We live in a generation that wants or demands an explanation for everything. But while we may operate by that policy, God does not. He operates strictly on a "need to know basis."

"Why me?" assumes an injustice has been done, one that demands redress. The "why me?" focuses only on the unfairness of the situation. We hardly ever ask, "Why not me?" because we think we certainly didn't deserve it.

Perhaps the fundamental reason we ask "why" is because we cannot live with mystery. When we ask why, we want a simple, pat explanation, thus avoiding the inconvenience of mystery. But still the mystery stands. Then one day while I was struggling to unmask this question, a thought struck me. "What if I'm asking the wrong question?"

What Now?

At this point Ron turns to the ninth chapter of John and the story of the man who was born blind, pointing out that the correct question to ask was not "Why?" he was born blind, which was what the disciples asked, but, "What now?" (See chapter 17 for the message, *What Now?*)

Asking the question, "What now?" allows us to step outside the prison of our "self-centered" universe to see ourselves, not as victims but as objects of God's divine attention. It breaks the trance of self-pity.

Silence

Ron Dunn wrote: The silence of God can be a terrifying thing. From his ash-heap, Job demanded that God read the charges against him. Surely he has the right to know for what crime he is being punished. But heaven is silent. As a matter of fact, when it is all over, Job still does not know why he has suffered. He is never informed of the conversation between God and Satan.

Finally, when God does speak, after thirty-seven chapters of silence, it is not to provide answers; it is to ask questions. And the questions He asks are totally irrelevant to what has been happening to Job. He takes Job on a nature hike. He flings the universe in Job's face, saying that He has the right to do what He does, to govern what He has created, and to say whether He is governing it properly.

God Has the Right

The first, and most difficult hurdle of all, is to settle the fact that, when we meet God, it is not to get answers to our questions, but it is to learn the right questions to ask. And the right question here is, "Does God have the right to do what He does?"

This was the first question I had to face the night we heard of Ronnie Jr.'s death. On his grave-marker are these words from Psalm 115:3: "But our God is in the heavens: he hath done whatsoever he hath pleased" (KJV). This is the verse that came immediately to mind that night.

God Has a Reason

Job said: "I know that you can do all things; no plan of yours can be thwarted" (42:2 NIV). Job may not have known what the purpose was, but it was enough to know that there was one. And this is one of the supreme lessons of the book of Job: Our suffering serves some larger purpose of God. This links our human lives with a divine purpose.

God Has a Reward

I love these words, "The Lord blessed the latter part of Job's life more than the first." I believe that is what the Lord wants to do for all of us. He always saves the best wine until last.

I like to imagine that God went looking for Satan afterward. I expect Satan had made himself scarce. I can picture him hiding behind a bush. "Come on out, Satan, and pay up. I told you Job would serve me for nothing, and I was right."

The Dark Side of Grace

Darkness, despair, depression—are these legitimate spiritual experiences? Isaiah thought so. "Let him who walks in the dark, who has no light, trust in the name of the LORD" (Isa. 50:10 NIV). Isaiah's portrayal is that of a man on a journey, and as he walks, suddenly the light is withdrawn and darkness rushes in. You feel forsaken and abandoned.

Theologians have a term for this: *Deus Absconditus*—the God who is hidden. This is when no light is thrown on the "why" of your suffering.

This is when the usual means of grace—prayer, worship, singing, God's Word—have no affect on the drooping spirit; when the tried and true formulas from books and seminars sound hollow; when you discover there are some things you cannot praise or pray your way out of. You can rebuke the devil, plead the blood, station angels, and wear garlic around your neck, but nothing moves the darkness. Saints through the ages have trod this dark road before us. "How long, O LORD? Will you forget me forever? How long will you hide your face from me?" said the psalmist (Ps. 13:1 NIV).

We think of the Psalms as being the hymnbook of the church. Then, why don't we sing Psalm 88? I'll tell you why. Listen: "O LORD, the God who saves me, day and night I cry before you . . . For my soul is full of trouble and my life draws near the grave . . . I am like a man without strength. I am set apart with the dead, like the slain who lie in the grave, whom you remember no more, who are cut off from your care" (Ps. 88:1, 3–5 NIV).

Try throwing that on your overhead next Sunday morning and see what it does to your praise service. I'm not advocating that, but it is real because it is in the Bible.

The darkness is ordained of God. Oswald Chambers said that God sometimes withdraws His conscious blessings to teach us to trust Him more perfectly.[26] When God withdraws the light, He is trying to teach us that there is something better than light—faith.

Closing Chapters

In the next several chapters Ron looked at the struggle many have with memories, and what to remember when you can't forget. One of Ron's powerful sermons, available from LifeStyles Ministries, is titled "What to Remember When You Can't Forget."

He went on to share the encouraging word that God judges us not by our achievements but by the ambition of our heart and, that when God says "no," it is not to deprive us of a blessing but to drive us to a better one.

Ron then looked at what he called the most unbelievable verse in the Bible—Romans 8:28. "And we know that God causes all things to work together for good to those who love God, to those who are called according to His purpose."

Ron Dunn wrote: I discovered that Paul is not saying that everything that happens to a Christian is good. A lot of bad things happen to us. We cannot say that what happens to us is best, but we can say that what happens will be worked out for our good, and that the things that do happen to us have no weight in thwarting the good God intends for us. And Paul does not mean that God works out all things for our comfort, convenience, health, and wealth. Whatever good Paul has in mind has to do with our salvation and our relationship to the God who saved us.

A Closer Look

The context of this verse is important. The primary reference to "all things," is the "sufferings of this time" in verse 18: "For I consider that the sufferings of this present time are not worthy to be compared with the glory that is to be revealed to us" (Rom. 8:18). But Romans 8:28 not only looks back to verse 18, it looks forward to verses 35–39 as well.

"Who shall separate us from the love of Christ? Shall tribulation, or distress, or persecution, or famine, or nakedness, or danger, or sword?" (Rom. 8:35 ESV). But in all these things we overwhelmingly conquer through Him who loved us" (Rom. 8:37).

Paul appears to be saying that all things, like those he lists, are used to profit those who love God. When the Bible says that all things work together for our good, it means that *all things work together for God's purpose.* God's purpose is good, the good of God's purpose.

If this is true, it means that the pain Kaye and I encountered when we buried a cherished dream—even that is destined for our good. If this is true, it means that if God subtracted one pain, one heartache, one disappointment from my life, I would be less than the person God wants me to be.

If this is true, it means that I can climb over those disappointments, over tears and heartaches, over the graves and sleepless nights, and stand on top of that ash-heap and declare, "All things God is working together for good!"

Providence and a Guy Named Joe

Ron began this book with Jacob, presenting him as a paradigm of God's dealings with His people—"a struggle till the break of day." He closed the book with Joseph as a summary of all he had said about God's silence and His strange ministers.

Ron Dunn wrote: With Joseph, God was silent for twenty-five years. And he had his share of strange ministers—his brothers, the Midianites, the Ishmaelites, Potiphar, Potiphar's wife, the butler and the baker, and famine. The brothers, themselves, brought about the fulfillment of Joseph's dreams, which they had hated. And, had they not thrown him in the pit, they would never have bowed before him in Egypt. But here's an even more fantastic thought: If those brothers had not done what they did, twenty-five years later, they would have starved to death as would have Egypt and the surrounding nations. You could say that their sin became their salvation.

Epilogue

I'm writing these final pages at Cape Cod. Kaye and I come here every year around Labor Day as the guests of dear Christian friends, Bill and Mary Lou McElmurray. It seems fitting that I should finish the book here because it was on our first trip to Cape Cod in 1986 that the darkness began to lift.

I'm always reluctant to finish a manuscript and mail it off, and I'm especially reluctant to let this one go because it has become so personal. I didn't intend it to be that way, but books, like mischievous children, have a mind of their own and often run off in their own direction. But I agree with Henri Nouwen, who says that the thing that is most personal is most universal.[27]

At the core of our being, down in the guts of our soul, we are all alike, fearing the same fears and desiring the same desires.

I am not an exception.

Neither are you.

That's the truth.

Honest.

I promise.

TESTIMONY: NELSON McKINNEY, MBBC DEACON

As Ron's friend and MBBC deacon, I was able to watch the price he and Kaye had to pay in family members, lost dreams, and broken hearts. Ron had that great humor and wit. He had that great mind and that great passion for God, but every bit of it had its pound of flesh in it. I've never seen a man suffer the way that man suffered. It's easy to think about his victories, but oh, at what cost. ❊

[2 5]

Will God Heal Me?[28]

I have read scores of books about evil in the world and suffering in the lives of Christians—and have even written a book on the topic myself—but this one is outstanding. Ron Dunn is not afraid to face facts honestly, nor is he inexperienced in applying God's truth lovingly. He himself has been in the furnace and found Jesus there with him, so pay attention to what he says.

—WARREN WIERSBE

The New God in Town

There's a new god in town—the god of Health and Fitness, the Bel and Nebo of our day (see Isa. 46:1).

And so, with a touch of humor, the kind that Ron did so well, he began to lay the foundation for what would follow, as he addressed one of the most controversial and divisive issues in the church today—Does God heal, and will He heal me?

The Health Obsession

Ron Dunn wrote: The followers of this *new god,* worship from dawn's early light to the shadows of evening, seven days a week, sometimes alone, often in small groups or large gatherings. Indoors and outdoors, on sidewalks, in parks, in homes and in offices, this determined congregation spans the generation gap and is oblivious to race, creed, or color.

Exercise is, of course, good for the body and great fun for the spirit, but what happens when sickness removes us from this scene; when suffering intrudes on our lives? We're never really prepared for this. It catches us by surprise and knocks us off balance.

The Fear of Ill Health

"What will it do to our future?" we ask. "How will others respond?" And underlying our fear of ill health is our insecurity about where God fits into the picture. Will He heal me, or will I have to live with it, or die with it?—questions common to us all.

As we address these tough questions, let's keep in mind Paul's magnificent words of hope: "Now to Him who is able to do far more abundantly beyond all that we ask or think, according to the power that works within us, to Him be the glory" (Eph. 3:20–21, author paraphrase). "To God be the glory!" There just may be more to suffering than the pain.

When Questions Come

It's easy to philosophize about suffering when you're not doing any, but when the beast crouches at your door, it's another ball game—the answers don't come as easily then, and the explanations often don't satisfy.

The Problem of Pain is one of the best books ever written on the subject. However, twenty years later, when C. S. Lewis's wife lay dying of cancer, he found no comfort in the things he had written. They were no less true, but he was less able to affirm them. When things happen that make us look as though we no longer believe, the problem is not faith but an inability to affirm it in the shroud of darkness.

My personal search into the subject began when my faith suddenly collided with sickness, suffering, and death. "Skin for skin," the devil said, and it was my skin and the skin of my family. Meanwhile, I was writing a book on the power of prayer, and I was preaching around the world on the victorious Christian life, while my own life had become a paradox. Folk would say: "You don't have enough faith to be healed." My problem was, I didn't have enough faith to stay sick, if that was how things were to be.

Some told me that healing was my divine right, that I and my family were suffering unnecessarily, and that we were probably under a curse because of something my father or grandfather did. Well, if I was missing something, I wanted to know about it. I thought I knew what the Bible taught, but pain can make you do strange things.

In Search of an Answer

I soon realized that finding the answer about *physical* healing would not be enough. The real question lay beyond the physical, and if I was going to get the right answer, I had to start asking the right questions. And when I did, I saw that physical healing was just the outer layer, a secondary issue. Job ultimately understood that. My friend, Manley Beasley, who suffered for years with three terminal diseases, when approached by a woman who wanted to pray for his healing, said: "Ma'am, I've long since passed that."

But believing in God can be a burden. If He can heal, why doesn't He? I would if I were God. Why must God's way often require pain? These are the same questions that have been asked for thousands of years, and we're no nearer the answer. Each generation has to ask them for themselves.

The Night Side of Life

In every battle there are losses, even for the victor. Illness is no exception. In fact the pain, suffering, and uncertainty of serious illnesses usually amplify the sense of loss experienced by both the patient and the loved ones. Loss of control over your body, loss of identity when people look at you differently and you realize you are no longer the person you used to be. But here's where we must walk a tightrope—we must not deny our illness, but neither can we allow it to define who we are: "That's the salesman with cancer." Or, "She's a wonderful mother but she has MS."

Gains in Suffering

Something that has impressed me as I talk to people with life-threatening illnesses is that they often say that the sickness is worth what they learned from it, about themselves, and about God. Often it is only after being confronted with a life-threatening illness we realize that the price tags have truly been switched, and that most of our previous labor has been in the junk business. Recovery may not be possible in every case, but renewal is.

Where Does Sickness Come From?

Philosophers, theologians, and ordinary folk like us have struggled for centuries to solve this puzzle. Some say: "When a person becomes sick, he has in some way violated the laws of health. That's a simple answer but not necessarily always true. We've known people who've eaten right, got plenty of sleep, exercised religiously, didn't drink or smoke, lived in a nuclear-free zone, who have dropped dead on the jogging trail.

Ron expressed concern for those who overemphasize that a sickness can be a result of a curse passed down from parents or grandparents, and that before healing or deliverance can be obtained, these satanic curses must be broken.

Then there are the superstitious, like the pastor Ron encountered at a conference in Kansas who wanted to buy a series Ron had recorded on *The Devil, Demons and the Occult.*

Ron Dunn continued: "How much is the whole set?" he asked me.

"Thirteen dollars," I said.

He paused for a moment. "Could I write you a check for twelve dollars and owe you a dollar?"

"Well, I guess so. Why?"

He hesitated, then said, "I don't like to write checks for thirteen dollars."

"This was a preacher. I determined he really needed the sermon series and I probably should have given the tapes to him, but I said:

"Tell you what—write the check for fourteen dollars and I'll owe you a dollar." And he did. Anything to avoid the number thirteen.

But by far, the favorite explanation for sickness espoused by those who believe that illness cannot be part of God's will is Satan. Sickness, they say, is caused by sin and delivered by Satan. Conclusion? *It is always God's will to heal.*

If Not . . . What?

Ron Dunn wrote: So then, from where does sickness come? I prefer to write *mystery* over the whole issue, but to prove that fools sometimes rush in where angels fear to tread, I will risk being simplistic and offer what I believe are the four basic sources of sickness.

1. **God.** That's right. I believe that God Himself is often the source of illness. To say He permits it but does not cause it is begging the point. Being sovereign, He could prevent it, and to the one suffering, it amounts to the same thing.

2. **Satan.** In Luke 13:11, Jesus healed "a woman who for eighteen years had had a sickness caused by a spirit."

3. **Our personal lifestyle.** Our bodies are so constituted that if we flagrantly disregard the laws of health, the body will react in illness.

4. **Being a human.** There is a natural process of decay going on right now in all of our bodies. Let's face it, sickness goes with the territory. We are part of a fallen race.

Absolute Sovereignty

The Bible teaches that God is sovereign over everything, even the devil. Satan can operate only within the limits God gives him. Witness the case of Job, or how God raised up Cyrus to accomplish His purposes (Isa. 45:1, 4–5). God can weave even the wicked into His design. The devil is under the power of God, so that while he is fighting against God, he is compelled to be the involuntary instrument of His purpose. A. J. Gordon once said: "The Lord sometimes allows His saints to be sharpened on the Devil's grindstone."

God has not promised that disaster will never find its way to believers, but He has promised us grace to bear it and to use it for our good and His glory. Or, as Augustine wisely observed: "God judged it better to bring good out of evil than to suffer evil not to exist."

The Seducers and the Seduced

After addressing his own battle with the black hole of depression that has been covered in section 4, Ron went on to look at why multitudes today are being seduced by seducers who are preaching the gospel of health and prosperity.

Ron Dunn wrote: If you dropped a lighted match into the gas tank of your car, people would run for cover. Why? Because there is something inside the tank that responds explosively to fire. You wouldn't get the same reaction if you dropped a lighted match into a tank of water because the match is only dangerous when there is fuel in the tank. And there is plenty of fuel in the tank of the human heart to make prosperity teaching powerfully attractive and to make possible the seduction of the sick.

What Do We Mean by Healing?
Are There Various Kinds or Degrees?

All healing, of course, comes from God. Whether through medication, surgery, proper diet and exercise, alternative medicine or divine intervention, the body receives its healing from the Lord who created it. The famous French surgeon, Ambroise Paré, is credited with saying, "I apply the dressing, but God heals the wound." Hanging on the wall of a doctor's office was this quip: "God does the healing. I charge the fee."

I do not claim that the following list is either medically exhaustive or scientifically satisfying, but it is at least will get us started.

Assisted Healing

There is healing that requires some kind of aid, whether medical treatment, therapy, change of diet, or taking two aspirin and going to bed. Nothing in the Bible discourages us from seeking qualified medical help. Luke was a *beloved physician* (either he was a very good doctor or he didn't charge much). It is not a lack of faith that sends us to the doctor.

Natural Healing

This is the body's ability to heal itself. Out of the dust of the earth God has fashioned an instrument with amazing recuperative powers, such as when you stop smoking or overeating, it may actually repair damage done.

Faith Healing

Here, I refer to "natural faith" that is native to our nature, the faith that we exercise when we sit in a chair or fly in an airplane. By "faith healing" I refer to the maintaining of a positive confession and attitude. Physicians agree that a positive mental attitude results in improvement. Cancer specialists see statistical evidence that patients who believe they will do well with certain treatments have a much better prognosis than those who are pessimistic about their chances for a cure. Conversely, all doctors have seen maladies whose symptoms appeared only because the patients thought they were sick, or sicknesses brought on by marked stress, resulting in a functional disorder of the body.

With these facts as a background, Ron went on to say that when those who present themselves as faith healers use high-powered, self-advertising campaigns, that build up impressive reputations, their claims can be believed by a highly "suggestible patient" and might conceivably be instrumental in curing these kinds of diseases.

Ron Dunn wrote: This kind of physical betterment has proven to be valid by doctors for years. In tests when patients are given "fake medicine" or "placebos," the recipient, thinking it is the real thing, begins to believe that healing is in progress, and this mentally conditions the patient to believe he is better and may actually allow the body's own chemistry a chance to unwind itself and begin to function properly.

Divine Healing

For our present purpose, divine healing is defined as the sovereign act of God in which He intervenes to heal the body without the use of human skills or means. When Jesus healed, there was no question a miracle had taken place. This is not true with many "miracles of healing" today. Unfortunately, however, questions that are raised concerning the validity of a healing miracle are often dismissed as lack of faith and a hindrance to the Spirit's work. But Jesus never shielded His patients from scrutiny. Asking for verification is not a sign of unbelief. *Truth does not fear investigation.*

I was not long out of seminary when the infant son of a young couple in the church I was pastoring suddenly became mysteriously ill. He was hospitalized in serious condition when the baby's fever rose to such a height that brain damage and even death was the prognosis. I visited the despairing parents every day in the child's hospital room, trying to comfort them. One day, as we gathered around the child's bed to pray, a strange thing happened. I was overcome with the presence of God. I knew God wanted to heal this little child. Never had I been so certain of anything. I placed my hand on the baby's burning head and asked God to heal him, and I thanked Him for doing it. Within a couple days the baby was released from the hospital, healed.

Since then there have been a number of similar incidents. On those occasions I don't sweat and strain to believe God for healing—it's easy for me to believe because this is a gift, a gift imparted by God to my heart that makes possible the "prayer of faith."

Handling Accurately the Word of Truth

Careful Bible study is vital to a faith that truly honors God. The apostle Paul, in his letter to his son in the ministry, cautioned young Timothy to, "Be diligent to present yourself approved to God as a workman who does not need to be ashamed, accurately handling the word of truth" (2 Tim. 2:15). Illumination by the Holy Spirit is essential to a correct understanding of Scripture, while an unsound approach thwarts the Spirit's work. Most of the confusion regarding God's perspective on sickness and healing could be eliminated by following the basic rules of interpretation.

A Plea for Open-Mindedness

Ron Dunn wrote: I do not wish to sound vindictive, but having been through the crucible of suffering myself, and having seen serious illnesses grip the lives of many wonderful friends who struggled with the question, "Will God heal me?" I must agree with John R. W. Stott who said: "We have to have the courage to reject the health-and-wealth gospel. It is a false gospel."[29]

Having laid the foundation to his treatise on *Will God Heal Me?* Ron provided five insightful and helpful rules, or guidelines, that should govern the interpretation of Scripture, then, following these, he addressed such issues as "Healing: The Same Yesterday, Today and Forever?" He asks and answers such questions as, "Are the miracles of the New Testament being repeated today?" and, "Are signs and wonders needed today?"

Ron then took a closer look at the healings of Jesus and the apostles, asking if they are valid models for modern-day healing? He pointed out that Jesus healed with a word and a touch. He healed everyone who came for healing. He healed without regard to faith. He healed instantaneously and completely, with no recorded relapses. And, as a rule, Jesus discouraged, and even forbade, the publicizing of His miracles.

Ron made clear that he was not suggesting that God does not heal today, but he emphasized that the healings of the New Testament are not models for healings today. God has a far different purpose in mind for us. In some cases healing may be His design for accomplishing that purpose. In other situations He may choose to wait or to say "no," in order to bring about that purpose. The question for us becomes, "Do I want my pleasure or God's purpose? On which should my heart focus?"

Did Christ Die to Make Us Healthy?

In this important section Ron examined other matters of concern such as, "Is Healing in the Atonement?" He leads the reader through an in-depth study of Old and New Testament Scriptures that form the basis for his conclusions before addressing the particularly challenging issue of why God heals some and not others.

When God Says "No"

Ron Dunn wrote: This question that plagues everyone, and to which there is no satisfying answer: Why does God heal some and not others? And when He says "no," we must recognize that there is no one who can overrule His decision, no higher court to which we can appeal. We must conclude that the answer to "Why does God heal some and not others?" is a mystery.

God Is Sovereign

When we question God, we are finite creatures with finite minds, trying to understand an infinite God. In many ways we judge Him by our standards, our definitions of goodness, justice, and fairness. Then, when we think we have God all figured out, we discover that He often colors outside the lines we have drawn for Him. We must never forget that . . .

God works on a different schedule than we do. We are time-space creatures. For God, there is only the present—the eternal now. And God invariably takes longer than we expect, as He did with Abraham and Sarah, and with Moses. With God, timing is more important than time.

God works with a different value system. For us, the words *good* and *blessing* signify comfort, convenience, and happy circumstances. But to God the same words may signify character and virtue and integrity. We think in physical and material terms; God thinks in spiritual terms. To Him, holiness is better than happiness. To God, character is more desirable than comfort.

Something Better than Healing (The God-Ultimate Purpose of Suffering)

I knew a man who taught me more about suffering than anyone I've ever known. To those who knew him, the only thing surprising about

Manley Beasley's death was that he actually died. Manley lived in great pain, for twenty years, yet I never heard him once complain about his pain or his seven illnesses, three of them terminal.

Manley was my best friend. He taught me more about faith than anyone I have ever known. He died about one year after I interviewed him about his life and ministry, and I'm convinced that he could have been healed years before had he chosen the healing option God gave him. He chose, rather, the way of suffering. Tough choice. But considering his life, ministry, and influence, I believe he made the right choice.[30]

Fear Not

Fear and anxiety haunt people from the cradle to the grave, and nowhere does this emotion express itself more forcefully than when we are confronted with sickness, suffering, and death. But I believe the answer to this fear is found in the words of Jesus—"Fear not." This was one of the most frequent greetings of Christ to His people. When the angel brought his message to Mary, he said, "Fear not." When Jesus called Peter to follow him, He said, "Fear not." When speaking of the enemies that would persecute His followers, He said, "Fear not." When speaking of sickness and death, He said, "Fear not."

Don't be afraid of life. To many people there are some things that are worse than dying—and living is one of them. To them, Jesus says: "Don't be afraid."

Don't be afraid of death. Christ controls death. "I have the keys to death and Hades," He said to John on the Isle of Patmos. Think of it. The devil doesn't even have the keys to his own house.

Don't be afraid of eternity. The "unseen world" is a good name for it, for we fear what we cannot see. But from that unseen world, Jesus says, "Fear not. Don't be afraid of what lies on the other side of the grave."

In closing, Ron tells of a personal "fear experience" he had when his Cub Scout den went to the Boston Mountains of Arkansas to learn how to read a compass. It was ten o'clock at night, and their assignment was to find their way back to the lodge where hot chocolate and Oreo cookies would be waiting. It was to take about an hour.

Clouds obscured the moon, so they had to depend on a flashlight to read their compass. Unfortunately, this was before bunny batteries, and the flashlight soon grew dimmer and dimmer, until it finally died. Not able to see the compass, their Scout leader led them in what he thought was the right direction.

"Suddenly the ground in front of us was even darker than the ground we had been stumbling over," recalls Ron. "We had come to a drop-off and we couldn't tell if it dropped off three feet or three hundred feet. We didn't move an inch. The tantalizing thing was that we now could see the lights of the lodge about one hundred yards ahead of us.

"We all waited for someone to volunteer to crawl over the edge of the drop-off to find out what was down there. It wasn't going to be me. The bravest thing I had ever done was light a match without closing the cover. Finally, the Boy Scout leader sat down on the edge and began to drag himself downward.

"We could hear him sliding through the brush, and then, nothing. Not a sound. Petrified, we waited. After what seemed to be an eternity, we heard a voice from the other side of the ravine. It was our Leader. 'It's okay boys,' he called. 'Come on. You can make it.'

"And we did. Hot chocolate and Oreo cookies never tasted so good. Someday we will all stand on that dark edge of the unseen world. And we may be frightened. But if we listen carefully, we will hear the voice of our Leader, calling: 'It's okay. Come on. You can make it.'" ※

Surviving Friendly Fire[31]

Prelude

Churches are full of hurting and wounded people—many of them hurt by friends and fellow believers. Ron observed this firsthand during his pastorates and subsequently when he began traveling in conference ministry. These observations caused him to begin thinking in terms of incidents that have become known as "friendly fire."

Friendly Fire

Ron Dunn wrote: I have held conferences in almost a thousand churches, big and little, city and rural, of this denomination and that, and have found them full of wounded, hurting people. It may have been yesterday or a lifetime ago, but it still ulcerates the heart and mind. And what makes this so tragic is that these wounds have come, not from enemies, but from friends. We expect our enemies to hurt us, but when it comes from one you trust, a pastor, a parishioner, a husband or wife, a parent or child, who can measure how deeply that wound buries itself in the soul?

Increasing numbers of people tell me that they are reluctant to share their hurts with friends or church members. When Jesus was on earth, however, troubled people ran to Him for refuge, while now, it seems that they are running from Him, or rather, from His church.

In trying to understand how Christians could lie, deceive, and literally betray fellow believers, I came to this conclusion: Before this kind of malicious behavior can live, something must first die—*Integrity*.

The Death of Integrity and Other Good Things

We read in Proverbs: "The integrity of the upright guides them, but the unfaithful are destroyed by their duplicity" (Prov. 11:3 NIV). Most people would agree that one of the greatest failures among leaders, and especially among politicians these days, is the failure of integrity.

In his book, *Integrity*,[32] Stephen Carter maintains that this is perhaps first among the virtues that make for good character because in some sense it is prior to everything else. The rest of what we think matters very little if we lack essential integrity.

A person with integrity believes that there are standards against which behavior can, and should be measured, even if sticking to those standards cost him personally.

God's Original Intention

God's original intention was that the world, His creation, live in fellowship with Him and one another. That's why He created us in His image. But the world failed. Man disobeyed God, breaking fellowship with Him, which led to brother killing brother.

But then, God made a new creation—the church. This new creation was to fulfill the intentions of the old creation. The church is supposed to be a microcosm of what God intended the world to be. But we too have failed.

After sharing several illustrations, Ron went on to say that friendly fire can come from a variety of sources, inflicting wounds that breed invisible tears—invisible to others, and sometimes, through denial, invisible to us. Yet, as he began to pinpoint and examine some of these sources, he stopped to admonish and encourage us: "Remember this," he said. "Friendly fire need not be fatal. You can survive it. God has made ample provision to carry you through to healing and victory."

Abandonment—a Source of Wounding

"Where is everybody?" If I were Jesus (I speak as a fool), I think the most disappointing day of my life would have been resurrection day. Why? Because not a single person was there to welcome Him back from the dead—none of His disciples, none of His friends. It wasn't that they were uninformed because Jesus had repeatedly told them that He would rise on the third day. But rather than being there to welcome Him, they were in hiding, huddled together around their fear and faithlessness, and they missed the dawning of a new day.

But actually, Jesus wasn't surprised at their absence. After all, they had forsaken Him during His hours of greatest needs, the hours of His passion. Peter had bragged how he would go to prison with his Lord. Empty words from an arrogant heart.

A View from the Pit

In 2 Timothy, the apostle Paul, writing from prison, spoke about those who had abandoned him during his great hour of need. "Demas," he said, "because he loved this world, has deserted me" (4:10 NIV).

The Greek word here means "to be left in the lurch." Paul encouraged Timothy to come as soon as possible to bring his cloak and his scrolls, especially the parchments. Paul felt alone and lonely, like a dying soldier lying forgotten on an empty battlefield.

I guess all those fine Roman Christians found it more convenient to be elsewhere on that day. I hate to admit it, but preachers know this all too well. That's where the expression, "Christians shoot their wounded," comes from. People want to be on the side of winners, the popular and the praised.

In contrast to this pattern, Paul told us that if one of our brethren is caught in a sin, "you who are spiritual should restore him gently," and we are to "do good to all people, especially to those who belong to the family of believers" (Gal. 6:1, 10 NIV).

But, just as it is a sin to abandon a brother or sister in their time of need, it is also a sin to become bitter over being abandoned. Paul showed us this when he asked God not to hold it against them.

Then, from his view from the pit, Paul discovered something else—although people may be fickle, the Lord is faithful. He said: "But the Lord stood by my side and gave me strength" (2 Tim. 4:17 NIV). The word *stood* in those days depicted a legal adviser who stood by the defendant, whispering advice to him. This is a picture of our Lord who stands by us.

Turning Your Pit into a Pulpit

In closing this passage, Paul declares: "The Lord will rescue me from every evil attack and will bring me safely to his heavenly kingdom" (2 Tim. 4:18 NIV). Paul, in describing his absence of friends, and the presence of the Lord who stood by and strengthened him, said, "So that through me the message might be fully proclaimed and all the Gentiles might hear it" (4:17 NIV). And so it is with us—nothing speaks louder and clearer of the sufficiency of God's grace than the trustful way we react in similar situations.

Invisible Tears

She was leaning against the wall in the auditorium, her body racked with uncontrollable weeping. This twenty-year-old woman just couldn't get assurance that God had forgiven her sin. Friends asked me to talk to her.

When she told me that she didn't believe God could forgive her, I said, "You need to see God as a father who loves . . ." Suddenly she shoved me back and cried out, "Don't use the word *father* to me!" I asked her what she meant. Between sobs, she related the years of abuse she had suffered from her father. The visible tears of God's unforgiveness were a subterfuge for the invisible tears of her father's abuse.

Her story tells of a double tragedy—the betrayal at the hands of one she loved and trusted and the trauma she has had to endure into her adulthood, invisible tears that may never dry up.

But Must the Past Determine the Present?

I have good news for all who have been hurt. Past hurts need not ruin your present or future happiness. Salvation is available; deliverance is within your reach, or more precisely, in the reach of Christ. In Colossians 2:15, writing of Christ's victory on the cross, Paul wrote, "And having disarmed the powers and authorities, he made a public spectacle of them, triumphing over them by the cross" (NIV).

Friendly Fire within the Church

Ron likened those who attack fellow believers to "spear throwers." Why would Saul try to pin David against the wall? He listed several reasons that could apply to what sometimes happens in the church today.

Jealousy—Saul was jealous of David's success and popularity.

Insecurity—The insecure person believes a man's life consists of the abundance of things he possesses, like the farmer in Luke 12 who built a bigger barn.

Mistrusted motives—Insecurity begets mistrust of others, thinking there must always be an ulterior motive. One of the results of the revival at MacArthur Boulevard was that the entire staff trusted each other. Ron pointed out that, though he sometimes made mistakes, they never questioned his motive.

Personal ambition—David was not after the throne, but Saul imagined that he was. Saul's world was defined by selfish ambition. He was determined to keep the throne at all costs, even if it meant killing his most loyal servant.

What to Do When Treated Unfairly

In the Galatian church they were, in Paul's words, "biting and devouring each other" (Gal. 5:15 NIV). "Biting and devouring" suggests wild animals engaged in a deadly struggle. I often hear people say, "If we could just get back to the New Testament church." Well, sometimes there's not that much difference between that church and ours. The real question is not, "Will I be treated unfairly?" but, "What should I do, or not do, when I am?"

Don't be surprised. "Dear friends," Peter advised, "do not be surprised at the painful trial you are suffering, as though something strange were happening to you" (1 Pet. 4:12 NIV). Mistreatment is not alien to the Christian. Remember the Beatitudes? The eighth and final one states, "Blessed are those who are persecuted" (Matt. 5:10 NIV). Trials are true to our calling, so don't be surprised.

Don't be vindictive. Our natural reaction is to get even, but Peter instructs us: "It is commendable if a man bears up under the pain of unjust suffering because he is conscious of God. But how is it to your credit if you receive a beating for doing wrong and endure it? But if you suffer for doing good and you endure it, this is commendable before God" (1 Pet. 2:19–20 NIV).

Don't be intimidated. "Who is going to harm you if you are eager to do good? But even if you suffer for what is right you are blessed . . . ; 'Do not fear; do not be frightened'" (1 Pet. 3:13–14 NIV). We may not know the Bible, but the Bible knows us. So its command is, don't be agitated, irritated, or intimidated. We are to respond as Christ would. "In your hearts set apart Christ as Lord. Always be prepared to give an answer to everyone who asks you to give the reason for the hope that you have" (1 Pet. 3:15 NIV).

Make Sure the Wound Is Not Self-Inflicted

I stood there with my legs spread slightly, my feet planted firmly, my left hand hanging loose at my side, my right hand hovering over the butt of the Colt .44 single-action Peacemaker resting in its holster. Though I had never done it before, I was considering an OLD WEST quick draw like Matt Dillon used to do in the TV series *Gunsmoke.* The man with the fastest draw won the battle. Matt Dillon always did!

Among gun enthusiasts "quick-draw" is a sport. I've met the champion. He could draw his gun, fire, hit the target, and have the gun back in the holster in four-hundredths of a second. The only problem for enthusiasts like me is that as you're pulling the pistol out of the holster, while at the same time cocking the hammer, your thumb can slip off the hammer, causing the gun to fire before you've completed the draw. The result? A .44 lead slug in the foot, a few missing toes, and a limp for the rest of your life.

In dry runs with an unloaded gun, my thumb slipped off the hammer most of the time, so I never tried a real "quick-draw." I didn't want to shoot myself in the foot. Of course, I have shot myself in the foot a number of times but not with a gun.

Our Own Worst Enemy

One pastor told me he had just recently realized that the problems he was facing in his church were of his own making. That's true of many of us, but this should be made clear—offending people will not always be avoidable. You can't preach the full counsel of God, including man's sin and Christ's cross, and not offend somebody. If a minister proclaims the gospel in the Spirit and love, if anyone is offended, he need not go to that person and apologize; he should praise the Lord that the gospel is still the power of God to those who believe.

Commit the Situation to God

The Christian life is largely a matter of reaction. Generally the world doesn't pay a lot of attention to how we act, but it is our reaction to adverse circumstances that catches their attention. Much of the Sermon on the Mount deals with reactions. "If someone strikes you on the right cheek, turn to him the other also. If someone wants to sue you and take your tunic, let him have your cloak as well" (Matt. 5:39–40 NIV). The apostle Peter urged us to follow the example of Jesus who, "when they hurled insults at him, he did not retaliate" (1 Pet. 2:23 NIV). The choice is yours. You may act with shock. You may act with hurt and humiliation. You may react with anger and desire vengeance or follow the example of Jesus and entrust yourself to Him who judges justly.

Contentment

Everyone is searching for it. Paul learned it in prison, having been falsely accused and betrayed by his colleagues. He wrote to the Philippians, "I am not saying this because I am in need, for I have learned to be content whatever the circumstances" (4:11 NIV).

The word *content* literally means "to be self-contained." It is to be independent of external circumstances. This attitude does not come easy, however. It has to be learned. I was hoping I could just pray for it and God would take a magic wand and zap me full of contentment. A person may know much about Christ but not have *learned* Him. Learning requires more thought and study than we're willing to give.

Look for the Unseen Hand of God—His Providence

The word *providence* comes from a Latin prefix and root. The prefix *pro* means before, and the root *videre* means "to see." These two put together, mean "to see beforehand." But the word indicates more than God's foreknowledge. "To see before" indicates "to see before and make provision." Providence performs in time what God purposed in eternity. R. C. Sproul puts it this way: "It is not merely that God looks at human affairs. The point is that He looks *after* human affairs. He not only watches us, He watches over us."[33]

Hiding from Saul, in a cave in the wilderness of En Gedi, David declared, "I will cry unto God most high; unto God that performeth all things for me" (Ps. 57:2 KJV).

Keep Humming!

Two things can pierce the umbrella of the wounded believer's peace—fretting over past hurts and fearing future ones. The present is crucified between the past and the future. But there is a way to plug the holes in the umbrella of peace, and it is meditating on God's providence. To many, meditation is a lost art or a suspicious practice associated with Eastern religions. But the Bible has much to say about meditating on the things of God. We are told that the person who *meditates* on the law of the Lord will be blessed (Ps. 1:2). The Hebrew word translated *meditate*, means "to ponder, to muse, or to hum."

Hum! I like that. In the same way, meditating, or humming, or pondering on the providence of God keeps us ready to sing His praises, no matter what problem suddenly arises.

Returning Friendly Fire

Alan Paton is credited with saying that there is a hard law, that when a deep injury is done to us, we never recover until we forgive. For us to forgive someone is to let go of a grudge, to abandon our desire for revenge, to dismiss our demand for repentance on his part.

We must always remember that forgiveness and reconciliation are not the same thing. You may forgive someone, and yet that someone may not change his attitudes toward you. In his book *Life Lines,* Forrest Church says, "When we forgive someone, we do not change them but ourselves. This doesn't reverse the past, but it changes the present and the future."[34]

So we forgive. Why? We forgive for the simple reason that God has forgiven us. Forgiveness is unilateral, all inclusive, and unconditional. It is "getting even," God's way.

A Closing Word

That's all I know about surviving friendly fire. Is it enough? I hope so. I think so. The alternative is to become a spear-thrower. If that is our intent, we should remind ourselves of how Saul summed up his life— "Behold, I have played the fool" (1 Sam. 26:21 KJV).

Getting to Know You

"Getting to know you, getting to know all about you," is the opening line to one of Rodgers and Hammerstein's hit songs from their musical *The King and I.* Not that we ever really get to know "all" about a person, but it is interesting to discover how similar or dissimilar personalities can be—how varied are our likes and dislikes. We all have our idiosyncrasies, and Ron had his share.

Have You Smelled a Book Lately?

Being the avid reader Ron was, many books passed through his hands, but few were ever read, if any for that matter, before he had opened the book and inhaled its aroma. Whether true or not, he claimed he could tell the publisher, or at least the printer, by the smell. Kaye testifies that, even when visiting a bookstore, before checking a book's content, he would open it up and deep-breathe. She laughs when wondering what book purchasers would have thought if they knew Ron Dunn had already had his nose in it!

Coffee with Cream and Sugar Please

Ron never drank coffee without an abundance of cream and sugar. When in restaurants he would tell the waiter to bring "plenty" of those little coffee-cream packets and sugar cubes. When he said "plenty," he meant just that. Whether he had an actual number in mind when "fixing" his drink, no one recalls, but what we do know is, by the time he was through, true coffee connoisseurs would have a problem recognizing the brew he drank.

Guns

Ron began collecting guns in his first pastorate. It was a country church, and "the folks" took him hunting and taught him to target shoot. Ron took to this sport, and it would not be long before he would be bit by the gun-collecting bug. One year, knowing how much Ron loved guns, Jimmy Robertson and the Milldale Bible Conference presented him with an Uzi. Ron was thrilled.

He carried his collection to the family farm in Arkansas each summer where both he, Kaye, and the children spent time target practicing. Ron also loved cleaning and oiling his guns, and he particularly enjoyed making his own ammunition.

In 1985, he was robbed and shot at by two men in a Holiday Inn parking lot in Little Rock, Arkansas. He was in Little Rock for his quarterly checkup with Dr. Ron Hardin, who was helping him with stomach problems that had at one point become debilitating. Ron happened to have part of his gun collection in the trunk of the car. He was in the process of carrying his collection to his room when these two men grabbed the bags out of his hands. The bag containing some of his guns also had three months of medication the doctor had given him. The next day the local newspaper headlined an article, "Preacher Robbed of Guns and Drugs."

During the trial the prosecuting attorney did an excellent job of explaining the gun collection and the medication (drugs). The man who shot at Ron received a sixty-year sentence for armed robbery. This was his fifth felony conviction.

Horses

Ron loved horses. He became interested in riding during the days of his rural pastorates. When Kim was fourteen, a family friend gave her a quarter horse. Though she soon lost interest in the horse, Ron took Trooper to the farm each summer where he enjoyed riding him, wearing a bandanna around his head, and his six-shooter on his hip, ever ready to whip it out of its holster to shoot a snake or any other critter he felt was a nuisance.

The Farm

Ron enjoyed spending summers and holidays on the 330-acre farm that his father had purchased in Greenwood, Arkansas, and where his parents and his brother Barry and his family lived.

"We loved our time together with them," recalls Kaye. "We would gather as a family each night for dinner, and then we usually watched *Wheel of Fortune,* played Charades, Pictionary, or some other family game. Those summers were when our families grew so close together.

"I remember how much Ron and the children loved to set up a trot-line in the evening and go out in the middle of the night to check it. Ron loved riding the tractor and mowing the pasture, and he always wore his six-shooter on his hip like he did when riding Trooper. He was always ready to pick off a snake. He was even known to shoot a fish or two!

"Since most of Ron's time at home was spent behind a desk, studying and writing, the weeks at the farm were a welcome retreat, though he did spend time reading, preparing sermons, and sometimes working on a book, usually when the rest of the family was asleep."

Thinking

Ron always claimed that one of his main hobbies was "thinking." He attributed this largely to the influence of J. P. McBeth. The times spent at the farm allowed him creative, reflective periods in which sermons and books were conceived. His first book, *Any Christian Can,* was completed while at the farm one summer, and Kaye had the privilege of typing and editing it for him—one of the joint efforts she really enjoyed over the years.

Ministry Philosophy

On several occasions over the course of Ron's ministry, he was approached by well-meaning Christian agent/promoters who felt that Ron was a marketable "product" and that they could help him expand his ministry. He, however, was convinced that God wanted him to follow the example of his mentor, Vance Havner, who never sought publicity or raised a hand to get a ministry engagement.

Nor did Ron ever put a price on his ministry. Big church or small church, he would never allow a monetary amount to influence his decision to accept or reject an invitation. He never allowed a church to discuss in advance what they thought they might do.

Michael Catt recalls talking to Ron one time about how, as a pastor, you feel you have failed if there is not a visible response at the end of the sermon. Ron's response was: "It's not your fault. Once you have been faithful in delivering what God has given you for the people, the response is in God's hands."

"But," Michael said, "they're hearing all this truth, and they're just standing there!"

Ron: "If you try to control it, you'll take the credit for it. The response is in God's hands. Let Him take care of it."

The Relationship of the Trusted Motive

This is how Ron described his relationship to his staff and deacon leadership. He trusted the staff God had placed around him to pursue the vision God had given them for their respective responsibilities at MBBC, while always being available to them for counsel. "And," recalls Nelson McKinney, deacon chairman, "Ron was not into committee meetings. He didn't feel he really had that much to contribute to them unless we felt we needed his input. 'If you need me, call me,' he'd say. He would much rather be spending his time praying and studying."

Simple Tastes

Ron was a man of simple tastes. He loved plain food. Give him a good hamburger, a steak, or spaghetti and meatballs, and he was a happy camper. He loved junk food. At night, Kaye recalls, "We would crawl up in the bed with our stack of books and a big bowl of popcorn, chips, or sweets and read. This was something he began doing while he traveled, and I fell into the habit quite happily whenever I traveled with him."

Michael Catt recalls one time when Ron invited him to his motel room for dessert after a service. "As I walked through the door, I was confronted with a counter full of junk food, including an angel food cake, and next to the cake lay his 9mm pistol. I said, "'Ron, do you leave that pistol sitting out like that all the time?' With as serious a look as he could muster, he said, 'Nobody's gonna steal my angel food cake!'"

Sports

Being from the Dallas area, Ron was a Cowboys fan. Though that interest waned some in later years, after Tom Landry left the team, he still enjoyed pro football games. Since he was on the road most Saturdays, he didn't get to watch much college football.

He and Kaye used to love to play tennis and enjoyed watching it on TV, especially Wimbledon. Kaye recalls that during the months he was laid up in bed, sometimes too weak even to study or read, they would watch any sport that would help pass the time.

Cars

Over the years Ron had several favorite cars, and among these was his little black Nissan 280Z and later a black 300Z. Since he spent so much time on the road, he found them to be great traveling cars. He'd pack them to capacity, mostly with books, then head off for a meeting. One time a porter at a Chattanooga hotel just sat down on the curb and watched as Ron loaded the car, declaring that he didn't think it could be done. It was . . .

The Dog

Years ago friends from the church gave the Dunn children a tiny, snow-white, toy poodle puppy. This was against Kaye's better judgment and desires. The children liked the puppy, but Ron fell in love with it, and it soon really became his. He suggested they name him Belshazzar since the dog was "weighed in the balances, and found wanting" (Dan. 5:27). They did, and for sixteen years Shaz and Ron were inseparable companions.

Money

Ron had an interesting thing about money. He didn't like to have a wallet in his pocket, and he wasn't interested in looking at their checkbook. As far as he was concerned, the personal money matters were Kaye's problem, and LifeStyle Ministries was for Joanne Gardner to care for. He knew he could trust God for whatever the needs were, and he left Kaye and Joanne to keep track of it all.

Humor

Stan Toler is credited with saying that "humor is to life what shock absorbers are to automobiles." This proved true for Ron over the years. He had the ability to see the humorous side of life and often even created it.

Jimell Badry, Ron's minister of music during his pastorate at MacArthur Boulevard Baptist Church, recalls walking into the pastor's office one day to discover a framed photo of Ron's Thunderbird car hanging on the wall. Around the car were photos of his five pastoral staff members, and at the bottom of the photo was this caption: My Rod and My Staff.

Ted Kersh will never forget an incident when Ron was with him in a meeting at Village Baptist Church in Oklahoma City.

"One of my deacons had offered Ron the use of a new Cadillac that he had just purchased. It was now the last service, and the deacons were about to take up the love offering. Ron was sitting in the front row, and the deacon, who had loaned Ron the car, was standing near Ron at the end of the row, ready to take up the offering. As I was finishing my challenge to give generously, I saw Ron lean over and say something to this deacon.

What he said was, "Does everything that goes in the offering plate belong to me?" When the deacon assured him that it did, Ron reached in his pocket, pulled out the keys to the Cadillac, and dropped them in the plate! The best part of the whole thing for me was the look on the deacon's face. It said: "I may have just given my Cadillac away!" Ron's humor was one of the many things that endeared him to us all. Ron taught me that, in the midst of the seriousness of ministry, it is alright to lighten up occasionally.

Illustrator

Ron was the consummate "illustrator." He knew that illustrations were windows to the soul, and most of Ron's stories were original with him, coming out of his own personal experience or from his fertile imagination. He could paint word pictures that were as tangible, simple, and real as anything you would see with your naked eye. Many testify to Ron's illustrations being so memorable that, after hearing one, all you needed, even years later, was for someone to say a key word, and immediately you'd recall not just the story but its application.

Cartoon Doodling

Ron loved to doodle. His interest in cartoon drawings led him to pursue a diploma course in cartoon art.[35]

Transparency

One of the more disarming things about Ron was his transparency and vulnerability. Though this kind of honesty was not often seen among evangelicals, it made Ron just that much more real to those who knew him best, to those who read his books, and to those to whom he preached. Ron's was an appropriate honesty that helped his hearers know he was not talking to them from an ivory tower, as someone who lived in 24/7 victory, but as one who identified with their struggles, with where they were. Testimonials to Ron's transparency are found throughout this account of his life, and in a day of rock-star ministries, it freed up others, who got to know Ron, to be more transparent and honest.

Humility

Going through the ministry records that Kaye and Joanne Gardner gathered into more than twenty-five annual scrapbooks, I've found many things that I had never heard about, things that could have become points of pride for Ron, temptations to name-drop, or reasons to be puffed up. But he never seemed to yield to those temptations, choosing rather to go about his calling, not having to make a public display of the many accolades he was receiving over the years. ✳

PART SEVEN

A "Prince" Among Preachers

❊ ❊ ❊

Before I formed you in the womb I knew you;
before you were born I sanctified you. . . .
You shall go to all to whom I send you,
and whatever I command you, you shall speak.

JEREMIAH 1:5A, 7B NKJV

I preach as never sure to preach again, and as a dying
man to dying men.

—RICHARD BAXTER, ENGLISH PURITAN

[2 7]

Quick Start

Preach the word! Be ready in season and
out of season. Convince, rebuke, exhort, with
all longsuffering and teaching.

2 TIMOTHY 4:2 NKJV

Preach the Word

We've a gospel to preach, we've a message to share.
God's eternal Word is what we declare.
It's the power to save, it's the Spirit's sword,
It's the heart of God, it's the Living Word.
We must study to learn and not be ashamed
To proclaim God's truth in the Savior's name,
With no compromise, but consistently,
We must preach the Word with integrity.

What is made by man will one day be gone,
But God's holy Word marches on and on.
Though the flower will fade and the grass will die,

The eternal Word ever will abide.
We must pay the price, we must take our stand,
With a heart on fire and God's Word in hand,
On the brightest day, in the darkest hour,
We must preach the truth in the Spirit's power.[36]

Ron was just fourteen years old in 1951 when he attended summer church youth camp in Siloam Springs, Arkansas. That was the year he began to sense a stirring in his soul regarding the ministry. The following year at the same camp, he knew for certain that God was calling him to be a preacher. He made this public at the close of one of the services when Dr. Carl Bates was preaching, and by the end of the camp he had put three sermons together. He laughingly confesses they were pretty pitiful, and he never did use them, but this was an indication of his total commitment to God's call on his life. He never looked back.

Ron was gung ho. He immediately began buying Bibles and books. He bought a loose-leaf Bible "just like my pastor had," and *101 Snappy Sermons*. Armed with these, he preached his first sermon three months later in the "drunk tank" of the Fort Smith city jail where the church's Brotherhood ministered on a weekly basis. The sermon was out of Isaiah 55:6–7.

"Our church Brotherhood had me do a good bit of preaching during those days in smaller towns and churches in the Fort Smith area. I preached my first revival at sixteen, a two-week, outdoor meeting, in Akins, Oklahoma that was billed as, "Hear the Gospel under the Stars." I had three sermons that were worth anything so I got down my books and began copying sermons and putting them in my loose-leaf Bible. I had no idea what one of the sermons was about, but I got up and preached it (read it), and strangely enough, God blessed it.

"One of the memories I have of that meeting was getting to meet the aunt of Pretty Boy Floyd.[37] She was a member of the church that was sponsoring the revival. It hadn't been all that long since that area of Oklahoma was outlaw country.

"I pastored my first church at the age of sixteen, while still in high school. We had fifteen members—fourteen women and one man. I had one deacon!"

Another memory Ron had of those early days was the Youth Revival held at First Baptist Church, Bowlegs, Oklahoma. At the time he was nineteen and a student of OBU. John (Johnny then) Bisagno was leading the music.

Ron had recently heard an evangelist preach on the home and thought it was a really good sermon so he decided to preach it. Before a packed-out sanctuary he enthusiastically told husbands how to love their wives, how to bring up their children, and all they needed to know and do in order to have a godly home. At the close of the service, a visiting pastor, after complimenting Ron on the message, said:

"By the way, how many children do you have?"

"Well," replied Ron. "None actually. I'm not married yet."

"Young man," the pastor said, "when you have children of your own, you'll throw that sermon away."

Thirty years later Ron was in a meeting at First Baptist, Chickasha, Oklahoma. At the end of one of the services, he was talking to folk at the front of the church when he looked up and saw a man walking toward him. Ron knew exactly who he was, though he hadn't seen him in thirty years.

"Have you thrown that sermon on the family away yet?" he asked.

"Yes sir. I have."

Ordination Day

Sitting on the front row of First Baptist Church, Fort Smith, Arkansas, sixteen-year-old Ronnie Dunn listens to J. Harold Smith explain the implications of God's call on his life.

"Now Ronnie, nobody wants you to be Billy Graham."

Ron thinks to himself, *There goes my first choice.*

"Now Ronnie, nobody wants you to be a W. A. Criswell."

Well, there goes my second choice.

"Now Ronnie, all anybody wants you to be is Ronnie Dunn, full of Jesus."

Reflecting on his ordination some time later, Ron thought to himself: *Who in the world would ever want to be a Ronnie Dunn?*

Testimony: Randy Bostick, Senior Pastor, Oakland Baptist Church, Corinth, Mississippi

Ron was the ultimate communicator. Much like Jesus did, Ron taught the profound truths of God's Word through everyday illustrations so that ordinary people could understand. After all these years I still remember many of his sermons.

Because Ron was not afraid to show his humanity in the pulpit, he preached to struggling people like a fellow struggler. I believe this was the primary reason Ron appealed to such a wide range of listeners, because people at every level struggle.

Ron preached in the church I still pastor, twelve years in a row. The greatest compliment to his effectiveness is that, even though Ron has been gone many years, I still hear my people pray things they heard Ron Dunn say. It's truly incredible!

TESTIMONY: DAN ROBINSON, PASTOR, HIGHLANDS CENTRAL BAPTIST, HIGHLANDS, NORTH CAROLINA

"The Ministry of the Thorn" was the first of Ron's sermons when I took notes. That was about thirty years ago, and I still have those notes. I learned from Ron that the problem is not that we're weak but that we're not weak enough. We pastors want to appear strong for our people, but true strength comes out of weakness. Ron pointed out that a "third heaven" experience and a "thorn" experience are often found in the same person. When you listened to Ron Dunn, you never had to worry what tangent he was running off on. As a preacher, he was careful exegetically. If you found yourself stuck at a point in your own study of a certain passage, you could turn to Ron Dunn without fear of getting off track. At the end of the day, as I have reflected on Ron, the thing that sticks in my heart is that he finished well. No embarrassment to the kingdom; he didn't sully the Lord's name. After all the research is in, the record will show a man who was transparent, who loved God, and who finished well. ✳

[2 8]

More Tributes to
"The Preacher"

Following are more testimonials, in alphabetical order, from ministry peers who were profoundly impacted by Ron's life and preaching. Some of these were shared in a *Friends of Ron Dunn* gathering at Sherwood Baptist Church, Albany, Georgia, in April 2011, and at a similar gathering at First Baptist Church, Euless, Texas, in September of the same year.

TESTIMONY: DAVID ALLEN: DEAN OF THE SCHOOL OF THEOLOGY, SOUTHWESTERN BAPTIST THEOLOGICAL SEMINARY, FORT WORTH, TEXAS

I had the privilege of being Ron and Kaye's pastor during the eighteen months prior to his home-going, though Ron Dunn's influence on my life began in 1975 when I moved to Dallas to go to college. Through the years I heard him preach on a number of occasions at conventions and conferences. Then, when I began pastoring, I listened to many of his sermons on tape. He made a great impact on my life and ministry.

It was, however, as early as the late sixties that preachers across the United States began listening to Ron's recorded sermons. My own pastor, Dr. Jerry Vines, of First Baptist, Jacksonville, Florida, where I grew up, regularly listened to Ron's messages.

Ron was a remarkable preacher. I recall when I was his pastor, during those last eighteen months, I would occasionally get together with him and question him about preaching, and he would share out of his many years of experience. Over the years Ron's impact has been felt worldwide, and I believe his real influence on preaching has yet to be told.

It's remarkable the influence Ron has had and will continue to have in the years to come. When I travel I still take CDs of Ron's messages with me. In recent years I've been studying his preaching from a homiletical standpoint, and as I teach preachers, year-in and year-out at SWBTS, I have the opportunity to pass on the remarkable wisdom and preaching ability of Ron Dunn. Though being dead he still influences and will continue to influence the lives of hundreds and thousands of young preachers.

TESTIMONY: JAY BADRY: PASTOR, FIRST BAPTIST CHURCH, WEWOKA, OKLAHOMA

As a teenager, growing up at MBBC under Ron's ministry was an incredible experience, partly because of Ron's pulpit ministry and the youth ministry with Ron Proctor. While in many other churches the youth were sitting on the back row writing notes, the MBBC youth were in the second and third rows taking notes.

Those days impacted my life in ways I don't have words to describe. I surrendered to the ministry under Ron Dunn's preaching. Initially, for the first twelve years I was in music, then I began to sense that God might be leading me more into a preaching-teaching ministry. I was struggling with that when I shared with Ron what I was going through. I'll never forget what he said.

"Jay, in the Old Testament there is the story about how they built the temple, without the sound of a hammer. What that means is, when they quarried the stone off-site, and numbered them, they were quarried with such precision that when they were brought on-site they didn't have to hammer or force them. The stones slipped effortlessly into place."

Ron told me that in his own life, when he had to force something, it was either not God's will or God's timing. "If this is God's plan for your life, Jay, it will happen without the sound of a hammer."

Twelve months later, when I was the music minister in a church in Augusta, Georgia, the pastor resigned. The deacons, not knowing anything about God's dealing in my life, asked me to be interim pastor. A few months later, I became the senior pastor, without the sound of a hammer.

I don't think I ever step into the pulpit without something of Ron's influence that impacts my message. I told him one time how I had observed that he was still preaching the same basic principles and truths he preached when I first heard him. I said, "Your doctrine has not changed."

"Jay," he said. "I'm first and foremost a theologian. During my early years of training, I took the time to diligently study the Scriptures and to settle my theology once and for all so that everything I preach, everything I teach, must conform to that basic truth. That's why I don't preach a different message today than I did twenty or thirty years ago."

Ron Dunn paid the price, and all who heard him preach were the beneficiaries of the price he paid.

TESTIMONY: MICHAEL CATT: SENIOR PASTOR, SHERWOOD BAPTIST CHURCH, ALBANY, GEORGIA

I always loved Ron's sermon taken from Paul's second letter to Timothy. It was written when Paul was in prison, and in the latter part of chapter 4 Paul says, "Go out of your way and get John Mark because he is useful to me" (see 2 Tim. 4:11). Ron said: "You know, Paul was lonely; he was cold, and he was bored." That was the first time I ever heard a preacher say that about Paul. I thought, *If it's alright for the apostle Paul to be lonely, cold, and bored, maybe it's OK for me to be lonely, cold, and bored sometimes.*

Ron pointed out in another message where Paul said, "Demas has forsaken me" (2 Tim. 4:10 NKJV), that he wasn't saying that Demas had forsaken the Lord. Ron said, "He probably went back to Thessalonica, sat on the back row, and never got involved again."

Ron talked about how hard it would have been to be on Paul's staff. And when Paul said, "Only Luke is with me" (2 Tim. 4:11 NKJV), Ron said Paul was saying "I'm down to just a doctor—Luke." Ron found nuggets in passages that most preachers just pass over.

Another sermon of Ron's that I'd like to preach is the one from Isaiah 45. That is one of those messages where Ron points us to the "God who causes darkness and creates calamity" (see v. 7). "Woe to the one who quarrels with his Maker" (v. 9). Ron reminds us that God uses our setbacks to become our salvation.

Ron said that we may sometimes feel that if God has hands, His fingers are all thumbs. You need to understand, in the story of Joseph, that the people of God did not think that deliverance was going to come the way it did, through the very one they got rid of. God was in the process of working out their deliverance, but it wasn't the way they had voted.

TESTIMONY: JIMMY DRAPER: PRESIDENT EMERITUS, LIFEWAY CHRISTIAN RESOURCES

I first became acquainted with Ron in 1970 through Jake Self, an associate pastor of mine when I was pastoring First Southern Baptist Church in Del City, Oklahoma. Ron at the time was pastor of MBBC, and Jake kept talking about Ronnie Dunn—my friend, Ronnie Dunn. I later found out that Ron considered Jake to be one of his mentors when he was in Oklahoma, during his college pastoring days.

When I was called to pastor First Baptist, Euless, Texas, I began to get to know Ron and Kaye. He was one of the speakers at our annual

Conference on Revival, along with Manley Beasley, Jack Taylor, Miss Bertha, and others.

A lasting impression I have of Ron is how God enabled him to preach out of his pain. I recall his sermon "What Do You Say When You Don't Know What to Say?" I can't remember all the points, but I do remember what the conclusion was—"You glorify God." Ron was always practical in what he said, and I always felt he was preaching right to me.

If someone were to ask me to pick a favorite Ron Dunn sermon, it would be like asking me to pick a favorite Scripture. I must admit, however, that "Chained to the Chariot" would probably be near the top of my list.

TESTIMONY: DAVID DYKES: PASTOR, GREENACRES BAPTIST CHURCH, TYLER, TEXAS

Ron's Bible-teaching ministry has had a huge impact on my life and ministry. In the early 1980s I remember first listening to a cassette of him preaching on staying "Chained to the Chariot" (2 Cor. 2:1–17). I was close to burnout as a young pastor, and his message of submitting to the yoke of Christ literally saved my life and ministry.

I was pastoring a rather small church in Alabama and didn't think there was any way Ron would come and preach for us. But I wrote him a letter and signed it by saying, "Chained to His Chariot." He called me the day he received the letter and said that my mention of being chained to Christ's chariot was the reason he would be willing to come.

Through the years it was my honor to invite him to share five or six times at the churches I served. God used Ron as a pure vessel to bring about healing, cleansing, and wholeness in the lives of people. His simple, humorous, life-application approach to teaching the Bible was unique. I will be eternally grateful for what Ron allowed Jesus to do through him.

TESTIMONY: MALCOM ELLIS: REVIVALIST, COLMESNEIL, TEXAS

Not a week goes by that I do not miss Ron Dunn and wish with all my heart that I could hear him preach one more time. His ministry was such a unique blend of wit, scholarship, and profound spiritual insight. He could open the Word of God in ways that left me breathless and astonished.

Brother Ron made, and continues to make, an indelible impression on my life, and I am grateful to God for every opportunity I had to sit under his preaching and for the privilege to know his friendship.

TESTIMONY: DUDLEY HALL: EVANGELIST-REVIVALIST, GRAPEVINE, TEXAS

When I was in college, I was privileged to sit under the expository preaching of my pastor, Gerald Jones. I asked him one day who he liked to listen to. One of the men he mentioned was Ron Dunn, so while in college I listened to Ron's messages. Then, when I began pastoring while in seminary, I continued to listen to Ron on the way to the hospitals, to my classes, wherever I was driving. He pastored me through his taped sermons. Ron soon became one of my heroes and eventually a close friend.

I feel that if he were with us today he would say, "Don't spend a lot of time entertaining, just preach the Word and let God do His work."

TESTIMONY: T. D. HALL: EVANGELIST-REVIVALIST, BEDFORD, TEXAS

Ron had a great influence on my life through his preaching. Though I was a member of another church, I would have Joanne send me all of Ron's sermons so, as I traveled, I heard two Ron Dunn sermons a week. Back then, when someone asked me who my pastor was, I'd say, "Well, I have two." Ron was my tape-pastor, and over the years his preaching and his books had a great influence on my life.

TESTIMONY: GEORGE HARRIS: FORMER SENIOR PASTOR, CASTLE HILLS FIRST BAPTIST CHURCH, SAN ANTONIO, TEXAS

I believe Ron Dunn stands like a mountain above all other mountains when it comes to preaching. He was focused on the Word of God and never allowed himself to be drawn away by fads. He never allowed himself to get caught up in the trivia of denominational politics. Humbled in his walk with God, he never allowed the accolades of man to go to his head. Ron loved one thing above all things, and that was to preach. Gone to glory, never to be forgotten, and most likely, never to be replaced.

I've known Ron since our seminary days, and as our ministries evolved over the years and we became closer friends, I saw how God was developing him into one of the greatest expositors of our day.

I believe the hurt and adversity Ron went through, he went through for all of us. Out of the pain, the questions, and the tears came life lessons that have helped thousands in the midst of their own testing times.

Part of the legacy of Ron Dunn is that he was real, he was honest, he was transparent, he was the genuine article, twenty-four-carat gold. What God worked into Ron, Ron worked out for all of us.

TESTIMONY: JIM HENRY: RETIRED, SENIOR PASTOR, FIRST BAPTIST CHURCH, ORLANDO, FLORIDA

It's not easy to put in words the impact Ron Dunn's life and ministry made on me and the congregation of First Baptist, Orlando. He touched us through his integrity, his humor, and his ability to see into the Scriptures in such depth and freshness. Then there was the incredible way he applied what he taught to our daily lives and the widespread net he cast in his teaching and preaching that reached people of all ages—all economic and social backgrounds, the church, the unchurched, the lost, and the saved. His teaching reflected his life. It was as fresh as the morning dew.

TESTIMONY: TED KERSH: SENIOR PASTOR, SOUTH TULSA BAPTIST CHURCH, TULSA, OKLAHOMA

I had the privilege of being in Bible conferences with Ron for twenty-five years. As a young pastor I began inviting Ron to do a Bible conference at my church. After writing and bugging him long enough, he finally came. That first conference was at Southwood Baptist Church in Oklahoma City. Our hearts soon linked, and we continued to have Ron over a period of twenty-five years, wherever I was.

Ron impacts me to this day. I don't think I prepare a message where, at some point, I don't ask myself, "I wonder what Ron would say? I wonder how Ron would do this?" He exemplified for me purity and holiness, a desire for God, and a love for His Word.

I remember back in those days how I would take a Scripture and feel I had milked it for everything that was in it; then I'd hear Ron preach out of that passage, and it was almost like I had never read it before. To this day, my wife, my children, and the church I pastor benefit from my having known Ron because of the challenge his life was to me.

TESTIMONY: D. L. LOWRY: FORMER PASTOR, FIRST BAPTIST CHURCH, LUBBOCK, TEXAS

Ron and I first met in 1958 at SWBTS in a Greek class taught by Dr. Curtis Vaughn. As the years passed, I would have Ron in the churches I pastored until, in my more mature years, Ron and I began to share a ministry in western North Carolina at the annual Bible conference at Grassy Branch Baptist Church in Asheville, North Carolina. Other churches in the Hendersonville area participated, along with students and faculty from the Fruitland Baptist Bible Institute. The highlight of those years for me was the ministry Ron and I shared.

We had so much in common. This included a passion for expository preaching as well as a longing to see the Lord's churches revived. Ron impacted my life by how he lived and what he preached.

TESTIMONY: STAN MAY: PASTOR, IMMANUEL BAPTIST CHURCH, OLIVE BRANCH, MISSISSIPPI

I can think of no other preacher who has more influenced my preaching style than has Ron Dunn. It was not so much a conscious emulation as it was captivation by his mastery of expository preaching. He wove humor into the message as few other preachers, brought out the truth of the passage with clarity, and then hammered home the main point with precision and finesse. I was singularly enriched by his life and ministry.

TESTIMONY: JOHN MEADOR: SENIOR PASTOR, FIRST BAPTIST CHURCH, EULESS, TEXAS

I kind of married into the Ron Dunn influence through my wife Kim while attending OBU. She was a woman of deep spiritual insight, and I would ask her, "Where have you learned all this?" I was a preacher's kid, but I sure didn't know the Word like she did. She'd say, "I listen to Ron Dunn tapes."

By the time we were married, Ron had resigned MBBC to go into an itinerate ministry, so I never did get to hear him there. When I was in seminary, however, I listened to Ron Dunn tapes as I delivered papers from two to five-thirty in the morning. My mother-in-law gave me three hundred of Ron's sermons. I ended up listening to two Ron Dunn tapes every day for two and a half years. I like to say that Ron Dunn didn't save my life, but he saved my mind because during those two plus years my mind was being renewed. The Holy Spirit met with me in that little VW Beetle as I listened to Ron expound the Scriptures. I was amazed, and still am, at the simplicity, yet the profound truths Ron uncovered in the Word.

As I got into the ministry and was preparing my own sermons, I would find myself asking. "What would Ron Dunn say about this? How did he find what he did in this passage?" I knew, of course, that he didn't find what he did through a method, as much as he did through the inspiration of the Holy Spirit.

I did get to know Ron on a more personal level between 1992 and 1999 when I pastored MBBC. I would occasionally take him out to lunch and ply him with questions. I sometimes felt that Ron did not realize how much he had to give to younger pastors like me, personally. He didn't think highly of himself in that way. I remember telling him how we needed to hear the wisdom he had gleaned through his own walk with the Lord. He began answering questions about life and ministry in a way that blew me out of the water. It was all from the overflow of his life. He didn't have to go and study for the answer.

TESTIMONY: JON MOORE: REVIVALIST, KELLER, TEXAS

Of all the series of messages Ron preached, the one out of Habakkuk continues to speak to us. In it he posed the questions: "What if it doesn't get any better than this? What if, years down the road, we look back and these were the good ole days? What will we do? Will we love God? Will we keep serving Him? Will we trust Him?" That question, "What if it doesn't get any better?" has continued to resound in my heart through the years. What if this is as good as it gets, what will you do?"

TESTIMONY: STEPHEN F. OLFORD: INTERNATIONAL EXPOSITOR, AUTHOR, FOUNDER OF THE STEPHEN OLFORD CENTER FOR BIBLICAL PREACHING, MEMPHIS, TENNESSEE

I want to testify to the blessing dear Ron Dunn was in my personal life. We ministered many times together, and I never failed to be challenged and blessed through his anointed, expository preaching of God's holy Word. I remember especially the years in England, both at the Keswick Convention and at Filey. His insights into God's Word, his holy humor, and especially his exemplary life were an impact to all who heard and saw him, especially to myself. I praise God for his life and look forward to the day when we will talk in glory about the times down here.

Note: Dr. Olford joined Ron "in glory" on August 29, 2004.

TESTIMONY: KENNETH RIDINGS: PRESIDENT OF FRUITLAND
BAPTIST BIBLE INSTITUTE, HENDERSON, NORTH CAROLINA
AND RETIRED PASTOR OF GRASSY BRANCH BAPTIST CHURCH,
ASHEVILLE, NORTH CAROLINA

We were always impressed by Ron's handling of the Word of God.
To us he was determined to be as prepared as he possibly could. He had
a unique ability to unfold the Scriptures and mine nuggets from familiar
passages I seemed to have missed or overlooked. His humble and sweet
spirit always showed in his preaching.

I'll never forget the Sunday morning, however, when the 11:00 a.m.
worship time arrived and no Ron. Kaye wasn't with him on that trip. I
went on down to the motel below the church where he was staying and
knocked on the door. By then it was 11:40. He came to the door squint-
ing his eyes.

"What time is it?" he asked. I said, "It's time for you to get your
clothes on and go to church."

"Do you mean I need to preach at this late hour?"

"Our people are waiting on you," I said.

I went back to the church to tell the folk that he was coming. He
finally slipped in the back door and, walking up to the pulpit, said:
"Whew . . . waking up is a terrible way to start a day." Ron's humor and
his love for the Word of God were contagious.

From that point on he endeared himself to the church, to Ann and
me, as well as to Fruitland Baptist Bible Institute, in Hendersonville,
North Carolina, where for many years he and D. L. Lowry were a part of
our annual conference and founder's days. What a man of God, what a
preacher, what a friend.

I will always be grateful for the many hours of fellowship we had with
Kaye and Ron when he was with us at Grassy Branch Baptist Church and
in our home. I know of no days in our spiritual lives that meant more to
us. I know of no friend I have missed more. Ron Dunn changed my life
and meant more to me than words could ever tell.

TESTIMONY: JIMMY ROBERTSON: PASTOR OF MILLDALE BAPTIST CHURCH AND DIRECTOR OF MILLDALE CONFERENCE CENTER, ZACHARY, LOUISIANA

Someone once asked me what made Ron Dunn such a great expositor. I said: "First of all, Ron was a great man. He was a great Christian. Ron's messages were not just hammered out in the study, but they were worked out in life experiences. I don't know anyone who could relate life's experiences so well to the Word of God. 'For to me, to live is Christ and to die is gain,' was one of his major themes and life verses. Christ was glorified through the great difficulties God took Ron through."

I've never heard a more honest man in his preaching and his writing. Ron poured out his heart and life. Preachers like me, who were going through difficulties, could identify with him because he was not afraid to share his own struggles. Thank God, Ron Dunn fought the fight, he kept the faith, he completed the course, and he finished well. But Ron's ministry is not over. History shows that the ministry of many of God's great servants did not end with their death, but their greatest impact was after they were gone. I believe Bro. Ron's life and message will continue on through his recorded sermons and the books he has written until Jesus comes.

TESTIMONY: RICK SHEPHERD: TEAM STRATEGIST—PRAYER/ SPIRITUAL AWAKENING, FLORIDA BAPTIST CONVENTION

I recall several moments of impact. The first was a conference at MacArthur Boulevard in May 1975, when I was in the midst of a spiritual famine. Ron's messages were anointed, food for the spirit. His cassette tapes traveled with me many places and were shared by many as I was in seminary in Fort Worth and then on staff at Southcliff Baptist Church. I remember wanting to be a preacher like Ron, in his clear and creative exposition.

His word was always fresh. His view of the Word impacted me, and I took to heart his high regard for the study of the Word, for no-nonsense teaching and preaching. He didn't use gimmicks. He approached the text head on and sought the heart of God as he unpacked each book, each chapter, each verse. He did not mind wrestling with the things we have difficulties with—the issues people face. Ron called for honest, open communication with the Lord. He didn't have all the answers but pointed us to trust in the God who does. The fruitfulness of Ron Dunn's ministry continues on to this day through the lives of those who were impacted by his life and ministry.

TESTIMONY: HAYES WICKER, SENIOR PASTOR, FIRST BAPTIST CHURCH, NAPLES, FLORIDA

Ron was both a Barnabas and an Apollos. He had eloquence, he was mighty in the Scriptures, he was a scholar, and he made young preachers want to study the Word. He dug, he exegeted, he did word studies; but when he delivered the sermon, he was not clunky, he didn't get bogged down in the Greek or Hebrew like some scholars do. Ron made the Word live for the common man while satisfying the intellectual.

I recall speaking in a meeting with Ron at First Baptist, Castle Hills, San Antonio, Texas, at a time when I was going through the most difficult period in my ministry because of a stand I had taken. After one of the evening services, out in the hallway, I began pouring out to Ron some of the struggles I was going through. I'll never forget his response. "Hayes," he said, "I know where you are because I've been to the bottom and found it to be solid rock. They may intend it for evil, but God is going to turn it out for your good and His glory, just like He did with Joseph."

TESTIMONY: KEN WHITTEN: SENIOR PASTOR, IDLEWILD BAPTIST CHURCH, TAMPA, FLORIDA

To me Ron Dunn was a heart preacher. He didn't just preach out of his intellect but he preached from the depths of his heart—sometimes out of brokenness, sometimes full of joy, but always consistent with where he was on his journey. Someone said that "the tongue in Ron's mouth and the tongue in his shoe always went in the same direction." He walked what he taught, and he taught what he walked.

One of the many messages of Ron's that have deeply impacted my life is "The Ministry of Failure," out of Deuteronomy 8, that anybody can identify with. Ron was so in touch with the emotional side of where people were—that every day is not a glorious and happy day because it wasn't for him either. There has to be a message of sufficiency for that, and the way Ron did it was preach it without telling them his personal story, and before you knew it you were saying, "Hold it. That's my story."

A lot of people today share that story, of feeling they have failed. Ron would tell them that that is the greatest thing that could ever happen because God did it to humble you, to make you hungry, and to make you holy. If you had not gone through what you've experienced, you would never have known what a great minister failure is.

The reason Ron was so good in conferences and with pastors, was because he lived where so many of them lived. How many have felt like resigning every Monday. And it wasn't just in the big revivals, the big conventions. Ron could get with a pastor whose church was running one hundred and make that pastor feel like he really mattered to the kingdom because Ron really did feel that he mattered. Ron never got drunk on, or enamored with, success.

During those years when Ron was preaching in self-defense, preaching to himself the truths he was needing to hear, what his hearers saw and heard was only the sermon, the "baby" he had birthed. Few there were who knew the birth pangs he went through while preparing what he preached during that period in his life.

Final Exegesis

During the months of Ron's final illness, he worked on an exegesis of the book of Philippians, focusing primarily on chapter 3. He preached six messages from that study at the Ron Dunn Encourager's Conference at MBBC in May and then preached the sixth message again at First Southern, Del City, Oklahoma, just weeks before his passing.

Soon after returning from Oklahoma, Kaye insisted that he go to the hospital, much against his will. Finally, he did, fully expecting to be released the next morning. That evening, from his hospital bed, he preached a seventh message from the Philippians series to Kaye, a message that he had been planning to preach that night at the MEF Conference in Colorado Springs, but now, a message no one else on earth would ever hear because that night he would be put in ICU for the last time. Kaye recalls telling Ron what a powerful sermon that was, and as she kissed him good-night and left for home, she had no idea that Ron had just preached his last sermon, to her.

Preaching in Heaven?

How often have you heard musicians chide preachers that there will be lots of singing in heaven but there'll be no preaching? Being a singer, I've been guilty of teasingly saying that to preacher friends, but as I've given it further thought, I'm wondering if there just might not be a Preachers Corner in heaven, something like the Speakers Corner in Hyde Park, London, England.

There's so much about heaven that we do not know, but can you imagine what it would be like to hear Abraham, Moses, David, Isaiah, the apostle Paul, Peter, John, John Bunyan, Spurgeon, John Wesley, Ron Dunn, Vance Havner, Martyn Lloyd-Jones, Manley Beasley—servants of God from every people group there has ever been, preaching the truth as it was revealed across the ages, preaching without any error or spirit of competition, in heaven's language, all to the glory of God the Father and to the Lamb, our Savior.

And there would be plenty of time to do it as no one would be watching the clock—all a part of heaven's worship. After all, if Scripture is the divine, Holy Spirit-inspired Word of God, will it not have a central place in heaven? It is there that God's Word finds its final fulfillment.

And so, to dream—just perhaps, Ron Dunn, the preacher, will get to preach his series from Philippians, including the message only Kaye has heard. And let us imagine who could be in the audience. The apostle Paul, who wrote the letter! Might this not be a part of Ron's offering of worship to the Lamb seated on the throne? After all, he did leave this world anxious to preach that last message at the MEF Conference in Colorado Springs.

TESTIMONY: WAYNE BARBER—SENIOR PASTOR, WOODLAND PARK BAPTIST CHURCH, CHATTANOOGA, TENNESSEE

Ron Dunn was one of the most influential people God has used in my life and walk with Jesus. His preaching was truly anointed of God, and the way he was gifted held me spellbound in every message I ever heard him preach. I'll never forget how God convicted me in the message Ron preached out of Job, "Will a Man Serve God for Nothing?" and how that changed my whole concept of ministry and what serving was all about.

I could go on and on about "being chained to the chariot and always being led in Christ's triumph," along with so many other messages that have impacted my life. But Ron was also my friend. Christ radiated through Ron in the gentle, caring, and kind way he always treated me and in the personal interest he took in me. Only heaven will reveal the eternal effectiveness that Ron has had on countless thousands. I'll never be the same because of how Christ used him in my life. ✳

[2 9]

Chained to the Chariot
2 Corinthians 2:12–17

❄ ❄ ❄

TESTIMONY: ROY FISH—DISTINGUISHED PROFESSOR
OF EVANGELISM, EMERITUS, SOUTHWESTERN BAPTIST
THEOLOGICAL SEMINARY, FORT WORTH, TEXAS

I remember the first time I ever heard Ron. I had become ill just before a chapel service at the seminary and had gone to the infirmary where the chapel program was piped in. I heard a voice I had never heard before. I asked the doctor who that was, and he didn't know. It was a fresh voice, and I heard this person talking about the Holy Spirit, something few talked about in those days. The more I listened to him, the more I knew I had to meet that man. It turned out to be Ron Dunn. As the years passed, I became convinced that Ron was not only perhaps the greatest Bible teacher in the SBC but one who walked his talk.

Note: Of the hundreds of sermons Ron preached, "Chained to the Chariot" has been at the top of the list of listener favorites over the years.

It was prepared during a period in which Ron said he had begun preaching to himself—around the time of Ronnie's death. He and Kaye were passing through the Valley of Baca (weeping), and it was only by God's grace and provision that their valley would one day become a place of springs.

Whose Photo Is That?

Ron Dunn wrote: Has it ever bothered you that there seems to be a great discrepancy between what the Bible says believers are and what we really are in our daily living? You read all of those great things in the New Testament about those of us who are in Christ. But when you turn to observe the lives of believers, you have to shake your head and say, "Well, I see the picture in the Bible of what you ought to be, but you don't look a thing like your picture."

Is this just a glamour photo God has made, where we're specially made over, and made up, so that we're not presented as we really are? Or is it something else? For instance, here's one picture the Bible gives of a believer. In Romans 8, Paul talks about all the terrible things that can happen to a person—all the fears and terrors that we face in life. He declares, "In all these things we are *more than conquerors* through him who loved us" (Rom. 8:37 NIV, emphasis added). That's the only time the words "more than conquerors" appear in the New Testament. It means we are *supra-conquerors*. We not only conquer, but we conquer by an overwhelming margin. And this isn't just a promise; this is a statement of fact. Simply because Christ loved us and that we know Christ, we win by an overwhelming margin.

By the Skin of Your Teeth?

I suppose every Christian believes we're going to win eventually. But they also think it's going to be close. They think the margin of victory will be narrow—that we're barely going to squeak by. In the last three seconds, they surmise, the Christians are going to kick a field goal and beat the devil 17 to 14. We're going to win, but it's going to be a slim, narrow victory. But that's not what the Bible says.

The Bible says we don't win by a narrow margin; we win by an overwhelming margin! We are *supra-conquerors* through Him who loved us! Well, I see the description in the Bible of what you're supposed to look like, but you don't look a thing like your picture!

In John 4, Jesus was talking to the woman at the well. He said, "Whoever drinks of the water that you have will thirst again. But whoever drinks of the water that I give him shall *not never* [notice the double negative] thirst again" (see John 4:13–14, emphasis added). In other words, Jesus said that whoever took a drink of the eternal life that He offered would never thirst again. And yet everywhere I go I find Christians who are thirsting and living lives that are filled with emptiness. I see in the Bible what you're supposed to be, but you don't look a thing like the picture.

The apostle John declared, "This is the victory that has overcome the world, even our faith" (1 John 5:4 NIV). I used to read that and think, *That's why I'm not overcoming the world. I don't have enough faith. If I just had more faith, I could overcome the world.* But then I realized that's not what John is talking about. John goes on to say, "Who is victor over the world but he who believes that Jesus is the Son of God?" (1 John 5:5 NEB). It's not how much faith you have, it's the kind of faith you have. It's faith centered on Jesus Christ.

Now if I were to ask how many of you believe that Jesus is the Son of God, I'm confident we'd get 100 percent affirmation. But the positive response would be much lower if I were to ask, "How many of you have overcome the world?" I believe the reason why we do not look like our photograph is that we are either ignorant of a certain truth, or knowing it, we have failed to obey it. Let's take a close look at 2 Corinthians 2:12–17.

Beginning in 2 Corinthians 2:12, and continuing all the way through verse 11 of chapter 6, Paul diverts from his main thought and defends and describes his apostleship. Some people were casting doubt upon his authenticity as an apostle. What we're about to read is an introduction to that entire section. Paul said:

> Now when I went to Troas to preach the gospel of Christ and found that the Lord had opened a door for me, I still had no peace of mind because I did not find my brother Titus there. So I said good-bye to them and went on to Macedonia. But thanks be to God, who always leads us in his triumphal procession in Christ and through us spreads everywhere the fragrance of the knowledge of him. For we are to God the aroma of Christ among those who are being saved and those who are perishing. To the one we are the smell of death; to the other, the fragrance of life. And who is equal to such a task? Unlike so many, we do not peddle the word of God for profit. On the contrary, in Christ we speak before God with sincerity, like men sent from God. (2 Cor. 2:12–17 NIV)

The Procession

I want to call your attention to the first part of verse 14: "But thanks be to God, who always leads us in his triumphal procession in Christ." In this statement Paul gives us the truth, the principle, the key, the secret to living the victorious life God has presented for us in the Bible.

The apostle does this in other places, of course, but here he does it in a special way. Notice the phrase "thanks be to God, who always leads us in his triumphal procession in Christ." Those words, "always leads us in triumphal procession" are the translation of one Greek word. This was a technical term for a custom that was common among the Roman armies of that day. When Paul wrote these words to the Corinthians and when they saw that word, they immediately knew what it was. They got the picture, they got the application, and they got the message.

But today we are so far removed from Paul's time that we miss what Paul is saying here. "Triumphal procession" refers to a custom that was common among the Roman armies. As soon as the soldiers had won the victory, they dispatched a herald runner who would run all the way back to the city of Rome. He would run through the streets of the city, announcing that the victory had been won. The word *preach* comes from that word *herald,* and that's what preaching is. It is going ahead of our conquering hero and announcing to everybody that the victory has been won.

When the people of the city heard the news, they began to make preparation for what they called a triumphal processional. It was a magnificent victory celebration. A particular type of incense was burned in the temples for those occasions. And that's why Paul refers to the perfume, or the fragrance. If you had been a citizen of Rome back then, and you had stepped out of your house one morning and breathed the air and smelled that particular incense, you would have said, "Hey, we're going to have a party! We're going to have a celebration. There's going to be a parade!"

When a commanding general—the conquering hero—returned to Rome, the people would line the streets, waiting for the appearance of their hero. The procession would be led by a priest swinging censors, burning that special incense. He would be followed by musicians and others. The main figure in that drama was the commanding general, the victorious military leader. He would be riding in a gold-plated chariot drawn by white horses. Right behind that chariot were the officers of the defeated army who were chained to that chariot. These men would later be executed, so they were being dragged to their death. The enemy soldiers who had been captured would be brought in later, and they would be enslaved.

When the people saw their hero in that chariot, they would cheer and shout. They would throw garlands and confetti into the air. But when they saw the officers of that defeated army chained to that chariot and being dragged along behind, they would really go wild. This was a demonstration of the power of their hero. Paul was referring to that custom when he said, "Thanks be to God, who always leads us in his triumphal procession." In other words, Paul was Christianizing that custom. He was saying there was a time when he was at war with Jesus Christ. There were hostilities between God and Paul. But the Lord Jesus had conquered him, and he had yielded to Him in unconditional surrender. He had put Paul in the chains of His lordship, and he was chained to His chariot. And everywhere Paul went, Christ led him in His triumphal procession.

The New English Bible brings it out well by saying, "Thanks be to God, who continually leads us about, captives in Christ's triumphant procession" (2 Cor. 5:14). Paul is saying, "I came to Jesus Christ; He overcame me, and I yielded to Him in unconditional surrender. He placed my hands in the chains of His lordship and chained me to His chariot. Now thanks be to God, everywhere I go I am being led in His triumphant procession."

Paul was wanting everybody to know this before he detailed his apostleship, because when you get over to chapter 4 of 2 Corinthians, he will speak about some bad things happening to him. He is saying in anticipation, "Now I'm going to tell you some things that some of you are going to think reveals failure and defeat. But I want you to know at the outset, thanks be to God, He always leads me in His triumph in Christ, and wherever I go, it may look like defeat to you; it may look like failure to you, But I'm chained to His chariot, and that means that everywhere I go I am following in his own triumphant victory in Christ!"

"But Paul—how is it that you can say everywhere you go there's victory?" Paul: "Because I've been conquered by Jesus Christ. I'm chained to His chariot, and I'm simply following along in the wake of His victory."

The Fourfold Secret to a Victorious Life

1. If you want to be a conqueror, you must first be conquered.
2. If you want to be an overcomer, you must first be overcome.
3. If you want to be a master, you must first be mastered.
4. If you want to exercise authority, you must first submit to it.

I was preaching in Florida a few years ago, and a man got to talking about my sermon. He said, "Preacher, that was a good sermon." I thanked him and told him I was glad he enjoyed it. But he went on to say there was one thing about it he didn't like. I asked what it was. "Well, I didn't like that idea of being chained to the chariot. I think if you would take that out, it would be a better sermon."

I said, "Brother, that *is* the sermon. That's the sermon right there! If I take it out, I don't have a sermon." He said, "Well, it just seems degrading and humiliating to be chained to a chariot." "Absolutely!" I replied. "And I know why you don't like it. I don't like it either. None of us like it because we want to ride up front with the Lord and help Him drag others along."

Heaven knows the Lord needs some help from time to time. Sometimes I say to Him, "Lord, why are we going so slow? Everybody else has passed us up. Can't You put the pedal to the metal on this thing?"

Other times I say, "Lord, why did You take this road? It's so bumpy, and it's got potholes in it. And we passed up a good superhighway." Sometimes I say, "Lord, I'm tired of traveling. Let's pull over at this roadside park and have a picnic." I like to help the Lord drive, don't you? That's where I want to be—up front.

But Paul says if you want to be a conqueror, you must first be conquered. And I say to you that you are only experiencing as much victory in Jesus as Jesus is experiencing in you. If there is an area of repeated failure in your life, that's a good sign there is an area of your life over which Jesus Christ is not yet Lord. If we are going to be conquerors, we must first be conquered.

The best illustration I've ever seen of this occurs in the encounter of Jesus and the centurion who had a sick servant. Let me paraphrase their conversation that is found in Matthew 8.

Centurion: "Lord, I have a sick servant."

Jesus: "I'll come to your house and heal him."

Centurion: "Oh, no, Lord, don't do that. I'm not worthy to have you come under my roof. Just speak the word, and my servant will live, for I also am a man under authority with soldiers under me. And I say to this one, go, and he goes. And to this one, do this, and he does it."

When Jesus heard what the man said, He marveled and said, "I have not found such great faith, not even in Israel" (Matt. 8:10 NKJV).

Now, I have great respect for the Word of God. But I must confess to you that for a long time I couldn't see what was so great about what that man said. I didn't understand it. What did he say? He said, "I also am a man under authority, having soldiers under me. And I say to this one, 'Go,' and he goes; and to another 'Come,' and he comes; and to my servant, 'Do this,' and he does it" (Matt. 8:9 NKJV).

Why was Jesus amazed at this man's faith? I couldn't see what the man said had to do with faith. But I got to thinking, *If it amazed Jesus, it ought to amaze me.* I would think it would take a lot to amaze Jesus. He was amazed twice in the Bible. Both times He expressed amazement at the faith of a Gentile. What could you show Jesus, or what could you tell Jesus that would amaze Him? He's seen it all! He made it all!

If this encounter with a Gentile amazed Jesus, it ought to do something to me. I thought to myself that I must be missing something. Let's look at their encounter again. Jesus told the centurion that He would come to his house and heal his servant. But the centurion replied, "Oh, no, Lord, don't do that. I'm not worthy to have you come under my roof. Just speak the word, and my servant will live, for I also am a man under authority." Now, I would expect his next words to be, "And if I am told to go somewhere, I go somewhere, and when I am told to do something, I do something." But that's not what the centurion said.

He said, "For I also am a man under authority with soldiers under me. And I say to this one, go, and he goes. And to this one, do this, and he does it." The centurion was saying, "I live under authority; therefore, I have authority." And he did. He had authority over one hundred soldiers. That's why they called him a centurion.

As long as that centurion was submitted to the authority of the emperor, he had the emperor's authority over those one hundred soldiers. If he rebelled against the authority of the emperor, he lost his authority over those one hundred soldiers. So that was the principle by which he was living. But that's still not what amazed Jesus. What amazed Jesus was one little word that the man said. Some translations say "also." Some say "too." And unfortunately, some translations leave it out. But it belongs there.

Now listen to me as I quote it: "He came to Jesus and he said, 'Lord, my servant is sick.' Jesus said, "I'll come to your house and heal him." The centurion said, "Oh, no, Lord, don't do that. I'm not worthy to have you come under my roof. Just speak the word, and my servant will live, for I also am a man under authority." In other words, "I don't have to run my own errands. If I want something done, I tell others to do it, and it's done for me. And Lord, I understand that You live by the same principle I live by." When he said, "I, too," or "I, also, am a man under authority," this is what amazed Jesus, that this centurion had such great insight into the truth that Jesus Himself lived by that same principle. He said, "I have never seen such faith."

The point I want you to get is that this was the principle by which Jesus Christ lived. He lived under the authority of His Father; therefore, He had His Father's authority. That's the principle by which the centurion lived. He was under the authority of the emperor; therefore, he had the emperor's authority. That's the principle by which Paul lived. That's the principle by which we should live if we want to experience victory in the Christian life. Let's look at three brief things about this victory.

This Victory Is God's Victory through His Son

This victory that Paul talked about is God's victory through His Son. Paul was saying, "Thanks be to God, who always leads us in His triumphal procession in Christ." It's not we who are triumphing; it's not we who are riding in that chariot. No, He doesn't cause us to triumph. He leads us in His triumph. It is God's victory through His Son. I'm trying to say that the responsibility for victory in the Christian life is not mine; it is God's. I realize that many of us use the expression, "win the victory." I've got to go out there and "win the victory," to overcome the devil, and win over temptation.

But I want you to know that there are no victories to be won. Christ Jesus won every victory two thousand years ago when He died for us on the cross! Every temptation you will face has already been overcome by Jesus. The responsibility for victory is not ours. It's important for us to know that because most Christians feel: "It's up to me. I didn't do good yesterday, but I'm going to do better today." So I climb out of bed, grit my teeth, tense my muscles, and say, "I'm going out there and win the victory today, if it kills me!" And it usually does! The responsibility for victory in the Christian life does not rest with us. It's not *our* victory; it is *God's* victory through Christ.

So, Whose Battle Is It?

I like the story of David and Goliath in 1 Samuel 17. They must have fought funny wars back in those days. Israel was fighting the Philistines. One day David's dad said, "David, here's a sack lunch. Your brothers are at war. Take them lunch." It just seems strange to me that David just walked into the war and said to his brothers, "Here's your lunch from home."

When he got to the front lines, David saw this giant mocking Israel and Israel's God. And Israel was hiding behind the bushes, scared to death. Little David said, "I want you to do something about that guy."

"Son," they replied, "just leave the lunch and go back home. Play your harp and write your poetry."

"Well, it's not right to let him get by with this," David said. "Why don't you do something about it?"

"You don't understand the situation. Go home. We'll handle it."

"Well, you're not handling it very well, it seems to me. I'm going to take care of him."

"Huh! You're what?"

"I'm going to take care of him."

"Go ahead and try."

They started to put Saul's armor on David. "Oh, no, I don't want Saul's armor," he cried. "It would just swallow me up. I don't need anything besides my slingshot and five smooth stones."

"Good-bye, brother. Been nice knowing you."

Do you remember what happened? Little David marched out to meet Goliath. He stopped and looked the giant straight in the kneecap. He said: "The battle is the LORD's and He will give you into our hands" (1 Sam. 17:47).

The battle was not David's—why, of course it wasn't. He wouldn't have been there if it had been! Neither was the battle Israel's. That's why the Israelite soldiers were hiding behind the bushes. The battle was the Lord's. What I need to learn to do is stand in front of the Goliaths in my life and say to them, "The battle is the LORD's and He will give you into my hands." The victory is God's, through His Son.

I'm a Southern Baptist, and in my denomination we have a bad habit of calling the church by the pastor's name. When I was pastor, people would say "Brother Dunn's church." Or last week I was at "Brother Ken's church!" We know it's not the pastor's church, but you hear that so much, and for so long, that you begin to think maybe it is. You're the pastor, and you've got all those people out there, and they're your responsibility. And you've got to take care of them. When they hurt, you've got to heal them. And when they're angry, you've got to soothe them. And you have to make sure you have more people in attendance this Sunday than you had Sunday a year ago, or it won't look good statistically. And you're behind on your budget. You're thinking, "This whole thing is mine. It's my church, and I'm responsible for it. I've got to build it. I've got to take care of it. It's just too much." That's why in our denomination we have about a thousand ministers a year quitting the ministry. "It's just too much."

Well, I was part of that club. That's the way I felt about *my* church. Once I was preaching through the book of Matthew, and I came to Matthew 16 where Jesus said, "On this rock I will build my church" (Matt. 16:18 NIV). I saw a little word there that I had not paid much attention to before—"MY," Jesus said, "I will build *my* church" (emphasis added).

I said, "Lord, do You mean to tell me this is Your church?"

"Yes, sir!"

"Welcome to it!"

I was never so glad to get rid of anything in all my life! A great weight was lifted from my shoulders. This is the Lord's church!

Then Jesus said, "On this rock *I will build my* church" (emphasis added).

"Lord, I thought I was supposed to build it. That's been one of my problems. You mean to tell me that You will build the church? This is Your church, and You will build it?"

"Yes."

What a deal! I don't know of anything that liberated me any more as a pastor than this. Now I understand that it is not *my* responsibility to get people to walk down the aisle and join the church. It's not *my* responsibility to get the people to give. It's not *my* responsibility to build the church. This is God's responsibility. I have a responsibility, but building the church is not it! This is the Lord's church, and He does the building. I do what God tells me to do as faithfully as I know how, and the rest is up to Him. This is God's victory through His Son.

You may be thinking that I'm preaching a religion of passivity. Not at all. We do have a responsibility, a great responsibility, but I think it's essential that we understand that it is God's responsibility to give the victory and to give the growth. We've got to understand that this victory is ours through submission.

This Victory Is through Submission

Now we come to our responsibility. This is God's victory through His Son, but it becomes mine through submission. How do I enter into this victory? By submission, by living chained to the chariot. You may say, "Oh, is that all?" Well, if you say that, I know you've never tried it.

We have a lot of "Houdini" Christians in the church who are slick at getting out of those chains. My number one responsibility is to make certain that moment by moment, day by day, I am living under His lordship, and I am living chained to His chariot. Every other responsibility I have flows from that.

A seminary student was interviewing several pastors in our area about their philosophy of ministry. One of the questions he asked me was, "What is your primary responsibility as pastor of this church?"

I looked at him and said, "Me. Write it down. M-E, me!" He looked back at me with this funny look on his face. I admit it did sound like an egotistical answer, and a very irresponsible one at that. Then I said, "You want to know what my top priority is as pastor of this church?"

"Yes."

"It's to me. Now, let me explain."

I went on to tell him that my number one priority as pastor of MacArthur Boulevard Baptist Church is not to the lost of our community. My number one priority is not to the members of this church. My number one priority is to me. To make certain I am living filled with Christ's Spirit, chained to His chariot, because when I'm filled with His Spirit and living under His lordship, then the lost of this community, and the members of my church, will be ministered to by the overflow of my life.

In 2 Corinthians 2, Paul makes this point very clear. These men who were chained were being led to their death. Paul put himself in that position: "Thanks be to God, who always leads [me] . . . in [his] triumphal procession" (2 Cor. 2:14 NIV). "Yes," you say. "But that's leading to death." Well, in chapter 4 he tells us what kind of death. He says, "I bear about in my body the dying of the Lord Jesus so that the life of Jesus might be made manifest through me. So then death works in me, that life may work in you" (2 Cor. 4:10–12).

Now I want you to focus on that. I bear about in my body the dying of the Lord Jesus. Why? So the life of Jesus that dwells in me can manifest itself through my mortal flesh.

The only thing that will bless anybody is the life of Jesus. When I stand to preach to my congregation, I cannot bless anyone. I may tell a few jokes and get a few laughs, and I may come up with two or three clever thoughts, but nobody's going to break out of their chains. No hearts are going to be healed. No wounds are going to be ministered to. No lives are going to be touched. The only thing I have to offer anybody is the life of Jesus that dwells in me. And the only way people are going to be ministered to is if somehow the life of Jesus, in me, manifests itself through my mortal flesh and touches their lives. That's what ministry is all about.

I must make certain you understand this. It's not the preacher. It's not me. I don't bless anybody. I don't minister to anybody. It is the life of Jesus in me. That's what people need. People don't need to hear my opinions or advice. What people need is to be touched with the life of Jesus. I must make certain that I live in such a way that His life can manifest itself through my human personality and touch others. It is then that people will be blessed.

Jesus said, "If anyone . . . come to Me and drink. . . . From his innermost being shall flow rivers of living water" (John 7:37–38 NASB). I like to think of myself as the riverbed and God supplies the river. Nobody's ever been blessed by an old, dry, crusty riverbed. No, it's the river running along it. So this victory is God's victory through His Son. It becomes mine through submission. But not only that. The victory is ours in any situation.

Victory in Any Situation

I want you to notice two phrases in 2 Corinthians 2:14. First of all, Paul said, "Thanks be to God, who *always . . .*" At the end of that verse he said, "[He] manifests through us the sweet aroma . . . of Him in *every place.*" So we have two things here—*always* and *every place.* Always—that's time. Every place—that's space. We are time/space creatures. Everything we do is in time and space. Here's what Paul is saying: "Thanks be to God who always, anytime, every time, all the time, leads me in His triumph in Christ. And it's in every place, all places, any place, you name the place."

Now I don't say this lightly. I've thought about this before saying it. If we can learn how to live *chained to the chariot,* there is no conceivable situation in life in which God cannot give us victory. But this may require us to redefine the word *victory.*

I won't say I've *learned* it; I'll say I'm *learning.* When I wake up and find myself in some trial, some difficulty, some adversity, the first thing I do is check to see if I'm *chained to the chariot.* I check to see if as far as I can tell, I'm still living under His lordship. And if I am, then I can say two things about that situation.

First, He led me into it. If I'm *chained to His chariot,* I couldn't have gotten there any other way! He led me into it.

Second, Jesus has already overcome it. Well, of course, because I'm following in the wake of His triumph. You may find this hard to believe, but when you live *chained to the chariot,* you walk on conquered ground. Every time you put your foot down, you place it on territory Jesus Christ has already conquered. He's leading you along, and you're simply following in His triumphant train! There is no conceivable situation in life in which God cannot give us victory.

A Creek-bed Lesson

When I was attending Oklahoma Baptist University, I pastored a little country church in the southeast corner of the state, about seventy miles from where my parents lived in Fort Smith, Arkansas. To get to Black Gum Baptist Church, I first took a main highway. It was a big superslab. But then, after a while, I turned off onto a secondary road, which was still not too bad—a nice, smooth, asphalt one. It was not long, however, before I got off on a road that had been acquainted at one time with asphalt. It was pretty rough. This finally led to a dirt road that wound through the Brushy Mountains for about three or four miles before it reached the church. Three times on this dirt road I had to cross a little, crystal-clear stream that was about an inch deep, and I never thought anything about it. I just splashed right on through.

One Sunday morning I was driving to the church after it had been raining all week. It was Easter, and God had given us a beautiful, sun-shiny day. I had on a new suit, a new pair of shoes, and I was driving my 1946 Ford. Back in those days, as I was driving to a preaching appointment, I would practice my sermon. I would try to make it last forty-five minutes because I figured that if I could go forty-five minutes in the car, when I got up before the people, I could at least make it last for twenty-five.

So there I was driving along, preaching my Easter sermon. As I recall, it was coming along pretty good when suddenly my car began to buck like it had hit a brick wall. Then it just stopped! Then I felt my feet getting wet. I looked down, and water was coming through the floorboard. It was then I noticed that this little stream that was usually about an inch deep was now about knee-deep. I hadn't even paid any attention to it. There wasn't anything for me to do except get out of the car, take off my new shoes, roll up my pants legs, and walk the last mile and a half to the church. OK, I can hear you saying, "Preacher, does this story go anywhere?" Yes sir, it does.

One day I came to Jesus Christ, I surrendered my life to Him, and He put me in the chains of His lordship, and He took off! And was I ever happy. Praise God. Hallelujah. It's fun to be a Christian! Just trust in Jesus every minute of your life! Praise God!

We went along like that for a while. Then we got off that big super-slab and got on that secondary road that wasn't quite as nice and smooth. But that doesn't bother me. Man, I'm chained to His chariot. Trust in Jesus. Bless God. Hallelujah! It's fun to be a Christian! Amen!

Then after a while we got on the third road that had a lot of potholes and bumps. But this doesn't bother me! I'm chained to His chariot! Praise God! Hallelujah! Trust in Jesus all the way. It's fun being a Christian! I'm having the greatest time of my life!

Finally, we got on that dirt road. Well, that doesn't bother me either. There's just a little dust in my eyes and grit in my teeth. And after all, I can sacrifice for Jesus—chained to His chariot! Bless God! Hallelujah! Praise the Lord! Amen! I'm having a wonderful time! It's fun being a Christian!

Well, after a while, I feel my feet getting wet. I look down, and I'm passing over one of those little streams. The water is about toe-high. Well, that doesn't bother me! Bless God! Hallelujah! Praise the Lord! Trust in Jesus all the way! Man, it's fun being a Christian!

I keep on going along. Then after a while the water is up to my knees. But that doesn't bother me. I'm chained to His chariot. Praise God! Hallelujah! Bless the Lord! Amen! It's fun being a Christian!

Then, suddenly, the water reaches my waist. Well . . . amen. And then the water gets to my shoulders. Oh, Jesus! And then the water rises to my chin, and I cry out, "If I don't get out of these chains, He's going to drown me!"

That's Victory!

Do you know what victory is? Victory is "staying" *chained to the chariot,* even when the water covers your head. Victory doesn't always mean that the Lord will lead you on dry land or drain the swamp. Sometimes He will take you into deep waters. Victory is staying *chained to that chariot,* no matter how deep the water gets, no matter where the chariot leads.

Remember what the apostle John said in his first Epistle? "Faith . . . is the victory" (see 1 John 5:4). He didn't say, "Faith brings the victory," or, "Faith gains the victory." He said, "Faith *is* the victory" (emphasis added).

You come into my office, and you say, "Preacher, I've got to have surgery. The doctor tells me I have a malignant tumor, and it doesn't look good." I ask you, "Do you still believe?" "Yes," you reply. *That's victory.*

Later I stand beside your bed. They've done the surgery, but all they could do was sew you back up and send you home to die. I ask again, "Do you still believe?" You reply, "Yes, I still believe." *That's victory.*

And then, as I stand beside your grave, I turn to your wife, and I ask her, "Do you still believe?" And she answers, "Yes, I still believe." *That's victory.* This is God's victory through His Son. It becomes ours through submission and remains ours in any situation. And if we learn how to live *chained to the chariot,* there is no situation in life in which He cannot give us victory.

Faith Is the Victory

Encamped along the hills of light, ye Christian soldiers, rise.
And press the battle ere the night shall veil the glowing skies.
Against the foe in vales below let all our strength be hurled.
Faith is the victory, we know, that overcomes the world.
Faith is the victory![38]

TESTIMONY: ADRIAN ROGERS—TRIBUTE MADE WHILE
PASTOR OF BELLEVUE BAPTIST CHURCH, MEMPHIS,
TENNESSEE

Ron Dunn is in a class by himself. I know of no preaching anywhere that stimulates me or encourages me like that of Ron Dunn. His messages are fresh and uniquely original. I prophecy that the impact of his life and ministry will be legendary. ※

PART EIGHT

Heading Home

And behold there was a very stately palace
before him, the name of which was Beautiful.

—John Bunyan: *Pilgrim's Progress*

[3 0]

Kaye's Medical Time Line

❈ ❈ ❈

2000

April—(Fourteen months before Ron's home-going.) Years ago, when I was going through a crisis, my mother suggested that I memorize Psalm 91. I did, and how I am needing that psalm these days. Our dear Kim has disappeared. We don't know where she is. No clues in her apartment. We have friends in law enforcement looking for her. Last night Ron thought he was having a panic attack. He went to see Dr. Grugle, who said it looked more like a heart attack. They did an immediate EKG. It's not the heart.

Ten days later—Kimberly called and asked me to meet her at Parkland Hospital in Dallas. We went out to eat before she checked herself in. The doctors put her through a series of tests. The results came back—Kim is bipolar. They're going to keep her in the hospital for two weeks while they adjust her medications.

May—Ron went to the emergency room with severe chest pains. Again they thought he was having a heart attack, but he checked out OK, and he has continued with his preaching schedule.

June—Ron is able to meet his preaching appointments in spite of weakness and chest pains.

July—While speaking at the MEF Conference in Colorado Springs, Ron began having chest pains again. We flew home and went immediately to the hospital where Dr. Feingold and Metzker met him. He was diagnosed as having heart blockage. Stayed there five days—heart catherization/stress test/Norvasc medication. Four weeks of heart rehab.

August—In and out of emergency rooms in almost every town where he's been preaching.

September 11—Ron's having difficulty breathing. Further tests scheduled for September 13.

September 13—Thalium stress test, sixty-four X-ray pictures. Heart is strong.

September 18—Emergency room in Cartersville, Georgia—severe pain in chest. Doctor thinks it is Tzieke's Syndrome. Gave Ron a shot of Toradal and Ativan and a prescription of Naprosyn.

September 22—Ron is coughing and is very weak. Went to Baylor Clinic in Irving. Saw Henry Pham who decided it was a cold virus. He gave Ron Z-pack and cough syrup. We're trying to decide if we should go to Sherwood Baptist in Albany, Georgia. Ron wants to go so badly to be with his friend Michael Catt.

September 24—We're in Albany: preached both morning services. Very weak. Doctor in the church took Ron to the Phoeby-Putney Hospital, and he ran tests. A pulmonologist was called in. Took CAT scan of lungs and determined there was an infiltrator in the right lung. Did a biopsy of lymph nodes that looked very enlarged.

Sent off several pathologies. All came back inconclusive. They were looking for a fungus or some kind of cancer. They could not determine what was causing the pulmonary fibrosis in his lungs. They had no explanation for the severe pain he was having. He was released from the hospital at the end of the week, and we stayed in Albany two more weeks for Ron to regain his strength enough to travel home.

Someone called today to share a Scripture with me concerning Ron. It was the very verse God had given me. I never doubted that he was going to make it through these times.

October 16—Traveled home. Ron woke up in the middle of the night gasping for breath. He went to his desk and sat down, but when he stood up, he was so weak that he blacked out and fell over his desk. I finally was able to get him back into the bed.

October 17—Called Dr. Palazolla in Albany. He said, "Get Ron to the emergency room right away."

October 21–November 9—Tests, tests, tests.

November 12—3:30 a.m. Ron's coughing up blood. Rushed to Baylor Hospital. Put on ventilator. No obvious cancer. Looking for a possible infectious disease. Checking for lupus, lymphoma, Wegener's Granulamatosis—increased steroids—back on Levaquin.

November 16–17—Negative for lupus and Wegeners. Doctor did a "bronch" to clear out air passages, then filled lungs with fluid and flushed them to see if there was fresh blood.

November 18—Seventh day in ICU and fifth day on ventilator.

November 19—Removed from ventilator—very traumatic. Got a phone call that Kimberly has been in a serious car accident. "Oh God!" Rushed to Parkland Hospital—one ankle blown to pieces like shattered glass. Risk of infection very great. Put pins in her tibia. Monday a foot and ankle team will install a metal rod. Barry, Ron's brother, is coming to help me.

November 21—Ron moved to Progressive Care Unit at Baylor Hospital in Irving while Kim is in ICU at Parkland, in Dallas, after going through three hours of surgery to remove as much of the shattered bone fragments as possible and to insert a steel rod. My sister Julie, and my mother have joined Barry to help me. We work in shifts. I'm with Ron first thing in the morning and the last thing at night. In between I go to Parkland to be with Kim while my family members and Joanne Gardner, Ron's secretary, stay with him.

November 25—Another negative test from Mayo. They still don't have a clue, apart from it being what they call a Hemorrhagic Disease. Ron still has the tubes from the biopsy in him and they are worried about air-leaks. He can't move from the bed to his chair without help. Just heard that Kim has a secondary infection.

November 28—Tonight the doctor walked away, shaking his head saying, "I'm at my wit's end."

November 29—Specific prayer today that a spot will open up for Kim to get into rehab.

December 4—Ron's nurse called me at 5:15 a.m. to ask me to go immediately to the hospital. They had given him Darvocet that made him disoriented, and he had a terrible night. She felt that I might be able to calm him down.

December 7—Ron moved to 4th floor yesterday. He begins rehab on the sixth floor. He actually walked with a walker down the hospital corridor and only had to stop twice to rest in his wheelchair.

December 11—Ron loves rehab. He says it makes him feel like a human being. Kim is enjoying hers too.

December 20—Brought Ron home today with oxygen, prednisone, Celebrex, etc. When I was helping him across the patio, he fell on me and he punctured his hand with the car keys, hit his head on the bricks, and cut his finger deeply. I rushed him to the clinic for a tetanus shot. What next?

Christmas: Ron is very ill and is not able to get out of bed. Vicki and Pat are here for two weeks to help. They asked Ron what he wanted for Christmas dinner. He said he wanted meatloaf, mashed potatoes, and green beans. They were gracious and gave him what he asked for, though it wasn't their idea of a Christmas meal. Stephen is with us, but Kimberly is still in the hospital having surgeries done on her leg. I'm trying to handle the two illnesses at the same time.

2001

January–February—Have been encouraged to take Ron to the Mayo Clinic in Rochester, Minnesota, though we've been waiting for almost seven weeks to get pathology test results back from them that had been sent from our doctor. Just discovered that the reason we had not heard from Mayo is that the tests had never been sent from Texas. The slides and blocks have been sitting in the pathologist's office, along with a note from the doctor, stating that he wanted them to be sent to Mayo Clinic. The office said the reason the tests had not been sent is that they were waiting for the name of a person at Mayo to send them to.

After we got that settled, I arranged to take Ron up to the Clinic. I wheeled him around their huge campus getting every test imaginable. Ron has been too weak to get out of his wheelchair. They think they have found the cause and have now sent us home with new medications and instructions to continue his lung rehab for three months, then to return to Mayo for re-evaluation.

All this time Kim has either been in the hospital recuperating from other surgeries or in a nursing home doing rehab. Ron has continued his rehab three days a week and has been mostly bedridden the remainder of the time. I'm keeping busy running between the two. Some of my family have stayed to help. I don't know what I'd do without them.

March—On March 9, I was rushed to the hospital. My small intestines had ruptured and I was in excruciating pain. I think this may have been caused by the physical stress I had put my body through the week we were at the Mayo Clinic. They did emergency surgery, and Ron pulled himself together enough to make it to the hospital, with his oxygen tank in tow, in order to be with me. He should really have stayed at home in bed, but he insisted on being by my side. They did additional tests while they had me under. The results came back a week later. I'll never forget hearing the doctor say: "You have lymphoma all over your body. We're going to need to begin chemotherapy right away."

April—My chemo treatments began just as Kim was having another surgery done to save her leg. I couldn't be with her because of the chemo, but Ron, again dragging his oxygen tank, insisted on being with his daughter. Friends of ours from the church drove him to Parkland. They operated, cleaned the wound, but now, two weeks later, they have had to amputate her leg four inches below the knee because a resistant staph infection has attacked the bone.

It's now the end of April, and Ron's brother, Barry, has taken him back to Mayo Clinic because I was too weak to make the trip due to the chemo treatments, and also, I needed to take care of Kim.

May—Ron's time at the Mayo Clinic carried over into the first few days of May. The doctors then sent him home with hope, saying they felt he was holding his own with the disease (whatever it is) and that he could begin traveling again as soon as he felt well enough. I'm thinking . . . travel again?

A week later Ron preached a Bible conference at MacArthur Boulevard. This was the first time he had preached in eight months. He preached six messages from Philippians that God had given him during the months he had been sick. He looked so weak as he'd make his way up the steps to the podium, but when he opened his mouth, God took over and anointed his words with supernatural power. Each evening after the service, he would stumble home, climb into bed, and stay there until the service the next night. But Kaye recalls how she'd never seen such joy on his face as when the services were all over and he knew he had been able to deliver the burden God had laid on his heart.

He now had a week to rest before his next scheduled meeting in Baton Rouge, Louisiana, but the day he was to fly, he felt so rotten that he had to cancel. This was very discouraging, but he was determined to make the next engagement, which was to preach the Sunday morning Memorial Day weekend service at First Southern Baptist, Del City, Oklahoma, where one of his dear friends, Tom Elliff, was pastor. ❄

[31]

One More Sermon!

On that 2001 Memorial Day weekend, nothing was going to deter Ron from driving those two hundred miles up Interstate 35 to Del City, Oklahoma, a suburb of Oklahoma City, located near Tinker Air Force Base. Though Kaye, still undergoing the chemo treatments, was too weak to accompany him, he persuaded her that he could make it on his own. He'd be fine. He promised that he would drive back on Sunday, right after he had preached and had lunch with Tom and Jeannie Elliff.

Knowing how much it meant to Ron to be back with this family of believers who had so faithfully prayed and supported them through the years, Kaye was not going to stand in his way, in spite of the risk she knew they were taking.

As she watched him drive off in his black Mark VIII, little did she, or Ron, realize that this would be his last trip here on earth and that the next morning, when he struggled up the steps to the platform and stood behind the pulpit of Del City's First Southern Baptist Church, he would be preaching his last sermon.

Introductory Remarks by Tom Elliff

This is a very special day for us because in one sense of the word we welcome back someone who is a part of our family, and in another sense we welcome someone who is fresh from the battlefield. He speaks to us from battlefield experience. As you know, we, as a church, have been following Ron's progress with the health issues he has been facing for many months and have been much in prayer for him, then for Kaye and her battle with cancer, and now, for their daughter Kim, who is still in the hospital following a tragic accident that resulted in her losing part of a leg.

Back during those days when Ron was spending so much time in intensive care and when he was barely able to speak, I told him that as soon as he got back on his feet I wanted him to come and share some of what God was doing in his life.

In Africa they say that, "When an old man dies, a library is burned." In other words, the volumes of information that have been deposited in him throughout his lifetime often die with him. We're grateful that God has spared Ron's life and that, this morning, we are going to have the privilege of checking out of the library of Ron's heart some of what God has been teaching him, lessons that will be a blessing to us all. Welcome back, Ron, to your First Southern family.

Ron began climbing the six steps to the platform . . .

Ron's Response

Thank you, Brother Tom. Those are the most steps I've climbed in a year. Let me catch my breath for a moment (pause). There are sixteen steps to my study at home. Unfortunately it is on the second floor, and I wasn't able to get up there for six months. But when I finally could climb those steps without stopping for breath, I figured that I was going to live.

It's a joy to be with you this morning. Actually, for me, it's a joy to be anywhere. During the time I was laid up for seven months, I thought I might never again be anywhere, at least here on earth. One night when I was in the hospital, I despaired of my life. No one thought I would make it. Then, on December 20, the day before our wedding anniversary, they released me from the hospital, but when I got home, I couldn't do anything but lie in bed. I couldn't even feed myself. I thought, *Well, I may not die, but I'll be an invalid for the rest of my life.* I figured that my preaching days were over, and I began to feel sorry for myself. I began to wonder if I would ever be of any value anymore to anyone.

Ever since I can remember, preaching has been my life. It has been my joy, the thing that has kept me going, and I wondered what I would do if I weren't able to preach the Word of God. I believe that's what God created me to do; it's what He ordained for me in eternity past. Then, after a few months at home, I began to feel like reading a little bit, and the Lord led me to Paul's letter to the Philippians. I began to study this letter, and I ordered every commentary on this book that I didn't already have. Though God began to speak to me out of the whole letter, there was one particular passage that He zeroed in on my heart, and that's what I'm going to share with you today. I'm going to talk to you about knowing God.

Sermon: *Knowing God* (Philippians 3:10)

I'm going to read the first 10 verses of Philippians 3. "Finally, my brethren, rejoice in the Lord . . ." (After reading the first ten verses, Ron continued.) Let me read verse 10 again because this is the verse God especially spoke to me from. "That I may know Him, and the power of His resurrection and the fellowship of His sufferings, being conformed to His death."

As I lay there in my bed, I began to wonder what value I now was to anyone, since I couldn't do anything for myself—I couldn't preach. Well, God both encouraged me and rebuked me out of this Philippian passage. We find here that Paul is looking back over his own life's story. He talks about all the things that were an advantage to him, things that would commend him to God. He lists his natural heritage: "[I was] circumcised the eighth day, [I am] of the nation of Israel, . . . the tribe of Benjamin, a Hebrew of Hebrews; as to the Law, a Pharisee; as to zeal, a persecutor of the church, as to the righteousness which is in the Law, found blameless." What he was saying here is that he had been counting on all of that commending him to God. He is saying: "I was certain that all these things would bring about my salvation."

All Things

But then, in a strong word of contrast in verse 7, he says: "But whatever things were gain to me, those things I have counted as loss for the sake of Christ." All the things Paul mentions in verses 5 and 6—his heritage, those religious things, all his achievements—he counted as loss. But then in verse 8, he says: "More than that, I count *all* things to be loss in view of the surpassing value of knowing Christ." He now has gone a step further. He's saying he counts *all* things as loss, not just those things that were religious, not just those things he mentions in verses 5 and 6, but everything; *all* things he counts as loss in view of the surpassing value of knowing Christ.

It was the "all things" that first attracted my attention, and as I lay there, I thought, *Of course, I have counted the loss of those kinds of things. I was brought up a Baptist. I was a Baptist before I was a Christian. I was baptized at the age of nine. I went to Sunday school and summer camp, but I've never counted on those things for my salvation.* But Paul is talking here about not just those things but *all* things. Whatever in my life I think might commend me to God, whatever I think might make me valuable to God, I am to count as rubbish.

I began to apply those "all things" to myself. I realized that those "all things" meant my health, my ministry. It meant my preaching, and not only was I to die to those things I thought would save me, which I had already done, but now it was those things that I had been engaged in, those things I thought somehow made me worthy, or somehow gave me my identification in God's sight. And as Paul comes to the culmination of this passage, he says all of this is "so I may know Him!" I now was beginning to realize that my vocation that for all these years I thought was preaching, was not preaching, or serving the Lord, but it was "to know Him!"

But didn't the apostle Paul already know Christ? Yes, but the meaning here is that he wanted to know Him more intimately, more completely. He wanted his relationship to deepen, to continue to grow until he would see Him face-to-face.

Knowing Christ is not just a matter of knowing Him in salvation, but it is a matter of growing in our knowledge and love of Him in our ever day life—knowing Him more intimately than we've ever known Him before. The ultimate goal of Paul's life was not his service, his ministry, or anything else; it was that he might know him in an ever increasing and intimate way.

As I lay there in bed, I realized that was what my vocation is. I began to realize that my worth is not contained in whether or not I can get up and walk around, whether or not I can serve the Lord, whether or not I can preach, but my worth is to be found in this—that I may *know Him.* And I began to realize that you can get to know Him in a deeper and more meaningful way lying flat on your back. If you are an invalid all your life, that doesn't keep you from knowing Him. Just as a wife or a husband get to know each other better and better, year after year, growing in knowledge of their ways, understanding more and more how they think, so we are to grow in our knowledge of Christ.

But there is more to what Paul is saying in verse 10. We find that there are two aspects to this knowing of Christ. In just a casual reading of this verse, you might say that there are three things Paul is wanting to know: (1) that I may know Him, (2) that I may know the power of His resurrection, and (3) that I may know the fellowship of His sufferings. But that's not the way the Greek text reads. It reads something like this.

"That I may know Him, and knowing Him means to experience the power of His resurrection, and to be a participant in His sufferings."

In other words, as you come to know Him in a deeper and more intimate way, you begin to experience the power of His resurrection, that life-giving power God has given us that enables us to live as Christ wants us to live. That enables us to overcome temptation and to overcome sin, that enables us to be all that God wants us to be. We are to know Him, and we cannot know Him without experiencing the power of His resurrection, the kind of power Paul talks about in Ephesians 1, the power that raised Jesus from the dead and "is now working in us" (see v. 19).

I tell you, it takes the same power to save a little child as it took to raise Jesus from the dead! And that kind of power is working in your life as you come to know Him. That's why we should want to be around new converts. Why? Because lightning has just struck there. Resurrection power has just lighted upon that newly born babe. And, by the way, it takes this same power for you to overcome temptation as it did to raise Jesus from the dead. So my question to you is, Are you enjoying that same resurrection power in your life today? Are you experiencing it in your own life? Are you conscious, on a day-by-day basis, that supernatural power is operating in you that is beyond anything this world can ever know?

But it's not only that. It is also participating in the fellowship of His sufferings. Paul is saying here that there is no knowing Christ as he wants us to know Him, there is no growing in Him without sharing in His sufferings.

Something began to strike me as I looked at those statements about the power of Christ's resurrection and the sharing in His sufferings. I thought, *How strange to put those two things together—resurrection and sufferings*. You would think a person who had the power of Christ's resurrection in them could rise above suffering. That he could refuse to go through any tribulation or trial.

A lot of people today in the Christian church see an inconsistency in having resurrection power and having to experience any suffering. They are what we call "triumphalists." They believe you can overcome anything—that you don't have to submit to anything. Why? Because they say you have the power of the resurrection working in you. But what we find here in Paul's letter to the Philippians is that he saw no inconsistency in having the power of Christ's resurrection while at the same time sharing in His sufferings.

Now I admit that I would never have put resurrection and suffering together. And yet, what the apostle is saying here is that the reason we are given the power of Christ's resurrection is so we'll have the power to share in His sufferings. What we find here is that you cannot know Christ, in the deep way the apostle Paul is talking about, without sharing in His sufferings. There is no other way. Those of us who would try to escape suffering, trials, and tribulations will never know Jesus in the way Paul wanted to know Him. It is only as we participate in those sufferings that we get to know Him.

So, as I lay there in my bed, I said, "Bless God, I'm participating in His sufferings. How about that." There I was, barely able to move. My daughter has just had part of her leg amputated, and my wife, Kaye, has lymphoma and is going through the whole chemo thing. I know you'd think God would be good enough to let one thing happen at a time. But all these have happened at once. And there, lying on my back, with an uncertain future, I thought, *Paul doesn't have anything on me. I'm participating in sufferings.*

I was wrong. I was participating in suffering all right, and I believe every Christian does to one point or another, but Paul is speaking of the sufferings of Christ. That's something more than just mere suffering. That's something more than just being sick. The sufferings of Christ.

Now Paul isn't talking about the redemptive sufferings of Christ as if to say Christ did not suffer enough to save us. We know He did. In Colossians 1 Paul writes, "I fill up that which is lacking of the sufferings of Christ." I want you to notice in Philippians 3:29 where Paul says, "For to you it has been granted for Christ's sake, not only to believe in Him, but also to suffer for His sake."

This is saying that suffering is as much a part of your salvation as believing. They are both gifts of grace. We all endure suffering, and if we think we can rise above it, we'll never know Him to the degree Paul is speaking. And then he goes on to talk about being conformed to His death. We'll never be conformed to the spirit and temper of sacrifice that was in Christ when He suffered without our own identification with His suffering.

The Sufferings of Christ

What are the sufferings of Christ that you and I are to enter into? To find this out, we need to go back to the main section of this letter. Everything before it and everything after it flows from this main section which is Philippians 2:5–11; this great hymn about Christ who humbled Himself and became a servant. In verse 5 we see that we are to have this "attitude (mind-set) . . . which was also in Christ Jesus, who, although He existed in the form of God, did not regard equality with God a thing to be grasped, but emptied Himself, taking the form of a bond-servant, and being found in appearance as a man, He humbled Himself by becoming obedient to the point of death, even death on a cross." Here we have a description of the sufferings Christ endured, and in it we find three main statements.

HE EMPTIED HIMSELF

This is where Christ's sufferings began. This word *emptied* means "to be made of no effect." It doesn't mean He emptied Himself of His deity or His divinity and became less than God. No, it doesn't mean that at all. It means He emptied Himself of all His privileges and prerogatives as the Son of God. Jesus, who was in the position He was in, could have used that position as a stepping-stone to gain even more glory than He already had.

When it says "He emptied Himself," it means He did not use His position or power to advantage Himself, but rather, He did not consider that something to be grasped or held on to. He refused to use His rights as the Son of God to gain more glory for Himself.

I thought of Hebrews 12:2 while I was studying this. It says that we are to "[fix] our eyes on Jesus, the author and perfecter of faith," Now watch this, "who for the joy set before Him endured the cross, despising the shame."

Now, most of the time when we read this verse, we interpret it as though the "joy" found here means it was the joy He knew He would have when He saw people redeemed by His blood—when He saw children and adults being saved, over the centuries, through the sacrifice He had made. Well, I'm sure that is true, but it is not at all what this verse is saying. Let me explain.

The little preposition "for" that precedes the word *joy*, is significant to the interpretation of this verse. The word *for* here is the same as the word *anti*, which means "against," or "instead of," or "in exchange of," a substitute for something, like in the word *anti-Christ*—a substitute for Christ, against Christ, instead of Christ. And the participle "set before Him," literally means, "lying at present," the things lying before Him "at present," or, "in the present," right now.

Williams' translation says this: "instead of the joy which lay before Him." In other words, Jesus was not going to the cross for the reward of seeing men and women coming to Him for salvation. No, that's not what the writer to the Hebrews is saying. He is saying that Jesus went to the cross "instead of" choosing the joy that was immediately in front of Him, in the present.

What was that joy? The joy of His fellowship with the Father. The joy of the worship of the angels. The joy of the glories of heaven. He could have held on to all those joys, but instead of that He endured the cross, despising the shame. That makes it a whole different matter. He could have clung to that joy, but instead of using His preeminent position as the Son of God, He instead chose the cross. He emptied Himself of His rights and chose suffering. And we are to share in that suffering by emptying ourselves.

In other words, you and I are not to use our power, our position, our influence, as a means to advantage ourselves. And this is even more clearly explained in Philippians 2 where He says in verse 4, "Do not merely look out for your own personal interests but also for the interests of others." And in verse 3, "Do nothing from selfishness or empty conceit, but with humility of mind regard one another as more important than yourselves."

Now this is contrary to everything this world believes, which says that you are to use every influence you have to advantage yourself. Only a fool would not use his position to do that. Oh no. If you and I are going to share in the sufferings of Christ, we'll not look on our own interests but on the interests of others and use our influence and position and whatever power and prestige we have not to advance our own cause but to advance the cause of others.

So we've seen how Christ emptied Himself. He made Himself of no effect. Now let's look at the second statement in this verse.

HE HUMBLED HIMSELF

When you think of it, this is what it means to be divine. This is what it means to be God. To be divine and to have the greatest power in the universe doesn't mean getting, it means giving. "He humbled Himself" (Phil. 2:8). This word means lowliness of mind. It means to take the lowest place—"He humbled Himself."

I'm not talking about this false humility that we see a lot of. You hear people saying, "Oh, I'm just no good. I'm of no value. I can't do anything. I don't have any talent. I'm . . ." That's not humility; that's pride. Nor does it mean the kind of servility that is always saying, "I'll do anything. I'm willing to serve," always focusing on what you are willing to do. That's not humility; that's pride.

But I think the most common form of that kind of humility is what I've already referred to, the kind that says, "Oh, I'm just nothing; I'm not worthy." Well we already knew that. You don't have to tell us that. You see, humility is not whipping yourself; humility is forgetting yourself. True humility focuses not on self but on others.

"He humbled Himself." This means He took the lowest position. That's why He became a slave, and for us to humble ourselves the way Christ did includes our becoming a slave, with no rights of our own, but rather serving our Master without question, without hesitation.

Jesus not only emptied Himself, He humbled Himself. These are the sufferings of Christ. But there is another statement in this verse I want to look at:

He Became Obedient unto Death

"Even death on a cross" (v. 8). If you're not careful, you will take that to mean He was obedient up until the time He died. All His life He was obedient. The only thing that cut off His obedience was His death. That's not what this passage is saying at all. What this is saying is that He became obedient to the point of death, even the death of the cross. In other words, Jesus' obedience to the Father meant death to Him. In essence He was saying, "I would rather die than be disobedient to my Father's will—obedient unto death." Then to make it even worse, the death of a cross, the most shameful and humiliating death of all deaths.

To share in the sufferings of Christ means that we will be obedient, even to the point of death. It means you and I had rather die than disobey our Father. Do you now see why we need the power of the resurrection? Let me tell you, knowing Jesus involves that.

Obedient, even to the point of losing friends? No matter what my friends say, I'm going to be obedient to what I know is God's will for my life, even though they drop me as a friend!

Obedient, even to the loss of a job? I'd rather lose my position or job than to disobey the Father. Obedient to the point of losing my church? I know a lot of pastors who have chosen to compromise in order to hang on to their churches rather than be obedient to the Word of God.

Obedient to the point of losing a second term as president? Obedient to the point of losing my seat in the House or the Senate? Regardless of what political correctness says, which I think is the most damnable doctrine that has ever come out of hell. I question that you can be politically correct and biblically correct at the same time because sooner or later you're going to run into a conflict between the two.

So here is a Christian who says, "I want to know Christ more than anything else, and I understand that this means I'll have to participate in His sufferings and be willing, if necessary, to be obedient to the point of losing my reputation, of losing my friends, of losing my job. I'm ready to die in order to get to know Christ—obedient unto death."

BEING CONFORMED TO HIS DEATH

There is one more phrase in Philippians 3:10 that I want to look at in closing. It is a phrase that explains everything else found in this verse. "That I may know Him and the power of His resurrection and the fellowship of His sufferings, being conformed to His death."

This means constantly being shaped and fashioned to His death. Paul is saying "that I might be like Jesus in His death, His spirit of self-sacrifice; His willingness to serve others; His willingness to do the Father's will in all things, being made conformable to His death." To know Christ is to be like Him in His death.

I'm not talking about physical death, although that might come as it has to many through the years. I'm talking about the same attitude, the spirit and the mind that led Christ to His death. That's why Paul said at the beginning of this great hymn in Philippians 2:5, "Let this mind be in you, which was also in Christ" (KJV). He's saying, let this same "mind-set" be in you which was in Christ.

Well, this is what God has been saying to me. He has been showing me that my value to God and to others is not in my preaching, my ministry, my service; but it's in coming to know Him in such a way that the power of His resurrection enables me to empty myself, to humble myself, to be obedient, even to the extremity of death.

As Tom Elliff lead the congregation in a time of response, Ron slowly made his way down the steps to the front row where he sat, exhausted, until the service ended. No one in attendance that morning could have known how significant were the last words they heard him speak: "Even to the extremity of death."

Did Ron have a premonition that this would be the last sermon he'd ever preach? Did he sense that he'd never again stand behind a pulpit? Did he realize how the last words of his last sermon would in just a few weeks become a reality, as God brought his earthly pilgrimage to a close—"obedient to the point of death" (2:8). ❋

[3 2]

Back Home

Because of how badly he felt when the service ended, Ron opted not to stay and eat lunch with Tom and Jeannie. Now, as he drove south on Interstate 35, he was becoming increasingly weaker, and when he finally reached home, he could barely stagger through the door. Kaye could see immediately how really rotten he felt.

He didn't improve much through the rest of the week, though he was able to continue his rehab, and when he could muster up enough strength, he would have Don Gardner take him to visit Kimberly in the hospital.

Ron kept trying to put up a good front, especially in front of Kaye, but she, who herself was weak from her chemo treatments, knew that as much as Ron hated the thought, he needed to go back to the hospital.

Kaye's Time Line Continues

June 6—Ron's been home for about a week since he returned from Oklahoma, and since Friday he's been feeling very bad. I'm insisting that we admit him to Baylor Hospital in Irving again. He's fighting me on that. He doesn't want to go. He phoned Joanne and told her that I was making him go but that he was alright. Well, he isn't. He's getting progressively worse each day. He's been having trouble breathing and is coughing a lot.

Joanne's Journal

Ron called me on June 6: "Joanne, Kaye's insisting that I go to the ER, but there's nothing wrong with me." He was looking for someone to vote with him!

Respecting their privacy, Don and I didn't go to the hospital immediately, but when we did decide to go, as we walked into the ER, Ron looked at us and said: "Don't worry, I'll see you. It will either be here or around the throne, and Joanne, you'll be saying, 'Where's that tape you promised to get to me?' He was laughing when he said that so we actually thought he was OK. It was not long before they came and took him upstairs where they induced a temporary medical coma.

Kaye was feeling so sick from her chemo during this period that she gave the hospital my number to call. We of course were with Ron every day. Then, one morning a week later, they called me and said, "We're taking Mr. Dunn to ICU, and we thought you should know that."

I said, "Have you called his wife?"

"No, should we?" They were confused. They had switched the numbers. They thought I was Kaye.

I said, "No, I'll call her."

I did, and Kaye said, "Joanne, you go. You can get there faster than I can because you're just six minutes from the hospital." So Don and I went immediately. When we arrived, they were taking him up the elevator to ICU. We ran over before the door closed, and when he saw us he asked, "Where is Kaye?" I told him that she was on her way.

Later, though he was on a lot of drugs, he called and said he wanted to get back to his room so he could watch the NBA finals game between the Lakers and the Sixers. That was the last thing I heard him say. Ron loved to watch basketball.

Ron Dunn was such a gentleman, such a godly man and so down to earth and "normal." There was no phoniness about him. He was real. USDA steak—no gristle.

Kaye's Time Line Continued

June 9—*They've put him in ICU. He's in much distress. Dr. Rosenblatt is talking about putting him on a ventilator, but Ron doesn't want them to.*

June 10—*They went ahead and put him on a ventilator. The doctor shocked me today. He said that Ron was too old to have a lung transplant. I had no idea that it was that serious.*

June 11—*I had another Rituxan treatment today and then went to Baylor to see Ron. They've put him in ICU where I heard what I never thought I would ever hear. Dr. Hydebrink told me that he didn't think Ron was going to make it. Not going to make it!*

The Shock

This was the first time in all those months that Kaye really understood the gravity of Ron's condition. They both had been expecting to be back on the road in the not-too-distant future. After all, only last month doctors at the Mayo Clinic told him he'd be traveling again soon, and it had not been that long since a Baylor Hospital doctor had intimated to them that Ron would have a good five more years to live and minister. When you've been as sick as Ron, that's wonderful news. You can do a lot in five years. But now Dr. Hydebrink was saying that Ron may not make it!

Kaye recalls how unprepared she was for Ron's death. "I had not planned on him dying. It was a complete shock. All through the ordeal

I always felt that he would get better and one day we'd be back on the road."

A Congregation of One

Thursday night, much to Kaye's surprise, she found herself being a congregation of one, as Ron, weak as he was, lying in his hospital bed, preached the final sermon of the series he had prepared out of the book of Philippians. It was the sermon he had planned to preach that week at the closing service of the MEF Bible Conference in Colorado Springs. Kaye recalls telling him what a wonderful message it was, and then, after kissing him good-night, she drove home.

Having been told that Ron was going to die, Kaye decided she wanted the medical staff who were attending Ron to know what he really looked like. She wanted them to know that he was not the person who looked so bloated by steroids and all the other stuff they were treating him with. So, when she got home, she found a picture of Ron that had been taken just eight months before—the one at Cape Cod when he looked as healthy as he'd ever been.

Early the next morning she took it with her to the hospital and put it on the bulletin board outside his room. "I was ready to tell the nurses, 'This is who you are treating. I want you to see who this man is,' but as I walked into the room, I knew it was too late. The crash unit was in the process of attempting to revive him. His heart had stopped. They succeeded in getting it going, but it stopped again. They asked me if I wanted them to keep trying. I said, 'If there is a chance that he will live, yes, but if not . . .'"

"But if not . . ." Moments later, the spirit of Ron Dunn—the preacher, the traveling pastor, loving husband, caring father, encourager, and friend—soared heavenward. His flight was recorded as having left earth at 7:45 Central Standard Time, on Friday morning, June 29, 2001. He was sixty-four, as earth calculates age. His arrival in heaven? Immediate, where time is no more.

As the nurses removed the tubes from what was now but the shell of God's servant, the doctor told Kaye that he was going to put Ron's body in a side room where she, her sister Julie, and Joanne, who were with her, would be able to take all the time they wanted to say their good-byes.

"He looked peaceful for the first time since he had been in the hospital," recalls Kaye. "I kissed and kissed his cheek. There was such a sweetness in the room as we prayed and sang.

"Oh, there were also tears, but strangely, it was a happy time. We talked about how wonderful Ron was, how God had used him over the years in so many lives. We remembered some of the things we had done and the special times we had had together. We talked about how happy he now was. How quickly that hour passed." ❋

[3 3]

Earth Grieved
as Heaven Rejoiced

Though it's not for us to question God's timing, our humanness still wanders and wonders what might have been. From our earthly perspective it seemed that Ron was called home prematurely; yet with God, we know that our times are in His hands.

> "But our God is in the heavens: He hath done whatsoever he hath pleased." (Ps. 115:3 KJV)[39]

Following are but a few of the hundreds of letters, e-mails, and telegrams received in response to Ron's home-going.

MESSAGE: ERIC ALEXANDER—INTERNATIONAL BIBLE TEACHER AND RETIRED PASTOR, ST. GEORGE'S TRON, GLASGOW, SCOTLAND

Dear Kaye,
I can still scarcely believe that Ron is gone from this world. You know, at least in part, how special he was to me personally, not only to me but to my family. His

sermon, "Will a Man Serve God for Nothing?" was life-changing for several of them.

To me there was no one in the same class as Ron. His passing is an unmistakable loss to the whole Christian world.

Greta and I send our love to you all as we continue to pray for your health and future.

Warmly yours in Christ,

Eric

MESSAGE: KEN WHITTEN: SENIOR PASTOR, IDLEWILD BAPTIST CHURCH, LUTZ, FLORIDA

When I received word that Ron had passed on, my heart grieved for Kaye and the family and for his close friends. I must admit, however, that I selfishly grieved for my own heart because I knew, as a pastor, that those life lessons Ron had been sharing out of brokenness were over. Since then, I've often wondered what the next message might have been, the next book he might have written, the next life lesson he would have taught, what he would have had to share with us preachers and the body of Christ.

MESSAGE: PHIL SOUTH—DIRECTOR OF THE UNITED KINGDOM'S ARM OF LIFESTYLE MINISTRIES

I found that I couldn't talk without tears flowing and my heart aching when I received the news of Ron's home-going. I hadn't realized how much of a friend he had become. I couldn't grasp that he had been taken from us.

MESSAGE: BILL STAFFORD—EVANGELIST, CHATTANOOGA, TENNESSEE

I got word of Ron's home-going while I was driving on the highway. I pulled over and wept.

MESSAGE: JEANETTE CLIFF GEORGE—ACTRESS, HOUSTON,
TEXAS

I was stunned. It's not the certainty of his eternal security that affects
me; it is Ron's "goneness." I loved him. He smiled deep into my heart.
Earth is now one smile short.

MESSAGE: MICHAEL CATT—SENIOR PASTOR, SHERWOOD
BAPTIST CHURCH, ALBANY, GEORGIA

I was at a loss to know what to say. Terri and I cried most of the way
home from Atlanta. Ron was my hero, my role model . . . more like a dad
to me than I can say.

As many of the condolences and tributes said, only eternity will reveal
the impact that this one man of God, born to preach, had on thousands
around the world.

The Memorial Service

Knowing that a memorial service had to be quickly put together,
Kaye started calling preachers; but since she could hardly function due to
the chemo treatments she was going through, Michael Catt and Jimmy
Robertson immediately got involved in helping bring it about.

Every contact they made was met with unbelief. Though Ron's
extended family knew he was very sick, no one felt his home-going was
that imminent. Years before, however, while eating in a restaurant, out
of the blue Ron asked Michael Catt to preach his funeral sermon. "The
thought cut through me like a knife," recalls Michael. Now the reality of
it was cutting even more deeply.

MacArthur Boulevard was being remodeled at that time and was
meeting in an equestrian center, so First Baptist Church, Euless, offered
their facility.

Joanne Gardner and Kaye's sister, Julie, took over the contacting of friends and relatives, putting together the obituary, etc., while Michael Catt and Jimmy Robertson contacted Ron's ministry peers and lined up those she wanted to participate in the memorial service.

A Mother's Dilemma

Kim was in a wheelchair. She had only been put in a nursing home the day before Ron died, and Kaye had to get her from the home in Grand Prairie to the funeral at First Baptist Church, Euless.

"The nursing home said they would bring Kim in a van. I told Michael Catt that Kim was going to be in a wheelchair with her leg propped up and that she would not be able to do that longer than an hour and a half, so 'whatever you do, the service can't be longer than that.'"

Ron would have seconded what Kaye requested. In fact, knowing Ron, if he could have attended his own memorial service, he might have told about the evening Kaye hit him with a most unexpected question. He wrote about this in his journal.

Journal Entry

We were in the den reading the newspaper. It was quiet and we were absorbed in what we were doing when, out of the blue, Kaye looks up and says, "What do you want written on your tombstone?" No preamble . . . no probable cause . . . just the question. "I don't know," I said. We ate out a lot after that!

Actually, Dad's illness has gotten me to thinking about what Kaye asked. First Timothy 4:6–7 talks about being a good servant of Jesus Christ, trained in the words of faith and sound doctrine. This is the touchstone, the ruler, by which I remind myself and judge myself.

That's what I'm here for. That's why God called me and what He has called me to do—to keep the faith—to fight the "good" fight, and to finish the course.

The Good Fight: *There are all kinds of fights a preacher can get into, but there's only one "good" fight.*

Finish the Course: *I love to watch the Boston Marathon. For most of the runners, winning is not the issue—finishing is. Demas, in looking at this present world, sold out for the moment, for the "now." We must hold out higher stakes than that. It's not how fast you run the race but whether or not you cross the finish line.*

Keep the Faith: *So far! I remember what the man in the little Baptist church in Krum, Oklahoma, said to me. "I first heard you fifteen years ago, and you haven't changed a bit." He meant it as a compliment and I took it as one. He was saying that I was not giving an "uncertain sound." Some folk jump at almost everything that moves theologically.*

I've decided on my epitaph, but should I tell Kaye yet? I want it to be taken out of 2 Timothy 4:6–7, which pictures life as a fight, a stewardship and a race. It also pictures death as a departure and as an act of worship. "For I am already being poured out as a drink offering, and the time of my departure has come. **I have fought the good fight, I have finished the race, I have kept the faith.**"[40]

A Synopsis of the Memorial Service Tributes

Jimell Badry, music director at MacArthur Boulevard Baptist Church when Ron was pastor, led the congregational singing. His brother, Jimell Badry, who had teamed with Ron in many meetings over the years, sang two solos. Jamall, also founder of the annual MEF Bible Conference in Colorado Springs, had had Ron preach every year from its inception until 2000, one year, almost to the day, before Ron's home-going. He always preached the closing message on Friday evening, and the message he shared with Kaye from his hospital bed the night before his spirit soared heavenward was what he had planned to preach that week in Colorado.

Testimonials were shared by some of Ron's closest friends and ministry associates. A brief synopsis of what was shared at the memorial service will suffice, as tributes by each of these are included throughout the book.

Ted Kersh: Yesterday morning I went to Ron's Web site to listen to his sermon, "Chained to the Chariot," a message he gleaned out of 2 Corinthians 2:12–17. Verse 16 speaks of being a fragrance of life to others . . . Ron Dunn was that kind of fragrance to me, and to so many others.

. **Jimmy Robertson:** Today, the storms are over for our Brother Ron. While we are here grieving over his departure, he is exploring the hillsides of glory, rejoicing with the saints of God who have gone before him. . . . But Ron's ministry is not over. History shows that the ministry of many of God's great servants did not end with their death, but for many their greatest impact was after they were gone. I believe this will be true of Bro. Ron's life and message.

George Harris: Psalm 1 is a description of Ron Dunn. . . . I asked Kaye what Ron's hobbies were. She said he really didn't have any except that he liked to read, study, prepare sermons, and preach. . . . Humbled in his walk with God, he never allowed the accolades of man to go to his head. Ron loved one thing above all, and that was to preach. Gone to glory, never to be forgotten, and most likely, never to be replaced.

Tom Elliff: What an incredible person and what a refreshing and transparent friend. . . . God hammered into Ron's life, through personal and painful experiences, the messages he shared with us. . . . Ron was a man of studied doctrinal balance and had the unique ability to find the center of truth.

Joanne Gardner: I went from being Ron's secretary to his assistant, and for thirty-five years I watched him live what he preached. It changed my life forever. . . . It seemed right that the last series of meetings he preached was at MacArthur Boulevard Baptist for the annual *Encouragers Conference* for pioneer pastors and wives that he started in 1975.

Ken Whitten: One of my heroes is gone. He permanently marked my life. . . . In John 12 the Greeks told Phillip that they wanted to see Jesus, and when Ron preached, I saw Jesus, and I wanted to be just like Him. . . . Good-bye Ron Dunn.

Bill Stafford: I've come to pay tribute to one of two great men who gloriously touched my life—Manley Beasley and Ron Dunn. Ron taught me how to respond in difficulty and storms and that God uses nobodies and that any old bush will do when God sets the bush aflame. . . . I always felt safe under Ron's preaching. You never went home wondering if what he preached was the truth or not.

Michael Catt: We are here to honor the Lord and to honor our friend and brother. . . . In our minds we can't help but think that Ron's passing was too soon. We were looking forward to the books he would still write, to the sermons he would still preach, to the Bible conferences he would still hold. Selfishly we were wanting to hear all the things Ron was going to be learning over the next twenty years of his life. We won't get that privilege, but we are here today to say that God has been so good in allowing us the privilege of knowing Ron Dunn.

Graveside

After the Memorial Service, family and a few friends went to the Oak Grove Memorial Gardens in Irving for the graveside service where Tom Elliff and Michael Catt presided. Michael read Scripture and prayed. Tom shared a brief word.

The nursing home van had driven Kim on to the cemetery, and, as Kaye recalls, this turned out to be a very difficult part of the day for her.

"I had to be with the casket, but they couldn't get Kim's wheelchair up to the graveside. I looked back and saw Kim in the background, wanting to be with Stephen and me, but she couldn't get her wheelchair across the ground. I didn't know what to do. I was so torn. Though she had some of the family with her, she belonged by my side. There was nothing I could do." ※

[3 4]

Will a Man Serve God
for Nothing?

Prelude

On one occasion after an extended phone conversation with Manley
Beasley, Ron told Kaye that he wished he had Manley's faith but wondered
whether he'd be willing to go through the kind of testing through which God
was taking Manley. But God would permit Satan to test Ron and test him
beyond what some, humanly speaking, would say was fair. Like Job, there
were times when one tragedy was piled on another. The years did prove, however, that Ron, who eventually could identify with Brother Manley, and with
Job, would say, "Though [God] slay me, yet will I trust him" (Job 13:15 KJV).

Sermon: *Will a Man Serve God for Nothing?*

Now there was a day when the sons of God came to present
themselves before the LORD, and Satan also came among
them. The LORD said to Satan, "From where do you come?"

> Then Satan answered the LORD and said, "From roaming about on the earth and walking around on it." The LORD said to Satan, "Have you considered My servant Job? For there is no one like him on the earth, a blameless and upright man, fearing God and turning away from evil." (Job 1:6–8)

These words found in the first chapter of Job are God's words, not Job's publicist, or his mother. And God repeated them later in the book. Satan replied by asking, "Does Job fear God for nothing?" (1:9).

The word *nothing* in the Hebrew means "out of favor." It speaks of an ulterior motive. In other words, the devil can't understand why anyone would serve God in the first place, so when he sees someone serving God, he's always suspicious of that person's motives. So he said, "Yeah, I know about Job. I know that You've blessed him. I know that You've increased his substance in the land. You've made him the richest man in the East. Not only that, but You've also built a hedge around him so that nothing can touch him or all that he has" (Dunn paraphrase).

The devil insinuated that Job wasn't serving God for nothing—there had to be a payoff. He thought God had given Job "the Midas touch" and protected all that He had given Job.

Satan thought he knew the truth about Job. Basically he told God: "If You were to stretch forth Your hand and touch all that he has and reduce him to nothing, You would find out the truth about Job, and he would curse You to Your face. Nobody will serve God if there's no payoff" (paraphrase).

I believe the theme of this book is not "Why do the righteous suffer?" but "Why do people serve God?" Will a person serve God for nothing if there are no blessings attached or no payoff? I have to confess to you that the devil has asked a legitimate question. It's a question that all of us must face and somehow try to answer. Why do you serve God? Why do you go to church on Sunday? Why do you tithe?

I remember when I was in seminary, a fellow pastor nearby was having a thirteen-week stewardship campaign. They would mail letters every week to every member of the church to encourage them to give. In every Sunday school class each week, someone would testify to the blessing of tithing. The pastor preached on tithing. The whole thing was capped off with a stewardship banquet, and everyone on the church roll was invited. A dynamic preacher came in and encouraged the people to tithe, and then they all signed the pledge cards.

I picked up this friend on the day after the banquet, and I could tell he wasn't very happy. He was frustrated with the preacher he had asked to speak at the stewardship banquet. His first words to the congregation were, "The only thing I can promise you if you tithe is that you'll have 10 percent less than you did before." The speaker proceeded by telling them they should tithe because God commands it, not because we want His blessings.

Of course, I believe God will bless us for giving, and I've always said that if God doesn't get it through the tithe, He'll collect it some way. Sometimes I tithe out of an unworthy motive, expecting that I'm going to get something back. Most of us believe that if we give to God and serve Him, that He's going to bless us. But my question to you is: What if He didn't?

What if, after you have said, "I'm going to start tithing," you go bankrupt and lose everything. What about that? Will a person serve God for nothing? Is there such a thing as "disinterested piety"? In other words, is there such a thing as a person worshipping God without any interest in the blessings that might come? Or is it true that we serve God knowing that, if we do, He's going to bless us? It's easy to be good when the good have the goods. It's easy to serve God when everything is going your way. But here's the question: Is God alone worthy of our service without any of His blessings?

The book of Job is a book of questions. In many ways it's a frustrating book because it's built of questions on top of questions. One question is answered by asking another one. I'm going to attempt to answer this question: "Will a person serve God for nothing?" and the way to answer that question is to ask three other questions.

Question 1: Will a Person Serve God When His Life Turns Tragic?

I'm using the word *tragedy* in the classical literary sense—tragedy, as opposed to regular suffering. Tragedy is when a good man or woman suffers undeservedly for no reason. Their suffering cannot be traced back to any cause, and it seems to serve no other purpose than to destroy the human spirit. Theologians call it radical suffering, as opposed to regular suffering. There is suffering that you and I deserve. But Job's suffering was undeserved.

We find this in Job 1:13–22 where Satan challenged God with a wager that if He ceased to bless Job and would allow Satan to turn God's blessings into tragedies in Job's life, taking away everything he had, that Job would turn against God and curse Him. God took Satan up on the bet and released the devil to attack Job. And he did with a vengeance.

Round 1

Satan used the Sabeans and Chaldeans to steal all of Job's animals, to wipe out his servants, and to kill his whole family except for his wife. But rather than Job cursing God for what had happened to him . . .

> Job arose and tore his robe and shaved his head, and he fell to the ground and worshiped. He said, "Naked I came from my mother's womb, and naked I shall return there. The Lord gave and the Lord has taken away. Blessed be the name of the Lord." Through all this Job did not sin nor did he blame God. (1:20–22)

Now this story has an interesting side to it. We always talk about our faith in God, but sometimes God has faith in us. God had faith in Job. God said to Satan, "You may take and do whatever you want with him, but I have faith in My servant that he will serve Me for nothing." So, the Lord won the first round.

ROUND 2

In Job 2:1–8, we again find Satan, having to admit that Job, in spite of losing all his wealth and family, still loved God. But the devil, never giving up, makes another wager with God, daring to allow him to touch Job's body, knowing that Job surely would finally turn on God and curse Him.

> "Skin for skin! Yes, all that a man has he will give for his life. However, put forth Your hand now, and touch his bone and his flesh; he will curse You to Your face." So the LORD said to Satan, "Behold, he is in your power, only spare his life." Then Satan went out from the presence of the LORD and smote Job with sore boils from the sole of his foot to the crown of his head. And he took a potsherd to scrape himself while he was sitting among the ashes. (2:4–8)

Another tragedy—one day we find Job sitting on the city council; the next day he is sitting on the city dump. *Ashes* is a delicate way of putting it—it was the dung heap, the sanitation fill. Everything was stripped from him, and he became an outcast.

When our first son died, we received an outpouring of support through cards and letters from people all over the country. One in particular caught my attention from a couple in Memphis. "Brother Dunn, we know that you are a man of God, and you have committed your life to serve Him and to preach His word, and we know that you are a faithful servant of God. We do not understand how something like this could happen to you."

I got the impression they were thinking, *We're just mere people. This kind of thing can happen to us, but you're a man of God.* I think the real fear that was in their hearts was this: "If this could happen to a man of God, what might happen to us?"

I don't understand it either. It looks like it ought to count for something that we're Christians who are serving God. Don't you believe we deserve some kind of special consideration in this matter? It seems there ought to be a few perks that go along with this job. You'd think that when God passes out calamities and disasters, He ought to keep in mind that I'm His child and His servant. What's in it for me? If there are no extra blessings or special protection or immunity, then why are we serving God?

The hard truth is that faith cannot be tested by prosperity. Anybody can praise the Lord as long as everything is going the way they want. Even a lost person can praise God. But what if the opposite is true? What if suddenly life is filled with tragedy that you don't deserve?

The prevailing theology of Job's day was that if a man truly served God, God would bless him physically and materially. In the Old Testament, salvation is depicted more in terms of physical and material blessings than in terms of spiritual blessings. In the Old Testament they had not yet developed enough spiritually to understand that the greatest blessings are spiritual blessings. When you read Psalms, most of the times the writers are thanking God for physical blessings.

When you come to the New Testament, however, you'll find the opposite is true. You won't find Paul thanking God for his "three-camel garage." He thanked God for the spiritual blessings he has in Christ Jesus in heavenly places.

> Those today who preach a health-and-wealth gospel base most
> of their teaching on Old Testament Scriptures.

I once got a newsletter from a colleague in the ministry who made this statement: "Your financial condition is a reflection of your spiritual condition." That sounds good at the Hyatt Regency ballroom here in the States, but I'd like to hear him preach that same message in Ethiopia or Rwanda.

Job even believed this Old Testament theology himself. It was as if God were treating him as an enemy. Scholars have come to believe that the name *Job* meant "enemy" in ancient times.

Question 2: Will a Person Serve God When He Has to Stand Alone?

Will a person serve God when his friends forsake him, when nobody understands him, and when he finds himself standing alone?

> Then his wife said to him, "Do you still hold fast your integrity? Curse God and die!" But he said to her, "You speak as one of the foolish women speaks. Shall we indeed accept good from God and not accept adversity?" In all this Job did not sin with his lips. (2:9–10)

Is that a testimony of faith or what? Then after Job's wife's discouraging statement, here came Job's three friends.

> Now when Job's three friends heard of all this adversity that had come upon him, they came each one from his own place, Eliphaz the Temanite, Bildad the Shuhite and Zophar the Naamathite; and they made an appointment together to come to sympathize with him and comfort him. When they lifted up their eyes at a distance and did not recognize him, they raised their voices and wept. And each of them tore his robe and they threw dust over their heads toward the sky. Then they sat down on the ground with him for seven days and seven nights with no one speaking a word to him, for they saw that his pain was very great. (2:11–13)

I'd find that incredibly comforting, wouldn't you? It reminds me of vultures perching on a limb, waiting for the fellow to expire. Finally, after the end of seven days and nights of silence, Job's friends came to a conclusion. All three of them said the same thing: "Job, you've sinned. You're going to have to confess and get right, or God is never going to return you to His favor."

You see, suddenly Job had to stand alone. Nobody believed in his innocence—not his wife or his three best friends. It's easy for us to serve

God and stay true to Him when surrounded by encouraging friends and loved ones. But what happens when you have to stand alone and no one believes in you? When everybody looks at you with great suspicion and casts doubt on your integrity?

We're quick to criticize Job's friends. But the fact of the matter is they had no other choice. Why? Because their theology said to. They either had to admit their theology was wrong, or they had to condemn Job. They chose to hang on to their theology.

We believe there is always a link between suffering and guilt. Job is a problem to a lot of people who believe that if you serve God and are right with Him, you'll be healthy and wealthy. Job's friends had the same problem and looked all over for a reason for Job's suffering.

We need to look back at verse 3 of chapter 2 to clear some of this up: "And he still holds fast his integrity, although you incited Me against him to ruin him without cause."

There was no reason in Job's life for God to have done this; God Himself said it. You could run a fine-tooth comb through the life of Job and find no reason for Job's suffering. God had a reason, of course, but not a reason as far as Job was concerned. Sometimes things happen for no reason—they just happen.

As a preacher, I am warmly received and encouraged by people all the time. I have great admiration for people who work in offices that are godless, where there is no Christian support or encouragement. I wonder if I would be as faithful to God as these are. I admire our Christian men and women who work in a godless world and yet still stand for Christ. It's not easy to stand for God when you're alone.

Note that Job wasn't only forsaken by his wife and his friends; he was also forsaken by God. Well, not really, but so it seemed to Job because God was treating him like an enemy. God wasn't answering any of his questions, so Job began to lash out against God. Job's problem wasn't with God's absence; his problem was with God's presence. It was an oppressive presence.

Suffering isolates you. Everyone else's world is in full color, but yours is in black-and-white. The loneliness will lead to bitterness. Look back at Job's words in chapter 7:

> Therefore, I will not restrain my mouth; I will speak in the anguish of my spirit. I will complain in the bitterness of my soul. Am I the sea, or the sea monster, that You set a guard over me? . . . I waste away; I will not live forever. Leave me alone, for my days are but a breath. What is man that You magnify him, and that You are concerned about him, that You examine him every morning and try him every moment? . . . Have I sinned? What have I done to You, O watcher of men? Why have You set me as Your target, so that I am a burden to myself? (7:11–12, 16–18, 20)

Job was speaking to God in those verses. Job was standing alone, in his mind, forsaken and abandoned by God.

Question 3: Will a Person Serve God When God Is Silent?

I believe this may be the most difficult question of all. God didn't answer Job for a while. He didn't give him any answers. I believe I can handle something for a while, as long as I have a reason for handling it. We feel that if God would give us an explanation we'd have something to hang on to, and we could handle the situation better.

My life is characterized by creative chaos. My wife's life is characterized by order; therefore, she takes care of our finances, and she handles our income taxes every year. One year she came across a change the IRS had made that would cost us an additional $800. She called them for further explanation. She talked to three different people, asking about the change, and every one of them answered, "I don't know." Well, I don't like to pay taxes anyway, but I'd sure like to have a reason behind an $800 increase—any reason, some explanation.

Why? is the most often asked question, and it's the most unanswered question. In 1986, I was in a conference with Elisabeth Elliot, the widow of Jim Elliot, one of the missionaries murdered in Ecuador in 1956. She said, "I do not know any better now than I did thirty years ago why God chose to work that way." That was astounding to me. You'd think that after thirty years she would have had insight from the Lord about His actions, but she didn't. A lot of times we want a word from God, a word of explanation or direction, but none comes. Will you still serve God? Well, God finally did speak to Job out of the whirlwind.

> Who is this that darkens counsel by words without knowledge? Now gird up your loins like a man, and I will ask you, and you instruct Me! *(I'm getting the impression this is not going to go Job's way.)* Where were you when I laid the foundation of the earth? Tell Me, if you have understanding, who set its measurements? Since you know. Or who stretched the line on it? . . . Have you entered into the springs of the sea or walked in the recesses of the deep? Have the gates of death been revealed to you, or have you seen the gates of deep darkness? Have you understood the expanse of the earth? Tell Me, if you know all this. . . . Can you lift up your voice to the clouds, so that an abundance of water may cover you? Can you send forth lightnings that they may go and say to you, "Here we are"? Who has put wisdom in the innermost being or given understanding to the mind? Who can count the clouds by wisdom, or tip the water jars of the heavens, when the dust hardens into a mass and the clods stick together? (Job 38:1–5, 16–18, 34–38).

What is God talking about? To Job, it wasn't relevant. Job wanted to know why he had lost his children and possessions, why he had sores all over his body, why he was suffering; and all God wanted to do was talk about nature. What Job discovered was this: When you finally meet

God, it's not to get the answers to questions but to discover the right questions. God was saying, "Job, I have a right to do whatever I do." He reminded Job of who He (God) was and who Job was. Job was creature and God was Creator. When we find ourselves in situations like Job, the first hurdle we have to get over is, "Does God have a right to do what He does?" The answer is "yes" because He is the Creator.

Not only does God have a right, but He also has a reason. Job finally realized that God had a purpose behind it all. While there may not have been a reason as far as Job was concerned, there was a reason as far as God was concerned. God had a purpose, and it couldn't be defeated.

"Then Job answered the LORD and said, 'I know that You can do all things, and that no purpose of Yours can be thwarted'" (42:1–2).

We may not know the exact purpose, but it's enough to know that there is one—that God has a divine purpose behind it all and that everything that is happening in our lives is to fulfill His eternal purposes. That gives us a sense of security and confidence. If I didn't believe that, then what use is there in going on? Even after it was all over, God never told Job why these things had happened. Job lived and died without the answer. It had to be that way for Job to trust.

In Conclusion

Finally, God had a reward for Job's faithfulness. "The LORD restored the fortunes of Job when he prayed for his friends, and the LORD increased all that Job had twofold. . . . The LORD blessed the latter days of Job more than his beginning, and he had 14,000 sheep, and 6,000 camels and 1,000 yoke of oxen and 1,000 female donkeys. He had seven sons and three daughters" (42:10, 12–13).

God gave Job twice as much as he had before. But, you say, the text says he had seven sons and three daughters, the same number he had before all the tragedies. Exactly! Now he had ten children in heaven and ten on earth because you never lose what you lose to heaven.

When Vance Havner's wife passed away, people would come up to him and say, "Dr. Havner, I'm so sorry to hear that you lost your wife." He would say, "No, I haven't lost her; I know right where she is. You haven't lost someone when you know where they are." Then he would quote this little saying:

> Death can hide, but not divide.
> She is, but on Christ's other side.
> She with Christ, and Christ with me;
> United still in Christ are we.

God has a reward. He is no man's debtor. No one will ever be able to stand in heaven and shake a fist at God and say, "You owe me."

I like to imagine what might have happened when this was all over. Don't you think the devil made himself mighty scarce? He lost a big bet. God probably had to go looking for him and perhaps found him hiding behind a bush somewhere.

"Pay up. I told you so. I told you Job would serve Me for nothing." ❋

Epilogue

✳ ✳ ✳

"Have you considered my servant, Ron—you know, the one who's pastoring MacArthur Boulevard Baptist Church in Irving, Texas? Have you observed how faithfully he is serving Me?"

"Yes—but look how you've blessed him. Already, at a young age, he has a beautiful family, pastors a great church, is in demand as a revival and conference speaker—no wonder he serves you. But you just let me at him."

And God Did

Unlike Job, however, Ron did not live to see all his "fortunes" restored in this life, but he has already seen Ronnie Jr. perfectly healed. He will one day see Kimberly physically whole. He will again be able to sit down with Stephen and discuss theology and archeology as he once so enjoyed doing. He will learn how God has provided for Kaye, the love of his life, the one who protected him, provided for him, and who faithfully stood by his side through the darkest of nights. He is now experiencing the meaning of the words of that old gospel song, "It Will Be Worth It All."

It will be worth it all when we see Jesus;
Life's trials will seem so small when we see Christ.

One glimpse of His dear face all sorrow will erase.
So bravely run the race till we see Christ.[41]

Yet, in spite of what we might consider an untimely home-going, Ron still saw the fulfillment of many of the dreams and desires he had expressed in a 1992 journal entry.

Journal Entry: The Desire of My Heart

On October 12, 1952, I preached my first sermon in the city jail at Fort Smith, Arkansas. I was on the outside looking in, by the way. So this October marks my fortieth year in the ministry. Kaye has been with me for thirty-five of those forty years. I couldn't have made the trip without her.

From the day I started preaching, I asked God to let me do two things: travel the country teaching the Bible and write books. That has been the desire of my heart from the beginning. And God has satisfied that desire a thousand times over. He has not only let us travel this country sharing the Word; He has taken us around the world to places we never dreamed of going, opening doors we couldn't have blasted open with an atom bomb.

Since leaving the pastorate in 1975, we have ministered in churches, colleges, seminaries, conventions, and conferences in most of the fifty states, Europe, Australia, Canada, South Africa, Central America, and the Caribbean Islands. God has also blessed our tape ministry more than we could have imagined. Everywhere we go, somehow the tapes have preceded us. We've yet to travel in a foreign country where someone has not told of being blessed by the tape ministry.

Earlier this year I believe God gave me a promise that the last years of our ministry would be greater than all the others. And that's the way I want it to be. Watching the Olympics last summer, I noticed that the runners in every race didn't slacken their speed when they caught sight of the finish line. No, that's when they went to afterburners and pushed the accelerator to the floor.

Afterburners

Kaye notes that God gave Ron almost ten years of additional, fruitful ministry and that during the last eight months prior to his death, as much as he could, he turned on the afterburners and pushed the accelerator to the floor.

Richard L. Morgan writes that, "as long as we keep our hopes and dreams alive, as long as we stay involved in life, our spirits will be renewed. There should be no wrinkles on the soul."[42]

Ron determined to allow no wrinkles on his soul! Though often in either a hospital bed or confined to his bed at home, he immersed himself in the book of Philippians, studying and preparing messages on "Knowing God." He never gave up hope that he would again be back on the road, preaching. He had, after all, been told by doctors, twelve hours before they put him in ICU for the last time, that he would be released from the hospital the following day. That very day he was put on a ventilator, never again to regain consciousness.

Life Goes On—Here and There!

Kaye continued living in their home in Hackberry Creek subdivision in Irving for six months before downsizing in a move to Flower Mound. In addition to continuing her chemo treatments for lymphoma, she did all she could to attend to the needs of Kimberly, who was adjusting to the many changes in her life resulting from the automobile accident. During this time Kaye's mother, who lived in Little Rock, was a great help. She assisted Kaye in making the move, but not long after that she had a stroke, and Kaye's sister, Julie, became her primary caregiver, with Kaye occasionally being able to help.

In addition to these responsibilities, there was also the matter of the ongoing work of LifeStyle Ministries. She, along with son, Stephen, and Joanne Gardner, began the assignment of keeping Ron's life and message alive. This, along with her church involvement, meant there was not much time left for anything else, that is, until the phone call.

The Phone Call

"Hi Dan. This is Kaye Dunn returning your call."

Little did Kaye realize where that phone call to Dan Robinson would one day lead.

She and Ron had ministered in Dan's church in Highlands, North Carolina, several times over the years, and when the church newsletter arrived, announcing his wife, Gwynn's, home-going, Kaye had written Dan a letter expressing her condolences and commitment to be praying for him and the family.

Then, at Thanksgiving, Dan phoned Kaye. She was not at home to receive the call but would return it several days later. That call would lead to another call, to another call, to a meal at Mimi's when Dan was in the Dallas-Fort Worth area, and Kaye didn't think there was anything more to these meetings than her simply encouraging a grieving friend.

But the phone calls continued and eventually became so frequent that Kaye sent Dan a six hundred-minute Costco phone card. Then, after almost four years of calls, letters, and several visits, they were married on May 27, 2007.

Since then, not only have they ministered together as pastor and wife, but Dan has walked by Kaye's and Joanne Gardner's side in the continuing ministry of LifeStyle. In addition to his being father to his own three children, Charis, Zach, and Seth, he has filled that role for Kimberly and Stephen. There has been a mutual bonding of love.

Dunn but Not Finished

"I may be Dunn, but I'm not finished," was something Ron used to enjoy saying, though little did he realize at the time how well this statement, though partially said in jest, would one day describe the legacy of his life. Now, years later, he, being dead, still speaks. He never fully knew the impact his life and ministry was making on thousands around the world, nor could he have imagined how his life and message would continue to minister to thousands, after his home-going, through his recorded messages, his books, and the faithful testimonies of those who would never be the same, having had their lives intersect with his.

The Ron Dunn Center for Biblical Studies

Kaye donated Ron's complete library to Sherwood Baptist Church in Albany, Georgia. Ron had preached at Sherwood's annual Fall Bible Conference from 1989 to 2000. According to Michael Catt, Ron helped shape Sherwood to become the church she is today.

Sherwood has recreated Ron's library-study, complete with desk, books, and pictures just as it was set up in his home for many years. His library is now a part of the Ron Dunn Center for Biblical Studies at Sherwood, and in addition to being open for tours, it is available to pastors, lay leaders, students, and study groups for research.

A Web site has also been developed for LifeStyle Ministries on which can be found a host of items including CDs, DVDs, Ron's books, podcasts, sermons to download, along with Ron's approach to exegeting the Scriptures.[43] ※

[APPENDIX 1]

Tributes and Testimonies

❄ ❄ ❄

SHERRY ANDERSON: FORMER MBBC SECRETARY AND DUNN FAMILY FRIEND

As I look back on my life, first as just a church member and then as a believer, I honestly can say that Ron Dunn was truly my "pastor." There are several reasons for this—first is that he was the one who showed me that just being a church member didn't cut it with God, and my "pastor" led me into faith and faithfully shepherded me in that faith.

Ron's authentic teaching, his love of the Word of God, his study habits, all have been a great incentive to me to be like that. I still use notes I took under his teaching, and those thoughts, examples, and vulnerabilities continue to minister to those I teach.

JIMELL AND CAROLYN BADRY: MINISTER OF MUSIC (AND WIFE) ON RON'S STAFF AT MBBC

I first met Ron in the late 1950s where I was serving a church in Oklahoma City. Our pastor invited a young man, then known as Ronnie Dunn to preach a youth revival. A few years later Ron began to have a profound influence on Carolyn's and my life. He was always careful, with few exceptions, to be in the pulpit on Sunday mornings, but when away on a Sunday evening, he would always fill the pulpit with strong preaching. When some church members began complaining about Ron preaching in other churches, Dr. J. P. McBeth told the staff what to say: "Tell them they could have called a man to be their pastor who nobody else wanted!"

T. D. Hall: Evangelist-Revivalist, Bedford, Texas

Ron and Kaye were dear friends. Sarah and I used to travel to the Southern Baptist Conventions with them. I recall one trip when we were stopped for speeding. Ron was driving, but the patrolman didn't give Ron a ticket. Instead, he told him to follow the patrol car, and he took us straight to court. Ron was always good at seeing the lighter side of situations, and on the way he said: "Maybe my testimony as a criminal will open up some doors!"

I recall a lesson I learned from Ron in the early days that had to do with giving. I had gone to hear Manley Beasley in a meeting at MBBC and when it was time for the offering, I knew I had a ten-dollar bill and two ones in my wallet. I decided to be real generous and give the ten. Then Ron said: "Wait a minute. Wait a minute. Don't give yet. Around here we give by revelation. Ask God what you are to give, and when you know what He wants you to give, you'll be worshipping the Lord and not giving to Brother Manley or a ministry; you'll be giving to the Lord."

So I bowed my head, and what the Lord told me was a good bit more than what I had in my pocket. I told the Lord that I didn't have that much. I sensed Him saying, "Well, they'll take a check." I looked at my billfold, and sure enough, there was a check. That was a lesson I've never forgotten. The amount was quite large, and as I began writing the check, I experienced a great thrill in my heart because I knew that what I was doing was in obedience to the Lord.

George Harris—Former Pastor, Castle Hills First Baptist Church, San Antonio, Texas

Those who tried to impress Ron Dunn didn't. Those who criticized him, he forgave. Those who tried to use him failed.

R. T. Kendall: Former Minister of Westminster Chapel, London, England

Ron Dunn is one of the few preachers I have wanted to listen to. I ordered all of his sermons I could get and listened to every one of them. I was edified beyond my ability to explain, and not only that, I found that my own preaching took on a different style that was not unlike his, without intentionally imitating him.

In Europe, Ron Owens first introduced me to Ron Dunn. I had no idea at the time what an enormous favor he was doing for me because it opened up not only a friendship but a wealth of preaching know-how which I never learned from anyone else. It was my privilege to minister alongside Ron in conferences in England, Austria, and Switzerland.

In my opinion Ron's greatest illustration was the story about his daughter's comment, "I didn't get a balloon," after Ron had spent a long hot day at Six Flags Over Texas. Little Kimberly could only think about what she didn't get that day. The last time I saw Ron Dunn was when he visited me in my vestry in London. He said, "Do you think that not seeing revival at Westminster Chapel is your balloon?" Strangely enough, it was.

Nelson McKinney: Deacon, MacArthur Boulevard Baptist Church

I've been a member of MBBC since 1960, and initially I did not realize the impact Ron was having on me and my family until I began to hear my son and daughter come out of the services saying things like, "Boy, did he fly today!" I couldn't have given that to my children personally, but my pastor could, and that influence is still in our lives to this day, thirty-five years later. His life and ministry continue to impact our whole family, and when we get together for a reunion, we'll find ourselves still quoting Ron. We'll be saying things like, "Do you remember when . . . ?"

At one point Ron asked me to lead the singles department, and we grew from a few to a few hundred. In those days you didn't have to beg folk to come. We had to expand by buying another building to make it into a meeting place for singles. They wanted to hear the Word of God.

CHARLES MOORE, MISSIONARY TO CENTRAL AMERICA

My wife, Judy, and I were members of MacArthur for several years, and from time to time Ron and I would meet for lunch at a Mexican restaurant where he would share some fresh discovery he had made in God's Word. I learned so much from Ron, and what he taught me was passed on to the young men whom I was personally discipling.

Ron loved to pull jokes on others, and I was able to return my share. A special memory of one of these occasions had to do with Ron and Kaye's praying for $1000 to go on a mission trip to Africa. I knew that Ron at one time had given Manley Beasley his love offering all in coins, so I decided to contribute the $1000 they were needing, in pennies.

On the first page of his book, *Don't Just Stand There, Pray Something,* Ron shares what happened when he found twenty sacks of pennies, each weighing forty pounds, stacked like a pyramid against his back door, and how conspicuous he felt, as pastor of the largest church in Irving, dragging twenty sacks, two at a time, through the bank lobby.

When Ron was a member of our Christians Sharing Christ board, he and his son, Stephen, made a trip with me to Costa Rica. I enjoyed translating many messages for him and especially the message that he preached in the open yard of Costa Rica's penitentiary. I was blessed twice when he preached—first by hearing him and then by repeating what he said. Ron Dunn was one of three men who have made the greatest spiritual impact on my life.

Jon Moore: Revivalist, Keller, Texas

During the year I traveled with Manley Beasley, I got to participate in a number of conferences where Ron preached. I got to know him on a more personal level, and I recall how he always made you feel comfortable around him—you never felt you were intruding on him. You sensed that he had time for you and that you mattered. In the mid nineties we were living in Oklahoma, and I was able to attend the noon services during a conference where he was preaching. At the time we were going through a difficult period, and Ron noticed that on my countenance. One day he suggested we go out to eat after the service rather than eat at the church. I'll never forget how he took three hours to minister to me.

Phyllis (Mrs. Jon) Moore—Women's Ministry

Jon was a pharmacist when God called him to preach at the age of thirty-two. I wasn't prepared for this, as I was not raised in church, so, as we went from conference to conference, I began watching the wives of preachers to help me learn what to do and how to act. Every time we were around the Dunns, I observed how Kaye was always right there by Ron, always looking gorgeous, and, though I knew she had heard those messages before, there was always that admiring look as Ron preached. As a "newly called" wife of a minister, things like that made a lasting impression on me.

Patricia Owens: (Mrs. Ron) Dunn Family Friend

One of the things that meant so much to me over the years were the wonderful illustrations God gave Ron that just lit up truth. I recall the simple but poignant illustration he used of the faucet in teaching us about always being available for God to use us. God gifted Ron with the ability to make truth live in a such a way you couldn't forget it as he opened up God's Word, something Ron never failed to do.

Jack and Fran Schoeppey: Former Staff Member with Ron at MBBC

Ron and I go back to the tenth grade. We played in the band, and a memory I have was how he signed his yearbook photo in which he was holding his cornet: "Hot lips, Dunn."

We've had a lot of experiences together, but the primary thing that impacted me as I watched him was his love for the Word of God. Ron loved books. His influence has caused me to love the Word. One of Ron's famous quotes is: "Studying the Bible is like walking ankle-deep in a fathomless ocean."

Judy Scoggins, Editor, *Fires of Revival*, Milldale Ministries, Zachary, Louisiana

When my first husband, Mel McClellan, started the Rocky Mountain Bible Conference in Rifle, Colorado, we invited Ron and Jimmy Robertson to preach. The first time Ron and Kaye came, it was my responsibility to meet them at the Grand Junction airport, sixty miles from Rifle. Though I had heard Ron and seen him and Kaye for many years at Milldale, I didn't know them personally, and I had put Ron on a pedestal.

All the way to the airport, I kept thinking, *What will I do to keep conversation going for a whole hour on the way back?* Little did I know what normal folks Ron and Kaye were. We laughed and talked incessantly, and over the four or five years they came to Rifle, we became good friends. They were such a blessing in the dry and thirsty land of the West, where churches are usually small and don't have the privilege of having people of their stature come to minister.

Carol Scott: *Music Evangelism Foundation* Office Administrator

From the viewpoint of someone who had been involved with the annual MEF Bible Conference in Colorado Springs from the beginning, and who knew Jamall from 1976 until God took him home, Ron Dunn was a cornerstone for the conference. He always preached the opening and the closing messages, with several others in between. No one wanted to miss hearing what he had to tell us. He was much loved, and we all felt that when Ron was in the building, everything was just fine. We all knew Ron was one of God's best friends.

BILL STAFFORD: EVANGELIST, CHATTANOOGA, TENNESSEE

I first met Ron when I was pastoring an independent Baptist church in Chattanooga, Tennessee. I had gone through many storms and heartbreaks. My wife, Sue, had had an emotional breakdown just before Manley Beasley came to preach. Then, shortly after that, I heard Ron Dunn preach a message on being more than conquerors. I learned for the first time who I really was in Christ. As a result, God taught us the principle of how to appropriate Jesus in those periods when you couldn't hear Him, when you didn't know what He was doing and you just had to trust Him. I learned that God's promise overrides my feelings and that by faith I could appropriate Him when I had no idea what He was doing.

CORNELIA SYNCO—FAMILY FRIEND, DOTHAN, ALABAMA

Ron, Kaye, and the children became like family to me. I would often stay with the children when Kaye was traveling with Ron. Ron taught me to listen to God speak through His Word. He taught me to trust God in the midst of adversity, to look for God's hand in all my circumstances. Another thing he said that has stuck with me is, "Jesus will never be all you need until He's all you've got." Ron, through his life and preaching, taught me how to live. He told me: "When dark times come, don't try to light your own candle. Wait on God."

JOHN B. WRIGHT: PASTOR EMERITUS, FIRST BAPTIST
CHURCH, LITTLE ROCK, ARKANSAS

During a span of forty years of close relationship with Ron, I discovered him to be a man with a passion for God unmatched by any man I have known. Ron communicated this both from the pulpit and in his personal life. He was a favorite pulpit guest in our church on a number of occasions. Sitting on the platform listening to him preach, I had the feeling I was listening to Spurgeon, the prince of preachers. He possessed all the qualities inherent in a great preacher. Space does not permit a delineation of these qualities. Prominent among them was his authenticity. He was real. In Ron Dunn there was no sham or affectation. The power of his preaching was reflective of the dynamic of a life fully committed to God. ❋

[APPENDIX 2]

Index of Tributes and Endorsements

❄ ✳ ❄

*(E. B.) Endorsements blurbs

Eric Alexander—305

David Allen—244

Sherry Anderson—329

Jimell and Carolyn Badry—235, 309

Jay Badry—245

Wayne Barber—259

Manley Beasley, Jr.—178

Richard Bewes—(E. B.) 71, 148

John Blanchard—(E. B.)

Julie Blevins—136

Randy Bostick—242

Michael Catt—(E. B.) 180, 246, 307

Shirley Calvert—34, 67

Michael Dean—(E. B.)

Jimmy Draper—(E. B.), 247

Barry and Janet Dunn—10, 127

Kimberly Dunn—133

Stephen Dunn—127

David Dykes—248

Tom Elliff—(E. B.) 288, 310

Malcom Ellis—217

Roy Fish—269

Joanne Gardner—36, 56

Jeanette Cliff George—307

Danny Greig—196

Pat Grossman—138

Phillip Hacking—136

Dudley Hall—249

T. D. Hall—248, 330

Ed & Marian Harris—56

George Harris—250, 310, 331

Gerald Harris—(E. B.)

Peter Harvey, UK—136

Vance Havner—175

O. S. Hawkins—(E. B.) 77

Jim Henry—250

Johnny Hunt—(E. B.)

R. T. Kendal—(E. B.), 331

Ted Kersh—220, 251, 310

D. L. & Alice Lowry—59, 251

J. P. MacBeth—33

Stan May—252

John McKay—(E. B.)

Nelson McKinney—49, 205, 331

Barbara McKinney—50

John Meador—252

Vicki Mitchell—137

Charles Moore—332

Don Moore—(E. B.) 171

Jon and Phyllis Moore—253, 333

Stephen F. Olford—253

Patricia Owens—333

Pastors, UK—139, 141

Ron and Della Proctor—180

Kenneth and Ann Ridings—254

Jimmy Robertson—(E. B.) 253, 310

Dan Robinson—243

Adrian Rogers—278

Maurice Rowlandson—141

Rick Shepherd—255

Jack and Fran Schoeppey—52, 334

Scripture Press—140

Judy Scoggins—334

Carol Scott—334

Phil South—(E. B.) 151–53, 306

Bill Stafford—179, 306, 335

Don and Anita Stanford—55

Cornelia Synco—335

Jack Taylor—(E. B.)

UK Tributes—154-156

Ken Whitten—179, 256, 306

Hayes Wicker—195, 256

Warren Wiersbe—(E. B.) 105, 206

John B. Wright—336

John L. Yeats (E. B.) 184

A Continuing Legacy

Sherwood Baptist Church, Albany, Georgia, maintains an official Ron Dunn Web site at *www.RonDunn.com*. Available resources on the site include: sermons, sermon outlines, devotionals, articles, and pages from Ron Dunn's personal Bible. Books and messages by Ron Dunn are also available for purchase from the site through Sherwood's *The Source Bookstore*. Sherwood also maintains Ron Dunn Facebook and Twitter accounts as a means of continuing his legacy through social media venues. Search "Rev Ron Dunn" on facebook, or follow @RevRonDunn on Twitter. ❈

Notes

❋ ❋ ❋

1. Jill Morgan, *A Man of the Word: Life of G. Campbell Morgan* (Eugene, OR: Wipf and Stock Publishers, 2010).

2. Senior pastor, retired, First Baptist Church, Houston, Texas.

3. See Photo Gallery.

4. Excerpted from Ron's first book, *Any Christian Can.*

5. Words by Ron Owens. Copyright © 1993, ICS Music, Inc.

6. Arthur Wallis, *In the Day of Thy Power* (Christian Literature Crusade, 2010, republished).

7. John Keith, "How Firm a Foundation," 1787.

8. This term originated with St. John of the Cross in his poem, *Dark Night of the Soul,* in which he addresses the feelings of being forgotten by the presence of the Almighty, a spiritual crisis that Christians, desirous of walking more closely with God, must pass through in order to truly learn to walk by faith and not by sight.

9. C. S. Lewis, *The Problem of Pain* (New York: HarperOne, 2001).

10. C. H. Spurgeon, *An All Round Ministry* (London: Passmore and Alabaster, 1900), 221–22.

11. David McCasland, *Abandoned to God, the Biography of Oswald Chambers* (Grand Rapids: Discovery House, 1993).

12. David Jeremiah, From Pathways, *Your Daily Walk With God* (June 29 reading).

13. Psychiatrists are medical doctors (MD) who specialize in the treatment of mental illnesses and emotional problems, whose medical training qualifies them to address not only the emotions but also the physical part of the anatomy such as body chemistry and blood disorders that affect the emotions and human behavior.

14. Ron Owens, "The Process."

15. Excerpted from an address Ron gave at the Rapha Luncheon during the 1991 Southern Baptist Convention in Atlanta, Georgia.

16. From *Christian Quotes*—Chuck Swindoll on family.

17. Frederick Buechner, *Now and Then* (New York: Harper & Row, 1991), 55–56.

18. Max Lerner, *Wrestling with the Angel* (New York: Touchstone Publishers, 1991).

19. Johan Christiaan Beker, *Suffering and Hope: The Biblical Vision and the Human Predicament* (Grand Rapids, MI: Eerdmans, 1994).

20. Max Lerner, *Wrestling with the Angel* (New York: Touchstone Publishers, 1991).

21. Ron Dunn, *Don't Just Stand There, Pray Something* (Nashville: Thomas Nelson, 1992).

22. An in-depth conversation between Ron and Manley Beasley is recorded in Manley's biography, *Manley Beasley: Man of Faith, Instrument of Revival,* chapters 15 and 16.

23. First published in 1976. Also published under the title, *Victory.*

24. First published in 1984. Republished in 2013 by B&H Publishing Group. Published in the UK under the title, *Don't Just Sit There, Have Faith.*

25. Ronald Dunn, *When Heaven Is Silent* (Nashville: Thomas Nelson, 1994).

26. Oswald Chambers, *My Utmost for His Highest* (New York: Dodd, Mead and Company, 1935), 305.

27. Henri J. M. Nouwen, *The Wounded Healer* (New York: Doubleday, 1972), 16.

28. First published in 1997. Republished in 2013 by B&H Publishing Group.

29. *Christianity Today,* January 8, 1996.

30. Interview included in the biography, *Manley Beasley: Man of Faith, Instrument of Revival,* available at www.ronowensbooks.com.

31. Ron Dunn, *How to Respond When You're Hurt by Someone You Trust.* Published in 2001, shortly after Ron Dunn's home-going.

32. Stephen L. Carter, *Integrity* (San Francisco: Basic Books, 1996), 7.

33. R. C. Sproul, *The Invisible Hand* (Dallas: Word, 1996), 17.

34. Forrest Church, *Life Lines* (Boston: Beacon Press, 1996), 98.

35. See a sample of Ron's cartoon drawings in the Photo Gallery section.

36. Words by Ron Owens. Copyright © 1993, Ronald J. and Patricia H. Owens. Dedicated to Dr. Stephen F. Olford.

37. Pretty Boy Floyd, murderer and notorious bank robber, was buried in Akins, Oklahoma, in 1934. It is estimated that his funeral attracted upwards of forty thousand people, making it the largest funeral in Oklahoma history.

38. John H. Yates, "Faith Is the Victory," 1891.

39. Epitaph on Ronnie Jr.'s gravestone.

40. Ron's epitaph in bold print.

41. Esther Kerr Rusthoi, "It Will Be Worth It All," 1951.

42. Richard L. Morgan, *The American Baptist,* September 1991, 15.

43. See "A Continuing Legacy" page 339 for details.

Photo Gallery

❋ ❋ ❋

The "Preacher"

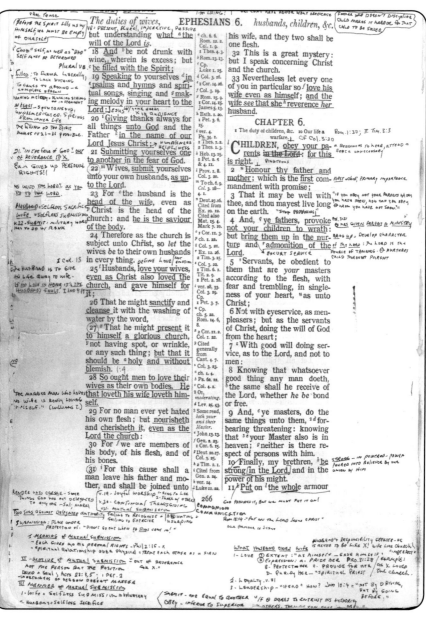

but understanding what *a the will of the Lord *is*.

18 And *b* be not drunk with wine, wherein is excess; but *c* be filled with the Spirit;

19 Speaking to yourselves *d* in *e* psalms and hymns and spiritual songs, singing and *f* making melody in your heart to the Lord;

20 *g* Giving thanks always for all things unto God and the Father *h* in the name of our Lord Jesus Christ;

21 Submitting yourselves one to another in the fear of God.

22 *m* Wives, submit yourselves unto your own husbands, as unto the Lord.

23 For *a* the husband is the head of the wife, even as Christ is the head of the church: and *he* is the saviour of the body.

24 Therefore as the church is subject unto Christ, so *let* the wives be to their own husbands in every thing.

25 *f* Husbands, love your wives, even as Christ also loved the church, and gave himself for it;

26 That he might sanctify and cleanse it with the washing of water by the word,

27 *g* That he might present it to himself a glorious church, *i* not having spot, or wrinkle, or any such thing; but that it should be *a* holy and without blemish.

28 So ought men to love their wives as their own bodies. He that loveth his wife loveth himself.

29 For no man ever yet hated his own flesh; but nourisheth and cherisheth it, even as the Lord the church:

30 For *j* we are members of his body, of his flesh, and of his bones.

31 *k* For this cause shall a man leave his father and mother, and shall be joined unto

his wife, and they two shall be one flesh.

32 This is a great mystery: but I speak concerning Christ and the church.

33 Nevertheless let every one of you in particular so *l* love his wife even as himself; and the wife *see* that she *k* reverence *her* husband.

CHAPTER 6.

1 *The duty of children, &c.* 10 *Our life a warfare.*

CHILDREN, obey your parents in the Lord: for this is right.

2 *a* Honour thy father and mother; which is the first commandment with promise;

3 That it may be well with thee, and thou mayest live long on the earth.

4 And, *b* ye fathers, provoke not your children to wrath: but bring them up in the nurture and *c* admonition of the Lord.

5 *d* Servants, be obedient to them that are *your* masters according to the flesh, with fear and trembling, in singleness of your heart, *u* as unto Christ;

6 Not with eyeservice, as menpleasers; but as the servants of Christ, doing the will of God from the heart;

7 *e* With good will doing service, as to the Lord, and not to men;

8 Knowing that whatsoever good thing any man doeth, *b* the same shall he receive of the Lord, whether *he be* bond or free.

9 And, *ye* masters, do the same things unto them, *d* forbearing threatening: knowing that *g* your Master also is in heaven; *g* neither is there respect of persons with him.

10 Finally, my brethren, *b* be strong in the Lord, and in the power of his might.

11 *c* Put on *d* the whole armour

Marginal cross references (center column)

a ch. 6. 6.
Col. 12. 2.
1 Thes. 4. 3.
b Rom. 13. 13.
c Cp.
Luke 1. 15.
d Col. 3. 16.
e 1 Cor. 14. 26.
f Col. 3. 19.
g Rom. 15. 9.
1 Cor. 14. 15.
h Esth. 1. 20.
1 Pet. 3. 6.
15.
v ver. 4.
Ps. 34.
1 Thes. 1. 2.
2 Thes. 1. 2.
b Heb. 13. 15.
1 Pet. 2. 4
& 4. 11.
i Prov. 1. 8.
Col. 3. 20.
m To ch. 6. 9.
Col. 3. 18—
4. 1.
d Deut. 27. 16.
Cited from
Ex. 20. 12.
Cited also
Mat. 15. 4.
Mark 7. 10.
v 1 Cor. 11. 3.
f ch. 1. 22.
g Col. 3. 20.
e Ex. 12. 26.
2 Tim. 3. 15.
b Col. 3. 22.
1 Tim. 6. 1.
Tit. 2. 9.
1 Pet. 2. 18.
v ver. 28, 33.
Cp.
1 Pet. 3. 7.
u Cp.
ch. 5. 22.
Rom. 14. 6.
e 2 Cor. 11. 2.
b Cited generally from
Cant. 4. 7.
c Col. 3. 23.
d ch. 1. 6.
b Ps. 62. 12.
c Col. 4. 1.
2 Or, *moderating.*
d Lev. 25. 43.
3 Some read, *both your and their Master.*
e John 13. 13.
f Gen. 2. 23.
1 Cor. 6. 15.
c Deut. 10. 17.
Col. 3. 25.
a 2 Tim. 2. 1.
k Cited from
Gen. 2. 24.
b ver. 14.
c Luke 11. 22.

266

Handwritten annotations (left margin, top)

ORAL TENSE
BEFORE THE SPIRIT FILLS US WE HIMSELF WE MUST BE EMPTY OF OURSELF

"GOOD" SELF, AS WELL AS "BAD" SELF MUST BE DETHRONED

PLURAL VB.

FILLED : TO FLRNALL LIBERALLY TO LACK NOTHING
TO CAUSE TO ABOUND - A COMPLETE PERSON

MAKING MELODY = PLUCKING STRING OF INSTRUMENT

IN HEART - SPONTANEOUS, UNPREMEDITATED. SPRINGS FROM INNER LIFE

THE FILLING OF THE SPIRIT MAKES VV 21-33 POSSIBLE.

21. "IN THE FEAR OF GOD" OUT OF REVERENCE TO X
EACH GIVES UP PERSONAL RIGHTS!!

AS UNTO THE LORD AS YOU DO IT TO THE LORD

HUSBAND = SELFLESS SACRIFICE
WIFE = SELFLESS SUBMISSION
V.22 - SUBMIT : MILITARY WORD HAS TO DO W/ RANK

1 Cor. 13
THE HUSBAND IS TO GIVE HIS LIFE AWAY TO WIFE -
IF NO LOVE IS HARD IT'S THE HUSBAND'S FAULT. 1 JNO 4.17,18

THE MARRIED MAN WHO LOVES HIS WIFE IS REALLY LOVING HIMSELF. (WILLIAMS T.)

Handwritten annotations (top right)

FATHER WHO DOESN'T DISCIPLINE CHILD MAKES IT HARDER FOR THAT CHILD TO BE SAVED

Handwritten annotations (right margin)

Rom. 1:30; II Tim. 3:3
Cf Col. 3:20

a REQUIRES TO HEAR, ATTEND & FORCE UNNECESSARY

FIRST &ONLY, PRIMARY IMPORTANCE

"IF YOU OBEY NOT YOUR PARENTS WHOM YOU HAVE SEEN, HOW CAN YOU OBEY @ WHOM YOU HAVE NOT SEEN."

"STOP PROVOKING"

Pst. 1:21
WE HAS GIVEN PARENTS A MINISTRY
BRING UP - DEVELOP CHARACTER
OF THE LORD : THE LORD IS THE SOURCE OF TRAINING - & NURTURES
BOURST SERVICE
CHILD THROUGH PARENT

STRESS - IN POWERED- POWER POURED INTO BELIEVER BY OUR UNION W/ HIM

GOD PROVIDES IT, BUT WE MUST PUT IT ON!

Handwritten annotations (bottom)

RENDER UNTO CAESAR - SOME THINGS GOD HAS NOT DELEGATED TO ANY ONE - SAL MORAL

TWO SINS AGAINST DELEGATED AUTHORITY :

V.19 - JOYFUL WORSHIP "SING A LIKE 2-TALK OF OTHER
V.20 - CONTINUAL THANKSGIVING
V.21 - MUTUAL SUBMISSION

1 SUBMISSION : PLACE UNDER
PROTECTION OF - "DONT GO OUT WHEN EG FLIES COME IN!"

I MEANING OF MUTUAL SUBMISSION
- EACH GIVES UP HIS PERSONAL RIGHTS - PHIL 2:15 - X
- SPIRITUAL RELATIONSHIP OVER PHYSICAL - TREAT EACH OTHER AS A SIGN

II MOTIVE OF MUTUAL SUBMISSION " OUT OF REVERENCE
NOT THE PERSON BUT THE POSITION &OUT OF X.
DAVID & SAUL : ACTS 23:3,5 ; 1 PEC. 2
- WORTHINESS OF PERSON DOESN'T MATTER

III MANNER OF MUTUAL SUBMISSION
1 - WIFE = SELFLESS SUBMISSION 2 VOLUNTARY
2 - HUSBAND = SELFLESS SACRIFICE

1 FAILING TO RECOGNIZE = ABDICATING
2 FAILING TO EXERCISE = USURPING

266 COMPANION COMMUNICATION
Rom 13:14 - "PUT ON THE LORD JESUS CHRIST"
OUR ARMOUR IS JESUS

WHAT HUSBAND OWES WIFE
HUSBAND'S RESPONSIBILITY GREATER - HE IS MEANT TO BE LIKE X! WIFE LIKE CHURCH!
1 - LOVE EXTENT : "AS HIMSELF - GAVE HIMSELF",
a EXPRESSION : a - PRIZE HER PRO. 31:28 EXAMPLE:
B. PROTECT HER C. PROVIDE FOR HER AS X LOVED
D - PURIFY HER - "SPIRITUAL PRIEST" THE CHURCH.

2. LOYALTY - V.31
3. LEADERSHIP = "HEAD" HOW? JNO 10:4 = "NOT BY DRIVING, BUT BY GOING BEFORE."

SUBMIT - ONE EQUAL TO ANOTHER "IF B DESIRES TO ENTRUST HIS AUTHORITY
OBEY - INFERIOR TO SUPERIOR TO OTHERS. THIS IS HIS OWN CHOICE"

December 21, 1956—Two became one

Ronnie Jr., Kimberly, Ron, Kaye, and Stephen

With Ronnie Jr.
Christmas, 1960

With Ronnie the night Ron surrendered to the ministry.

A fun moment with Ron's parents.

Ron with Barry
and his mother.

Riding Troope, packing his six-shooter.

Ron target shooting at the farm.

Ron with Kim and Stephen.

Ron and Kaye

Ron with his dad at the farm.

Kimberly: "I love you
Dad."

Vacationing on Cape Cod

Ron on Cape Cod

Kaye with Joanne Gardner, friends
and ministry partner.

Loading up with books for
another trip.

Ron and Stephen ski-bobbing in Switzerland.

REVIVAL!

You Can't Afford to Miss-

8 Great Days

with these 2 men of God!

RONNIE DUNN
EVANGELIST

at the

JOHNNY BISAGNIO
MUSICIAN

First Baptist Church

BOWLEGS, OKLA.

JANUARY 1st. - 8th.

Ron with Kenneth and Ann Ridings and D. L. Lowry.

Ron with Jimmy Robertson
and Manley Beasley Jr.

Ron with Adrian Rogers.

Ron and Kaye at their 40th
ministry anniversary celebration.

Ron with Bill Stafford at the 40th
anniversary celebration.

Ron with his friends Michael Catt, Tom Elliff, and
George Harris at the 40th anniversary celebration.

Ron and Kaye with Marthé Beasley and Michael and
Terri Catt at the 40th anniversary.

Ron with George Duncan at English Keswick.

Ron with Richard Bewes, Rector, All Souls Church, London.

Ron will Phil South, director of Lifestyle Ministries, UK.

Award ceremony for "Don't Just
Stand There, Pray Something"

1980 English Keswick Convention speakers—Alan
Redpath (3rd from left) and Ron (3rd from right)

Cartoon art by Ron Dunn

Ron and Kaye with Goofy at Disney.

Ron and Michael Catt at Disney.

Ron's study at Sherwood's Ron Dunn Center for Biblical Studies.

Ron and Patricia Owens with Dan and Kaye Robinson in
Highlands, North Carolina.